Issues in American Politics

D1408100

This wide-ranging book provides readers with a reliable and lively guide to contemporary American political practices, processes and institutions.

Chapters cover phenomena such as the Tea Party upsurge in the Republican Party, Obama's health care reforms, recent changes to campaign funding emanating from the key Citizens United Supreme Court decision, US foreign policy after the War on Terror, Obama's presidential strategy, and issues relating to polarization and partisanship in US politics.

This work is essential reading for all students of American politics and US foreign policy.

John Dumbrell is Professor in the School of Government and International Affairs, Durham University, UK.

'Featuring contributions from leading commentators on contemporary US politics, this book is an excellent guide to understanding the Obama Administration and the domestic challenges it has faced'.

Mark Phythian, *University of Leicester, UK.*

'John Dumbrell has brought together a collection of first rate scholars to review President Obama's first term. Whether you agree or disagree with the Obama policy agenda, this book will enable you to understand his presidency from a sophisticated perspective'.

James P. Pfiffner, *George Mason University, USA.*

'This collection of essays, edited by one of Britain's leading authorities on America, is essential reading for those wishing to understand the Obama presidency and the polarized political culture in which he has tried to lead'.

Mark White, *Queen Mary, University of London, UK.*

'John Dumbrell has pulled together an outstanding set of essays on modern American politics. These not only illustrate how polarized the United States has become in the age of Bush and Obama. They also reveal – once more – what a fascinating and exceptional country America remains. This is by far the most penetrating and wide-ranging volume on the key issues now facing the US in the opening decades of the 21st century'.

Michael Cox, *London School of Economics, UK*

Issues in American Politics

Polarized politics in the age of Obama

Edited by
John Dumbrell

Routledge
Taylor & Francis Group

LONDON AND NEW YORK

First published 2013
by Routledge
2 Park Square, Milton Park, Abingdon, Oxon OX14 4RN

Simultaneously published in the USA and Canada
by Routledge
711 Third Avenue, New York, NY 10017

Routledge is an imprint of the Taylor & Francis Group, an informa business

British Library Cataloguing in Publication Data
A catalogue record for this book is available from the British Library

Library of Congress Cataloging in Publication Data
Issues in American politics : polarized politics in the age of Obama / edited by John Dumbrell.
pages cm
Includes bibliographical references and index.
1. United States—Politics and government—2009- 2. United States--Social conditions—21st century.
3. Obama, Barack. I. Dumbrell, John, 1950-
JK275.I87 2013
320.60973—dc23
2012042043

ISBN: 978–0–415–69094–2 (hbk)
ISBN: 978–0–415–69095–9 (pbk)
ISBN: 978–0–203–52438–1 (ebk)

Typeset in Times New Roman
by Swales & Willis Ltd, Exeter, Devon

Printed and bound in the United States of America by Publishers Graphics, LLC on sustainably sourced paper.

To the memory of Alan Grant
(former chair, American Politics Group)

Contents

Figures

Tables

Contributors

Edward Ashbee is Professor in the Department of Business and Politics at Copenhagen Business School, Denmark. His recent books include *The US Economy Today* and *The Bush Administration: Sex and the Moral Agenda.*

Daniel Béland is Canada Research Chair in Public Policy and Professor at the Johnson–Shoyama Graduate School in Public Policy at the University of Saskatchewan, Canada. His books include *The Politics of Policy Change: Welfare, Medicare, and Social Security Reform in the United States* (2012, with Alex Waddan).

Philip John Davies is head of the Eccles Centre for American Studies at the British Library. Formerly of De Montfort and Manchester Universities, UK, he was Chair of the American Politics Group between 2006 and 2012. He is the author of numerous publications on the subject of American elections.

John Dumbrell is Professor of Government at Durham University, UK. A former Chair of the American Politics Group, he is author of *Rethinking the Vietnam War* (2012). His book *President Lyndon Johnson and Soviet Communism* received the Richard E. Neustadt book prize (awarded by the American Politics Group and the US Embassy, London) in 2005.

George C. Edwards III is University Distinguished Professor of Political Science at Texas A&M University. He is Winant Professor of American Government at Oxford University, UK in 2012–13. His numerous books include *On Deaf Ears: The Limits of the Bully Pulpit* and *Overreach: Leadership in the Obama Presidency*; he is also editor of *Presidential Studies Quarterly.*

Clodagh Harrington is Senior Lecturer in Politics at De Montfort University, Leicester, UK. Her published research focuses on the politics of American political scandal, including the legislation of ethics. She is currently Vice-Chair of the American Politics Group.

Jon Herbert is Lecturer in American Politics at Keele University, UK. He has published extensively on the US presidency, including recent studies of George W. Bush and 'Revisiting Arthur Schlesinger's *The Imperial Presidency*' (I. Morgan and M. A. Genovese, eds, *Watergate Remembered*).

Emma Long is a member of the School of History at the University of East Anglia, UK, specializing in US constitutional and legal history. She is the author of *The Church–State Debate: Religion, Education and the Establishment Clause in Postwar America* (2012).

Dean McSweeney is Principal Lecturer in Politics at the University of the West of England. He has published widely on American election campaign funding and is co-author of *The*

Republican Takeover on Capitol Hill and *American Political Parties*. He was for many years Treasurer of the American Politics Group.

Iwan Morgan is Professor of United States Studies and Head of US Programmes at the Institute of the Americas, University College London. His book *The Age of Deficits: Presidents and Unbalanced Budgets from Jimmy Carter to George W. Bush* was awarded the Richard E. Neustadt book prize in 2010.

John E. Owens is Professor of United States Government and Politics at Westminster University, UK. He is a former Chair of the American Politics Group and has published numerous articles in leading political science journals on the politics of the US Congress. He has been a Visiting Fellow at the Brookings Institution and the Congressional Research Service.

Clive S. Thomas is a Senior Fellow at the Thomas S. Foley Institute for Public Policy and Public Service at Washington State University, having previously taught for 30 years at the University of Alaska in Juneau. He has published widely on American national and state politics, including Alaskan politics, intergovernmental relations and political parties. He also runs the political consultancy firm APAS – Alaska Political Advocacy Strategies.

Alex Waddan is Senior Lecturer in American Politics and American Foreign Policy at the University of Leicester, UK. He specializes in the development of American social policy, and his books include *Clinton's Legacy? A New Democrat in Governance* (2002) and *The Politics of Policy Change* (2012).

Andrew Wroe is Lecturer in American Politics at the University of Kent, UK. He was Vice-Chair of the American Politics Group between 2005 and 2011. His research focuses on trust in government, particularly the reasons for its decline and its effects on the wider American polity. He is the author of *The Republican Party and Immigration Policy*.

Introduction

Issues in American politics: Polarized politics in the age of Obama

John Dumbrell

This collection of original essays reflects the key themes in American domestic politics in the years after 2008. The contributions are dominated by two major concerns. Firstly, the chapters deal with issues relating directly to the presidency of Barack Obama: his presidential strategies, policy achievements, problems and priorities. Secondly, the chapters examine the political environment in which Obama operated following his election: essentially a political environment of polarization and a resurgent conservatism. The chapters survey this territory from a variety of methodological and attitudinal perspectives. They provide a snapshot of the American national political landscape under a Democratic president, a Congress which shifted dramatically in its political orientation after the Republican gains in the 2010 midterm elections, and a finely balanced Supreme Court. They depict an electoral environment of apparently acute ideological division and (following a key Supreme Court decision of 2010) a high degree of financial deregulation.

In 1990, Robert Williams, introducing an earlier collection of essays emanating from the work of the American Politics Group, described the meetings of the Group as the site of 'most of the serious British discussion of American politics'.[1] The tradition continues. The American Politics Group is a constituent body of the Political Studies Association, the leading focus for the serious academic study of politics in the United Kingdom. The American Politics Group held its inaugural conference in January 1975 at the University of Keele, when it welcomed Archibald Cox (special prosecutor in the Watergate investigations) as first keynote lecturer. Over the years, the Group has established itself as one of the leading European forums – possibly *the* leading one – for the study of the politics of the United States. The Group organizes an annual residential conference and an annual day-long colloquium, usually held at the US Embassy in London, along with many other events and activities. In recent years it has attracted support from, and worked in tandem with, the British Association for American Studies, the American Political Science Association, and the Eccles Centre for American Studies at the British Library. The current collection is designed to showcase the work of the American Politics Group, which includes scholars working in continental Europe and the US as well as in the United Kingdom.

The collection is dedicated to the memory of Alan Grant, a stalwart supporter of the Group, a leading European student of American politics, and author of a much-read text on American government.[2] Sometime chair of the American Politics Group, Alan was a long-serving county councillor as well as an expert on issues such as US electoral campaign funding, Republican Party politics, and federalism. His presence at American Politics Group meetings is deeply missed by all his friends and colleagues.

President Obama and policy change

The legacy of President George W. Bush to President Obama was extraordinarily problematic. Controversial White House responses to the terror attacks of 2001 were implicated in globally negative perceptions of American power. Bush also bequeathed to his successor the direst economic conditions to face any incoming president since Franklin Roosevelt in 1933.[3] Crises, of course, do generate opportunities. In 2008, presidential candidate Barack Obama was able to develop the theme of necessary, if inevitably rather vague, 'change'. As the nation's first African American president, Obama embodied 'change' in his person as well as articulating the need for it in his speeches. However, evaluations of the presidency were soon regularly prefaced by wistful (and often *faux naïf*) references to the hopes and expectations of 2008. Political opponents such as Sarah Palin were soon asking whatever had become of 'that hopey-changey thing'. From the liberal side of the political aisle, Paul Krugman introduced his critique of Obama's economic strategy in the following terms: 'What happened to the inspirational figure his supporters thought they elected? Who is this bland guy who doesn't seem to stand for anything in particular?'[4] Reviewing Jonathan Alter's book *The Promise* in 2010, Frank Rich concluded: 'The Obama of Hope and Change was too tough an act for Obama, a mere chief executive, to follow.'[5]

Our first five chapters deal explicitly with Obama's domestic record and policy challenges. George C. Edwards III situates Obama in the paradigm of the 'strategic presidency'. Successful presidents, from the perspective of the 'strategic presidency', should not put all their eggs in the basket of persuasion, 'going public', and the presidential 'bully pulpit'. Rather, they can facilitate change by understanding their electoral and institutional environments, and grasping such opportunities as these environments present.[6] For Edwards, Obama put far too much faith in public persuasion – 'going public' – and in the possibility of bipartisanship in Congress. Such success as Obama did enjoy, notably healthcare reform (passage of the Patient Protection and Affordable Care Act in March 2010), derived from traditional party-oriented leadership, not from bipartisan 'persuasion'. Obama's governing strategy of 2009–10 (according to Edwards) came aground in the 2010 midterm elections, effectively shutting off the chance of domestic policy success in 2010–12. Engaging directly with Edwards's concept of the 'strategic presidency', Jon Herbert offers an alternative approach. He presents a more positive analysis of Obama's domestic policy record, tying the president's successes to complex strategies to attract the support of conservative (so-called 'Blue Dog') Democrats. Herbert sees the presidential strategy of 'going public' as multi-faceted, not least in the way it can impact on wavering presidential supporters in Congress. The debate between Edwards and Herbert thus leads us directly back into major controversies within presidential scholarship: controversies associated with the work of Samuel Kernell on 'going public' and indeed of Richard Neustadt on the degree to which presidential power ultimately is the 'power to persuade'.[7]

Daniel Béland and Alex Waddan analyse Obama's healthcare changes, concentrating on their convoluted legislative history and explaining the complex challenges to successful implementation. They conclude that the Patient Protection and Affordable Care Act has the potential to transform American social policy and to become the central plank of Obama's domestic legacy. It survived a major Supreme Court challenge in June 2012. However, even following that decision, major doubts remained about its prospects for survival and for thoroughgoing implementation. Obama's domestic policy 'change' agenda and its limitations are further explicated in Edward Ashbee's contribution. His focus is on economic regulation and obstacles to change. He deals with the concepts of presidential agency and 'strategic choice', emphasizing the structurally blocking role of business interests. Such interests, according to Ashbee, have, since the onset in 2007–08 of the Great Recession, been pulled back from accommodation to 'reformed' or 'welfare capitalism', and towards a more anti-statist, individualist capitalism. The economic context of the contemporary presidency is further analysed by Iwan Morgan, who offers an expert, panoramic focus on America's problems of growth, deficit and renewing prosperity. Morgan thus advances yet another perspective on Obama and the possibilities of change. The central problem for contemporary policymakers becomes one of reconciling the ultimate need for deficit reduction with the possibility of growth, always recognizing that the state can play a positive role.

Politics and institutions in an era of polarization

It has become axiomatic that contemporary American politics and government are beset by intense partisanship and ideological polarization. This is most obviously apparent at the elite congressional level. Announcing his retirement from the US Senate in February 2010, Senator Evan Bayh (Democrat of Indiana) referred to the US Congress as being trapped in an 'endless cycle of recrimination and revenge'. American government, according to Bayh, was the prisoner of 'brain-dead partisanship'.[8] To many commentators, America by 2010 seemed gripped by partisan passions on a scale not seen since the nineteenth century. Analysts varied in their assessment of the degree to which partisanship and polarization affected elite and mass opinion equally. Various explanations for the phenomenon were put forward: from the continuing 'culture wars' to the rise of new media and the role of partisan redistricting in the House of Representatives. Less than a year into his presidency, it was almost universally accepted that Obama's promise to move to a 'post-partisan age' had come to nothing.[9]

Andrew Wroe addresses directly the issue of elite versus mass polarization. Wroe contrasts the widespread acceptance of deep elite cultural and social divisions with comparative uncertainty about mass polarization. Wroe presents new research on the increased saliency of cultural issues at the mass level, arguing that the polarizing 'culture wars' – liberal versus conservative – do indeed define political attitudes for both elites and the general public. John E. Owens, drawing on detailed original data, deals with the accelerating partisan polarization of the US Congress, with the two parties now more polarized than at any time since the termination of Reconstruction in the 1880s. Owens emphasizes that such polarization is 'asymmetrical', with congressional Republicans moving farther in a conservative direction than the Democrats have moved in a liberal one.

Recent upsurges in (especially populist) American conservatism are examined in our next two chapters. Clodagh Harrington discusses the Tea Party movement, analysing it as a contemporary aspect of the 'paranoid style' in American politics. She examines the roots of the upsurge, including economic and social grievances, and considers the interplay between grassroots protest and corporate sponsorship. She concludes that the movement is likely to collapse into the political mainstream – albeit a mainstream itself structured around polarized politics. Clive Thomas analyses the Sarah Palin phenomenon, situating the political rise of the Republican Party's 2008 vice presidential candidate in terms of exceptionalist American political culture. Thomas draws on his long personal engagement with politics in Alaska. He sees Sarah Palin as a political enigma, both shaping and drawing on the wider polarization that is so central to the American political landscape.

Our final three chapters consider the contemporary condition of elections and the role of the Supreme Court in this era of polarization. Contemporary American elections show a high degree of balance between the two parties, with a high degree of uncertainty about how recent legal changes in the funding environment will affect the voting environment. Philip John Davies discusses the roots of divided government, focusing particularly on the polarizing 2010 midterms. He reviews recent elections and considers the possibility for any alleviation of the divided, ideologically polarized status quo. Dean McSweeney examines the atypical American system of funding election campaigns. Addressing the issue in comparative perspective, McSweeney points out the extraordinary impact of American conditions of demand and supply of campaign money. He delineates the context for elections held in the wake of the Supreme Court's landmark 2010 *Citizens United* decision, with an expected rise in corporate funding sure to have a significant impact on the politics of polarized America. Emma Long concludes our collection with a study of the Court's potentially path-breaking (but still difficult to read) interventions in the arena of church–state separation, itself a key issue in polarized 'culture wars' debates. Under Chief Justice John Roberts, the Court has emerged as an unpredictable but potentially decisive force in adjudicating fundamental disputes generated in a conflicted American polity.

The American Politics Group is proud to present this collection of interconnected and illuminating essays, dedicated to the memory of Alan Grant.

Notes

1 Robert Williams, 'Introduction' to Robert Williams, ed., *Explaining American Politics* (London: Routledge, 1990), p. 2.
2 Alan Grant, *The American Political Process*, 7th edn (London and New York: Routledge, 2004) (first edn 1979).
3 See Iwan Morgan and Philip John Davies, eds, *Assessing George W. Bush's Legacy: The Right Man?* (New York: Palgrave Macmillan, 2010); Michael Grunwald, *The New New Deal: The Hidden Story of Change in the Obama Era* (New York: Simon & Schuster, 2012).
4 Quoted in Bronwen Maddox, 'The $14.3 Trillion Question: Is America Broken?', *The Times*, 22 April 2011.
5 Frank Rich, 'Why Has He Fallen Short?', *New York Review of Books*, 19 August 2010, 21; Jonathan Alter, *The Promise: President Obama, Year One* (New York: Simon & Schuster, 2010).
6 See George C. Edwards III, *The Strategic President: Persuasion and Opportunity in Presidential Leadership* (Princeton, NJ: Princeton University Press, 2009).
7 Samuel Kernell, *Going Public: New Strategies of Presidential Leadership* (Washington, DC: Congressional Quarterly Press, 1982); Richard E. Neustadt, *Presidential Power: The Politics of Leadership from FDR to Carter* (New York: Wiley, 1980) (originally published 1960).
8 Evan Bayh, 'Why I'm Leaving the Senate', *New York Times*, 21 February 2010.
9 See also Thomas Mann and Norman Ornstein, *It's Even Worse than You Think: How the American Constitutional System Collided with the New Politics of Extremism* (New York: Basic Books, 2012).

1 Barack Obama and the strategic presidency

George C. Edwards III

In 2008, America suffered from war and economic crisis. Partisan polarization was extraordinarily high, while faith in government was exceptionally low. In such times, the reflexive call is for new – and better – leadership, especially in the White House. Barack Obama answered the call, presenting himself as a transformational leader who would fundamentally change the policy and the politics of America.

Even though both the public and commentators are frequently disillusioned with the performance of individual presidents and recognize that stalemate is common in the political system, Americans eagerly accept what appears to be the promise of presidential leadership to renew their faith in the potential of the presidency. Many Americans enthusiastically embraced Obama's candidacy and worked tirelessly to put him in the White House. Once there, the new president and his supporters shared an exuberant optimism about the changes he would bring to the country.

There is little question that Obama was sincere in wanting to bring about change. So were his followers. Yet, a year into his administration, many were frustrated – and surprised – by the widespread resistance to his major policy proposals. The public was typically unresponsive to the president's calls for support. Partisan polarization and congressional gridlock did not disappear. As a result, the promised transformation in energy, environmental, immigration, and other policies did not occur. When the president succeeded on health care reform, it was the result of old-fashioned party leadership, ramming the bill through Congress on a party-line vote. Even worse, from the Democrats' perspective, the 2010 midterm elections were a stunning defeat for the president's party that would undermine the administration's ability to govern in the succeeding years.

How could this bright, articulate, decent and knowledgeable new president have such a difficult time attaining his goals? Did the president fumble the ball, making tactical errors in his attempts to govern? Although no president is perfect, the Obama White House was not severely mismanaged, politically insensitive or prone to making avoidable mistakes. Ineffective implementation of a strategy was not the explanation for the lack of progress in transforming policy and politics.

Instead, the problem was in the strategies themselves – in the belief that they could succeed. A common premise underlying the widespread emphasis on political leadership as the wellspring of change is that some leaders have the capability to transform policy by reshaping the influences on it. The Obama White House believed in the power of the bully pulpit. The president and his advisers felt that he could persuade the public to support his programme. They also believed that the president could obtain bipartisan support in Congress through efforts to engage the opposition. As a result of these premises, the White House felt comfortable advancing an extraordinarily large and expensive agenda.

Presidential power is *not* the power to persuade, however. Presidents cannot reshape the contours of the political landscape to pave the way for change by establishing an agenda and persuading the public, Congress and others to support their policies. Instead, successful presidents *facilitate* change by recognizing opportunities in their environments and fashioning strategies and tactics to exploit them.[1] In other words, presidents who are successful in obtaining support for their agendas have to evaluate the opportunities for change in their environments carefully and orchestrate existing and potential support skilfully.

These conclusions lead us to predict that governing strategies dependent on employing persuasion to create opportunities for change will fail. The Obama administration provides an excellent test for these predictions, because it adopted two governing strategies highly dependent upon persuasion: going public and bipartisanship in Congress.

Before analysing these strategies for governing, we need to consider the nature of the president's agenda. The more ambitious the president's agenda, the more likely it will meet with intense criticism and political pushback. A White House strategy built on the assumption of persuading the public or members of Congress to support the president's programmes can lead to an overly ambitious agenda that lacks the fundamental support it needs to weather the inevitable attacks from the opposition.

The Obama agenda

Given the policy environment he inherited, the president often declared that he did not have the luxury of addressing the financial crisis and issues such as health care, education or the environment one at a time. 'I'm not choosing to address these additional challenges just because I feel like it or because I'm a glutton for punishment', he told the Business Roundtable. 'I'm doing so because they're fundamental to our economic growth and ensuring that we don't have more crises like this in the future.'[2] He wanted a more sustained approach than patching the economy until the next bubble, like the technology bubble of the 1990s and the housing bubble of the 2000s.[3]

In Obama's view, it was impossible to deal with the economic crisis without fixing the banking system, because it was not possible to generate a recovery without liquid markets and access to capital. He insisted that the only way to build a strong economy that would truly last was to address underlying problems in American society like unaffordable health care, dependence on foreign oil, and underperforming schools. Reducing dependence on foreign oil required addressing climate change, which in turn required international cooperation and engaging the world with vigorous US diplomacy. His appointment of five prominent White House 'czars' with jurisdictions ranging across several departments reflected this syncretic outlook.

Moreover, the president had little patience for waiting to act. 'There are those who say these plans are too ambitious, that we should be trying to do less, not more', he told a town hall meeting in Costa Mesa, California on 18 March 2009. 'Well, I say our challenges are too large to ignore.' The next day in Los Angeles he proclaimed:

> It would be nice if I could just pick and choose what problems to face, when to face them. So I could say, well, no, I don't want to deal with the war in Afghanistan right now; I'd prefer not having to deal with climate change right now. And if you could just hold on, even though you don't have health care, just please wait, because I've got other things to do.

Later, on *The Tonight Show with Jay Leno*, he repeated his standard response to critics who charged he was trying to do too much: 'Listen, here's what I say. I say our challenges are too big to ignore.'[4]

There was also an element of strategic pragmatism in the president's view. For example, Obama felt that health care was a once-in-a-lifetime struggle and a fight that could not wait. To have postponed it until 2010 would have meant trying to pass the bill in an election year. To have waited until 2011 would have risked taking on the battle with reduced majorities in the House and Senate.[5] Even when the administration began running into resistance to its health care plan in the summer of 2009 and White House chief of staff Rahm Emanuel went to Obama and pushed for a pared-back approach that would focus on expanding coverage for lower-income children and families and on reforming the most objectionable practices of insurance companies, Obama persisted in his comprehensive approach.[6]

Obama's top strategists, including David Axelrod and Emanuel, repeatedly defended the administration's sweeping agenda by arguing that success breeds success, that each legislative victory would make the next one easier.[7] In other words, the White House believed success on one issue on the agenda would *create* further opportunities on additional policies.

There were some efforts to set priorities, of course. The White House and congressional Democrats deferred fights over tax policy, despite the impending expiration of many of the George W. Bush tax cuts. The White House also opposed a high-profile commission to investigate Bush administration interrogation practices and declined to engage in hot-button debates over gays in the military (until late 2010) or gun control.[8] The administration also did not make immigration and union card check legislation priorities.[9]

Assessing opportunities: public support

Public support is a key political resource, and modern presidents have typically sought public support for themselves and their policies that they could leverage to obtain backing for their proposals in Congress. It is natural for a new president, basking in the glow of an electoral victory, to focus on creating, rather than exploiting, opportunities for change. After all, if he convinced voters and party leaders to support his candidacy – and just won the biggest prize in American politics by doing so – why should he not be able to convince the public or members of Congress to support his policies? Thus presidents may not focus on evaluating existing possibilities when they think they can create their own.

Barack Obama entered the presidency with an impressive record of political success, at the centre of which were his rhetorical skills. In college, he concluded that words had the power to transform: 'with the right words everything could change – South Africa, the lives of ghetto kids just a few miles away, my own tenuous place in the world'.[10] It is no surprise, then, that Obama followed the pattern of presidents seeking public support for themselves and their policies that they can leverage to obtain backing for their proposals in Congress – especially since it was commonplace at the beginning of his term for commentators to suggest that the president could exploit the capacity for social networking to reach people directly in a way that television and radio could not and harness this potential to overcome obstacles to legislative success.

The Obama White House believed in the power of the presidential pulpit. More importantly, it believed that the president was an irresistible persuader. According to the president's top counsellor, David Axelrod, 'I don't think there's been a President since Kennedy whose ability to move issues and people through a speech has been comparable.'[11] This faith in presidential persuasion underlay the administration's decision to try to move a large agenda simultaneously and its response to political problems.

Going public is a common strategy in recent presidencies. Yet it is a mistake for presidents to assume they can lead the public. There is nothing in the historical record to support such a belief. Research tracking the opinion leadership of Bill Clinton and Ronald Reagan on a wide range of policies and efforts to defend themselves against scandal found that public opinion rarely moved in the president's direction. On most of Clinton and Reagan's policy initiatives, pluralities, and often majorities, of the public *opposed* the president. Moreover, movement in public opinion was typically *against* the president.[12] Analyses of George W. Bush's and Franklin D. Roosevelt's efforts to lead the public also found that these presidents typically experienced frustration and failure.[13]

Thus it is critically important for presidents to assess accurately the potential for obtaining public support. Adopting strategies for governing that are prone to failure wastes rather than creates opportunities.[14] Relying on going public to pressure Congress when the public is unlikely to be responsive to the president's appeals is a recipe for failure.

There are two fundamental components of the opportunity for obtaining public support. First is the nature of public opinion at the time a president takes office. Does it support the direction in which the president would like to move? Is there a mandate from the voters in support of specific policies? Is there a broad public predisposition for government activism? Are opposition party identifiers open to supporting the president's initiatives? A second facet of the potential for public leadership focuses on the long run. What are the challenges to leading the public that every president faces?

I have analysed the latter in detail in *On Deaf Ears*.[15] In what follows I will explore the White House's view of the opportunities for change and then offer my own, quite different, evaluation. We will see that, by analysing the opportunity for obtaining public support for Obama's initiatives, it is possible to understand and predict the challenges President Obama faced in going public and the relative utility of this strategy for governing.

The view from the White House

Barack Obama was all about change. Calling for change was at the centre of his campaign strategy, and he spoke tirelessly of fundamental reforms in health care, energy, the environment and other policy areas. Once in office, the president and his aides embraced the view that the environment offered a rare opportunity for the changes they espoused. They reasoned that the crisis atmosphere would galvanize the country, perhaps even generating bipartisan support for the president's initiatives. Thus, they viewed the economic crisis as an opportunity, as a catalyst for action, rather than as a constraint. White House Chief of Staff Rahm Emanuel articulated this strategy most succinctly when he declared that one should 'Never let a serious crisis go to waste.'[16] In other words, the new administration concluded that the economic crisis had heightened the desire for change that voters expressed in November, creating a once-in-a-generation opportunity for bold policy shifts.[17]

The new president quite sensibly concluded that he had to promote economic recovery as his first order of business. Moreover, his proposal for recovery called for continuing the late Bush term's massive subsidies to keep the banking and automobile industries afloat, and adding a staggeringly expensive programme to stimulate the economy. These expenditures and tax cuts produced by far the largest deficits in American history. In addition, passing them required the president to spend his political capital in the early days of his presidency, difficult legislative battles in which he could not attract bipartisan support. A politically costly battle over his budget followed directly, with similar legislative results.

An alternative analysis of the policy environment might have viewed the economic crisis as a constraint. Obama could have justifiably argued that he would have to scale back his agenda, that the economy was in such a fragile state that he should focus all his attention on nursing it back to health as soon as possible. He also could have explained that, given the amount of money the government would be pouring into the economy, the country could not afford for the moment a costly overhaul of health care nor an ambitious initiative to combat global warming that included a controversial cap-and-trade system and energy taxes. Instead, he would work to overhaul the financial services industry, whose excesses triggered the crisis.

The White House was aware of the challenge it faced in dealing with the economy. According to senior adviser David Axelrod, 'We came to office and immediately walked into a fiscal crisis, a financial crisis, and an economic crisis. It required some very difficult decisions, and it required everyone to spend some political capital.'[18]

Nevertheless, the administration moved aggressively to propose the most ambitious domestic agenda since Lyndon Johnson's Great Society. Obama decided that he would convey the idea that the nation's problems, from the retreating economy to falling student test scores, were intertwined as he pressed for action on a host of fronts simultaneously.[19] The president often argued, for example, that the country had to address the cost and availability of health care and lessen its dependence on foreign oil before there could be a real economic recovery. From a policy-analytic standpoint, the White House had a good case. Politics rarely defers to analysis, however.[20]

Even after the frustrations of his first year in office, he declared in his State of the Union message in January 2010:

> From the day I took office, I've been told that addressing our larger challenges is too ambitious; such an effort would be too contentious. I've been told that our political system is too gridlocked, and that we should just put things on hold for a while. . . . For those who make these claims, I have one simple question: How long should we wait? How long should America put its future on hold?[21]

The president's mandate

New presidents traditionally claim a mandate from the people, because the most effective means of setting the terms of debate and overcoming opposition is the perception of an electoral mandate, an impression that the voters want to see the winner's programmes implemented. Indeed, major changes in policy, as in 1933, 1965 and 1981, rarely occur in the absence of such perceptions.

Mandates can be powerful symbols in American politics. They accord added legitimacy and credibility to the newly elected president's proposals. Concerns for representation and political survival encourage members of Congress to support the president if they feel the people have spoken.[22] As a result, mandates change the premises of decision. Perceptions of a mandate in 1980, for example, placed a stigma on big government and exalted the unregulated marketplace and large defence budgets, providing Ronald Reagan a favourable strategic position for dealing with Congress.

Barack Obama won the presidency with nearly 53 per cent of the popular vote, the first time a Northern Democrat had won a majority of the popular vote for president since Franklin D. Roosevelt's victory in 1944 – and only the third time any Democrat had won a majority of the vote in those 64 years. Democrats won additional seats in both houses of Congress, and the historic nature of the election of the first Black president generated an enormous amount of favourable press coverage. Furthermore, the new president had emphasized change, not continuity, in his campaign and promised bold new initiatives.[23] Thus it was easy for Democrats to overinterpret the new president's mandate for change.

Obama seemed to have a realistic interpretation of the nature of his victory, however, as we can see from his response to a question about his mandate in a press conference on 25 November 2008:

> But I won 53 percent of the vote. That means 46 or 47 percent of the country voted for John McCain. And it's important, as I said on election night, that we enter into the new administration with a sense of humility and a recognition that wisdom is not the monopoly of any one party.[24]

The president-elect had it about right. An ABC News/*Washington Post* poll taken shortly before his inauguration found that, although most people felt Obama had a mandate to work for major policy changes, 46 per cent of the public felt he should compromise with Republicans in doing so.[25]

By inauguration day, however, the new president took a more expansive view:

> Now, there are some who question the scale of our ambitions, who suggest that our system cannot tolerate too many big plans. Their memories are short, for they have forgotten what this country has already done, what free men and women can achieve when imagination is joined to common purpose, and necessity to courage. What the cynics fail to understand is that the ground has shifted beneath them, that the stale political arguments that have consumed us for so long no longer apply.[26]

Apparently, he concluded that the contours of the political landscape had shifted in such a way as to expand the opportunities for major liberal change.

Support for government activism

Major expansions in public policy also require public support for, or at least toleration of, government activism in the form of new programmes, increased spending and additional taxes. It appears as though the White House concluded that Obama's victory indicated the electorate had turned in a more liberal direction and that the economic crisis had increased the public's demand for more government.

There was reason for scepticism, however. The country's partisan balance had shifted more than its ideological balance. The broad repudiation of President George W. Bush propelled the Democrats to their widest advantage over Republicans in party identification in decades, but the public's ideological alignment did not change nearly as much. More Americans identified as conservatives than as liberals, for example (Table 1.1). In both 2009 and 2010, 40 per cent of Americans described their political views as conservative, and only 21 per cent as liberal; 36 and 35 per cent, respectively, identified as moderates. The number of conservatives increased since 2008, reaching its highest level in the entire time series. The 21 per cent calling themselves liberal was in line with findings throughout the decade. Equally significant, the number of moderates, potential supporters of Obama's agenda, was at its lowest point since the time series began in 1992 (when moderates were 43 per cent of the public).

Table 1.1 Trends in ideological identification

Year	Conservative (%)	Moderate (%)	Liberal (%)
1992	36	43	17
1993	39	40	18
1994	38	42	17
1995	36	39	16
1996	38	40	16
1997	37	40	19
1998	37	40	19
1999	38	40	19
2000	38	40	19
2001	38	40	20
2002	38	39	19
2003	38	40	20
2004	38	40	19
2005	38	39	20
2006	37	38	21
2007	37	37	22
2008	37	37	22
2009	40	36	21
2010	40	35	21

Source: Gallup poll.

Despite the Democratic Party's political strength in representation in Congress, a significantly higher percentage of Americans in most states, even some solidly Democratic ones, called themselves conservative rather than liberal. No state had a majority or even a plurality of people who called themselves liberal, with the conservative advantage ranging from 1 percentage point in Vermont, Hawaii and Massachusetts to 35 percentage points in Alabama. (Washington, DC has a plurality of liberals, 36 per cent.)[27]

We can also see the dominance of conservatism if we disaggregate opinion by political party. While 72 per cent of Republicans in 2009 called themselves conservative, only 37 per cent of Democrats identified as liberal. Thirty-nine per cent of Democrats said they were moderates and another 22 per cent saw themselves as conservative. Among Independents, 35 per cent said they were conservative, and only 18 per cent identified as liberal. Between 2008 and 2009, there was an increase of 6 points in the percentage of Independents calling themselves conservative.[28]

Ideological identification is not determinative, of course, and there is a well-known paradox of the incongruity between ideological identification and issue attitudes.[29] Scholars have long known that only a fraction of the public exhibits the requisite traits of an 'ideologue'.[30] Nevertheless, many more Americans are able to choose an ideological label and use it to guide their political judgements than in previous decades.[31] Scholars have found that ideological self-placements are influential determinants of vote choice,[32] issue attitudes[33] and views toward government spending.[34]

There are other indicators of conservatism aside from ideological identification. For example, in December 2009, Pew found that Americans had become more conservative on abortion, gun control and climate change.[35] Similarly, Gallup found that, at the end of August 2009, 53 per cent of Americans said the government should promote 'traditional values', while 42 per cent disagreed and believed the government should not favour any particular set of values. The previous year, Americans were divided down the middle, with 48 per cent taking each position.[36] The shift in attitudes came primarily from Independents, whose views showed a dramatic turnaround, from a 55 per cent to 37 per cent split against government-promoted morality in 2008 to a 54 per cent to 40 per cent division in favour of it in 2009.[37]

The public also increased its traditional scepticism about expanding government's role. For example, in November 2008, 54 per cent of the public said it was the responsibility of the federal government to make sure all Americans had health care coverage. A year later, this figure had decreased to 47 per cent, while 50 per cent said it was not the government's responsibility. At the same time, there was an increase of 12 percentage points in the number of people rating health care coverage in the US as good or excellent.[38]

More broadly, when asked whether it preferred smaller government offering fewer public services or larger government offering more services, the public chose the former. Support for larger government was modest when Obama took office, and was down to 38 per cent support a year later (Table 1.2). Meanwhile support for smaller government grew somewhat during his first two years in the White House.

The general state of the economy encouraged caution about bold innovation in public policy. With unemployment around 10 per cent and a stock market plunge that threatened retirement savings, Americans started spending less, saving more[39] and adopting a more measured approach to change.

In March 2009, Gallup found that only 13 per cent of Americans both approved of the government's expansion to address the economic crisis *and* wanted that expansion to be permanent. Another 39 per cent favoured the expansion but wanted it to be cut back once the crisis was resolved. A plurality – 44 per cent – of Americans opposed the expansion from the beginning.[40]

Overwhelming Republican opposition to government activism should surprise no one. But, by July 2009, 66 per cent of Independents thought Obama's proposals to address the country's major problems called for too much government spending, and 60 per cent said his agenda called for too much government expansion.[41] They supported fiscal discipline over economic stimulus by 56 per cent to 41 per cent.[42] By February 2010, 56 per cent of the public preferred smaller government providing fewer services to 34 per cent wanting bigger government providing more services.[43]

Another obstacle to change was paying for it, which is especially problematic in bad economic times. In August 2009, Gallup found that 68 per cent of Americans expected their

Table 1.2 Support for larger government

Poll dates	Smaller government, fewer services (%)	Larger government, more services (%)	No opinion (%)
29 October – 1 November 2007	50	44	5
12–15 June 2008	50	45	5
13–16 January 2009	53	43	4
18–21 June 2009	54	41	4
12–15 January 2010	58	38	4
22–25 April 2010	56	40	4

Question: 'Generally speaking, would you say you favour [smaller government with fewer services] or [larger government with more services]?'

Source: ABC News/*Washington Post* poll.

federal income taxes would be higher by the end of Barack Obama's first term as president. Nearly half of these people (35 per cent) expected their taxes would be 'a lot higher'.[44] The rise in expectations that taxes would increase probably was a reflection on Obama's ambitious domestic agenda, which began with a $787 billion economic stimulus plan and then focused on a roughly $1 trillion health care reform bill. Although Obama regularly reiterated his pledge not to raise taxes on all but the wealthiest Americans, most Americans remained sceptical that the administration could pay for health care reform and its other programmes without raising their taxes.

Americans were also markedly cynical about the amount of waste in federal spending. At the end of the summer of 2009, on average, Americans believed 50 cents of every tax dollar that went to the government in Washington, DC was wasted, an increase from 40 cents in 1979.[45]

The public's resistance to government activism should not be surprising. In their sweeping 'macro' view of public opinion, Robert Erikson, Michael MacKuen and James Stimson show that opinion always moves contrary to the president's position. They argue that a moderate public always gets too much liberalism from Democrats and too much conservatism from Republicans. Because public officials have policy beliefs as well as an interest in re-election, they are not likely to calibrate their policy stances exactly to match those of the public. Therefore opinion movement is typically contrary to the ideological persuasion of presidents. Liberal presidents produce movement in the conservative direction and conservatives generate public support for more liberal policies.[46]

Public polarization

A primary reason for the difficulty of passing major changes in public policy is the challenge of obtaining support from the opposition party identifiers among the public. We know that partisan polarization reached record levels during the presidency of George W. Bush.[47] The election of Barack Obama did not diminish this polarization and presented an obstacle to the new president obtaining support from Republicans. We can start with the election results to understand better this context.

The 2008 election

In 2008, party-line voting was 89.1 per cent, the second highest level in the history of the American National Election Studies (ANES), which go back to 1952. This level was surpassed only by the 89.9 per cent level in 2004. Moreover, Obama's electoral coalition contained the smallest share of opposite-party identifiers of any president elected since the advent of the ANES time series, just 4.4 per cent.[48]

Republicans and Republican-leaning Independents not only did not support Obama. By Election Day, they perceived a huge ideological gulf between themselves and the new president and viewed him as an untrustworthy radical leftist with a socialist agenda. Forty-one per cent of McCain voters judged Obama to be an 'extreme liberal', further left than Republican voters had placed any previous Democratic candidate. Moreover, they placed him further to the left of their own ideologies than they had placed any previous Democratic candidate.[49]

Thus the Republicans' campaign to brand Obama as a radical socialist[50] out of touch with American values resonated with many McCain voters. An African-American candidate was also likely to exacerbate right-wing opposition,[51] as were his Ivy League education and somewhat detached manner. The fact that he spent part of his childhood in Muslim Indonesia and that his middle name was Hussein provided additional fodder for those willing or even eager to believe that he was outside the mainstream. Republican voters did not simply oppose Obama; they despised and feared him.

Identifying the states that deviated from Obama's share of the nationwide vote (about 52.9 per cent) by 10 percentage points or more reveals that there were more 'polarized' states than in any election in the past 60 years.[52] A few states (Figure 1.1) – Vermont, Rhode Island, Hawaii and the District of Columbia – were polarized in favour of Obama. Most of the polarized states, however, voted for Republican John McCain. The majority of these states form a belt stretching from West Virginia, Kentucky and Tennessee through Alabama, Mississippi, Louisiana and Arkansas over to Oklahoma, Kansas and Nebraska. In addition, Wyoming, Idaho, Utah and Alaska were strongly in the Republican camp. Never before had many of these states voted so heavily against a victorious Democrat.

The polarization of the 2008 campaign and the nature of the opposition to Obama laid the groundwork for the intense aversion to Obama and his policies that appeared shortly after he took office. His initial actions of seeking the release of additional Troubled Asset Relief Program funds and promoting a historic economic stimulus bill confirmed to conservatives that he was indeed a left-wing radical who needed to be stopped at all costs and, along with the president's support of health care reform, fuelled the emergence of the Tea Party movement.

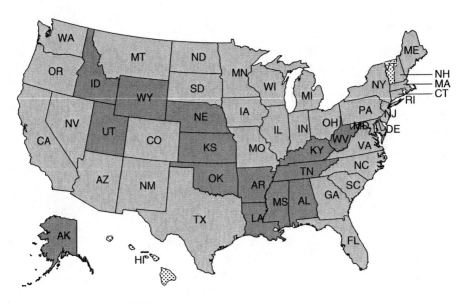

Figure 1.1 Polarized voting, 2008

Key:
Dark = polarized voting for McCain.
Dotted = polarized voting for Obama.

Note:
States with polarized election results in the 2008 presidential election: *Republican states*: Alabama; Alaska; Arkansas; Idaho; Kansas; Kentucky; Louisiana; Mississippi; Nebraska; Oklahoma; Tennessee; Utah; West Virginia; Wyoming. *Democratic states*: District of Columbia; Hawaii; Rhode Island; Vermont.

Party and ideological divisions in the public

The polarization evident in the 2008 election results did not end on Inauguration Day. Instead, it persisted in the underlying partisan and ideological divisions of the country. Indeed, there has been an increase in partisan-ideological polarization, as Americans increasingly base their party loyalties on their ideological beliefs rather than on membership in social groups.[53]

When President Obama took office, he enjoyed a 68 per cent approval level, the highest of any newly elected president since John F. Kennedy. For all of his hopes about bipartisanship, however, his early approval ratings were the most polarized of any president in the past four decades. Gallup reported that there was an average gap of 65 percentage points between Democrats' and Republicans' evaluations of the president in his first year, greatly exceeding the prior high of 52 percentage points for Bill Clinton.[54]

The Democratic political organization Democracy Corps concluded from its focus groups that those in the conservative GOP base believed that Obama 'is ruthlessly advancing a "secret agenda" to bankrupt the United States and dramatically expand government control to an extent nothing short of socialism'.[55] By June 2010, Democracy Corps found that 55 per cent of the public found Obama to be 'too liberal' and the same percentage thought 'socialist' was a reasonably accurate way of describing him.[56] In July 2010, 41 per cent of Republicans clung to the false belief that Obama was not born in the United States.[57] A poll the next month found that 31 per cent of Republicans thought he was a Muslim.[58] Another poll in the same month found that 52 per cent of the Republican respondents said it was definitely (14 per cent) or probably (38 per cent) true that 'Barack Obama sympathizes with the goals of Islamic fundamentalists who want to impose Islamic law around the world.'[59] These views represented a profound sense of alienation.[60]

Contributing to this polarization was the insulation of the opposition. Sixty-three per cent of Republicans and Republican leaners reported that they received most of their news from *Fox News*.[61] The president's initial actions were grist for commentators on the right, especially those on radio and cable television. They aggressively reinforced the fears of their audiences and encouraged active opposition to the White House.

Public perspectives on issues

As the Obama administration and Congress wrestled with how to fix the country's economic problems while at the same time dealing with the longer-term impact of those efforts, tensions between the two were inevitable. Differences in party and ideology inevitably result in different policy priorities and trade-offs between policies among the public. By June 2010, 63 per cent of Democrats thought the government should do more to solve the country's problems, but only 13 per cent of Republicans (and 32 per cent of moderates) agreed.[62]

In mid-2009, Gallup reported that Republicans and Democrats viewed the economic issues facing the country at the time from substantially different perspectives (Table 1.3). Republicans were much more likely than Democrats to express worry about issues that represented *consequences* of attempting to fix economic problems: the federal government's expanding ownership and regulation of private business and industry, increasing federal and state taxes, and the increasing federal budget deficit. Democrats, on the other hand, were much more likely to be worried about the societal problems that the increased spending and regulation were designed to address, including the increasing numbers of Americans without health insurance, and, to a lesser degree, about the rising unemployment rate, the increasing cost of health care, and decreasing pay and wages for the average worker.[63]

Table 1.3 Partisan concerns about economic issues

Issue	Concerned Republicans/leaners (%)	Concerned Democrats/leaners (%)	Democrats minus Republicans (percentage points)
Increasing numbers of Americans without health care insurance	65	90	25
The rising unemployment rate	82	91	9
The increasing cost of health care	82	89	7
Decreasing pay and wages for the average worker	74	81	7
Increasing problems Americans have with personal debt and credit cards	75	74	−1
The increasing price of gas	79	76	−3
Increasing problems state governments have funding their budgets	84	79	−5
The increasing federal budget deficit	90	75	−15
Increasing state income taxes	78	59	−19
Increasing federal income taxes	86	62	−24
The federal government's increasing regulation of business and industry	78	40	−38
The federal government's expanding ownership of private corporations	82	42	−40

Question: 'Please tell me whether you, personally, are worried about each of the following:'

Source: Gallup poll, 23–24 June 2009.

Another poll, conducted at the end of July 2009, also showed the differences between the parties on their priorities in making trade-offs between spending and reducing the budget deficit (see Table 1.4). The biggest partisan difference – 40 points – was over health care. Nearly three-quarters (72 per cent) of Democrats saw spending more on health care as the priority, while 23 per cent placed a higher priority on deficit reduction. By contrast, 63 per cent of Republicans put deficit reduction ahead of increased health care spending, while 32 per cent favoured such spending over trimming the deficit. Just over half (54 per cent) of

Table 1.4 Budget trade-offs by party

Higher priority	Republicans (%)	Democrats (%)	Independents (%)	Republicans minus Democrats (percentage points)
Spending more on health care	32	72	54	−40
Reducing the budget deficit	63	23	42	+40
Spending more on education	43	69	56	−26
Reducing the budget deficit	54	26	40	+28
Spending more on new energy technology	29	48	42	−19
Reducing the budget deficit	67	43	53	+24
Spending more on economic recovery	43	68	47	−25
Reducing the budget deficit	52	23	43	+29

Source: Pew Research Center for the People and the Press poll, 22–26 July 2009.

Independents placed a higher priority on health care spending, while 42 per cent said deficit reduction was more important. Democrats stood apart from both Republicans and Independents in saying that stimulus spending was a higher priority than deficit reduction. By a 68 per cent to 23 per cent margin, Democrats saw spending to help the economy recover as more important than reducing the deficit. By contrast, Independents were split about evenly (47 per cent placed a higher priority on economic stimulus, 43 per cent on deficit reduction), and a slim majority (52 per cent) of Republicans saw deficit reduction as the bigger priority.

In March 2010, the public said it was more important to develop US energy supplies than to protect the environment by a 50 per cent to 43 per cent margin. Several weeks after the massive oil spill resulting from the explosion of a BP oilrig in the Gulf of Mexico produced the biggest oil spill in American history, priorities shifted in favour of environmental protection, by a 55 per cent to 39 per cent margin. Support for the environmental protection option increased by 15 percentage points among both Democrats and Independents. In contrast, Republicans' opinions did not change at all in response to the environmental disaster and continued to prioritize energy production over environmental protection by a 2-to-1 margin.[64]

Summing up

Despite the historic and decisive nature of his election, Barack Obama did not enjoy an especially favourable environment for making major changes in public policy. The election results did not signal a mandate for change, an increase in support for government activism, or an end to extreme partisan polarization. In addition, the long-term constraints on opinion change remained firmly in place.

Assessing opportunities: bipartisan congressional support

Every president needs support in Congress to pass his legislative proposals. We have seen that it is natural for a new president, basking in the glow of an electoral victory, to focus on creating, rather than exploiting, opportunities for change. It may seem quite reasonable for a president who has just won the biggest prize in American politics by convincing voters and party leaders to support his candidacy to conclude that he should be able to convince members of Congress to support his policies. Thus Obama lost no time to begin, as he put it in his inaugural address, 'the work of remaking America'.

As with leading the public, presidents may not focus on evaluating existing possibilities when they think they can create their own. Yet, for example, assuming success in reaching across the aisle to obtain bipartisan support is fraught with dangers. There is not a single systematic study that demonstrates that presidents can reliably move members of Congress, especially members of the opposition party, to support them.

The best evidence is that presidential persuasion is at the margins of congressional decision making. Even presidents who appeared to dominate Congress were actually facilitators rather than directors of change. They understood their own limitations and quite explicitly took advantage of opportunities in their environments. Working at the margins, they successfully guided legislation through Congress. When these resources diminished, they reverted to the more typical stalemate that usually characterizes presidential–congressional relations.[65]

A primary obstacle to passing major changes in public policy is the challenge of obtaining support from the opposition party. Such support can be critical in overcoming a Senate filibuster or effectively appealing to Independents in the public, who find bipartisanship reassuring. The *Washington Post* reported that the Obama legislative agenda was built around what some termed an 'advancing tide' theory:

> Democrats would start with bills that targeted relatively narrow problems, such as expanding health care for low-income children, reforming Pentagon contracting practices and curbing abuses by credit-card companies. Republicans would see the victories stack up and would want to take credit alongside a popular president. As momentum built, larger bipartisan coalitions would form to tackle more ambitious initiatives.[66]

From the beginning, Barack Obama tried to strike a bipartisan pose. On the night of his election, he implored Democrats and Republicans alike to 'resist the temptation to fall back on the same partisanship and pettiness and immaturity that has poisoned our politics for so long'. In his press conference on 25 November 2008, the president-elect declared:

> it's important . . . that we enter into the new administration with a sense of humility and a recognition that wisdom is not the monopoly of any one party. In order for us to be effective . . . Republicans and Democrats are going to have to work together.[67]

Moreover, the president and his aides believed that a fair number of Republican lawmakers would rally behind the nation's first African-American president at a time of crisis.[68] They saw his liberal programmes drawing on Americans' desire for action and also counted on Obama's moderate, even conservative, temperament to hurdle the ideological obstacles that had paralysed Washington.[69]

The president made repeated and serious efforts to engage Republicans and win their support.[70] Just how realistic was the prospect of obtaining Republican support?

The prospect of Republican support

Perhaps the most important fact about Congress in 2009 was that polarization was at a historic high.[71] According to *Congressional Quarterly*, George W. Bush presided over the most polarized period at the Capitol since it began quantifying partisanship in the House and Senate in 1953. There had been a high percentage of party unity votes – those that pitted a majority of Republicans against a majority of Democrats – and an increasing propensity of individual lawmakers to vote with their fellow partisans.[72] Little changed in 2009, as *Congressional Quarterly* found extraordinarily high levels of party-line voting even in the first weeks of the Obama administration.[73] By the end of the year, 57 per cent of the votes in Congress were party unity votes, just above the 56 per cent average for the previous two decades.[74]

This polarization should not have been surprising. Republican constituencies send stalwart Republicans to Congress, whose job it is to oppose a Democratic president. Most of these senators and representatives were unlikely to be responsive to core Obama supporters. They knew their constituencies, and they knew Obama was unlikely to have much support in them. Thus few of the Republicans' electoral constituencies showed any enthusiasm for health care reform. The partisan divisions that emerged in Congress on the health care issue were firmly rooted in district opinion and electoral politics.[75] Moreover, conservative Republicans were the group of political identifiers least likely to support compromising 'to get things done'.[76]

In the 111th Congress (2009–10), nearly half of the Republicans in both the House and the Senate were elected from the 11 states of the Confederacy, plus Kentucky and Oklahoma. In each chamber, Southerners were a larger share of the Republican caucus than ever before. At the same time, Republicans held a smaller share of non-Southern seats in the House and

Senate than at any other point in its history except during the early days of the New Deal.[77] The party's increasing identification with staunch Southern economic and social conservatism made it much more difficult for Obama to reach across the aisle. Southern House Republicans, for instance, overwhelmingly opposed him, even on the handful of issues where he has made inroads among GOP legislators from other regions. Nearly one-third of House Republicans from outside of the South supported expanding the State Children's Health Insurance Program, but only one-tenth of Southern House Republicans did so. Likewise, just 5 per cent of Southern House Republicans supported the bill expanding the national service programme, compared with 22 per cent of Republicans from other states.

The Republican Party's losses in swing areas since 2006 accelerated its homogenization. Few Republicans represent Democratic-leaning districts. As a result, far fewer congressional Republicans than Democrats must worry most about moderate public opinion. Fully 31 of the 40 Republican senators serving in 2009 (31 of 41 in 2010), for example, were elected from the 18 states that twice backed Bush and also opposed Obama. Five other senators represented states that voted for Bush twice and then supported Obama. Just six Republican senators were elected by states that voted Democratic in at least two of the past three presidential elections. One of these lawmakers, Arlen Specter of Pennsylvania, switched parties to become a Democrat.

Table 1.5 shows the impact of these constituency cross-pressures on the voting of Republican senators in 2009 and 2010. Most Republican senators represented reliably Republican states, and these senators voted in a considerably more conservative direction than their party colleagues from states that were more likely to support Democratic presidential candidates. At the time of the vote to repeal 'Don't ask, don't tell', there were 11 Republican senators from states President Obama won in 2008. Of these, seven voted for repeal, three voted against, and one did not vote. On the other hand, only one of the 31 senators from states John McCain carried in 2008 voted for repeal.[78]

In addition, Republican members of Congress faced strong pressure to oppose proposals of the other party. Senators Max Baucus and Charles Grassley, the leaders of the Senate Finance Committee's negotiations over health care reform, both confronted whispers that they might lose their leadership positions if they conceded too much to the other side. Iowa conservatives even threatened that Grassley could face a 2010 primary challenge if he backed Baucus. In a similar vein, the executive committee of the Charleston County, South Carolina Republican Party censured Republican Senator Lindsey Graham because 'U.S. Sen. Lindsey Graham in the name of bipartisanship continues to weaken the Republican brand and tarnish the ideals of freedom, rule of law, and fiscal conservatism.'[79] Two months later the Lexington County Republican Party executive committee censured him for his stands on a range of

Table 1.5 Senate Republican conservatism by partisanship of state, 2009–10

Number of times states voted Republican in 2000–08 presidential elections	2009		2010	
	Number of senators	Average conservative score*	Number of senators	Average conservative score*
0	3	60	3	63
1	2	69	2	71
2	5	73	5	71
3	31	82	30	83

* Calculated by *National Journal*, which ranks members along a conservative-to-liberal continuum.

Source: Ronald Brownstein, 'Serving behind Enemy Lines', *National Journal*, 24 April 2010; Ronald Brownstein, 'Pulling Apart', *National Journal*, 26 February 2010.

policies, which it charged 'debased' Republican beliefs.[80] When asked in 2010 if he would be as bipartisan if he were facing re-election that November, Graham replied, 'The answer's probably no.' Similarly, he understood that John McCain had to win his primary for renomination in Arizona and thus could not take bipartisan stances.[81]

In January 2010, 55 per cent of Republicans and Republican leaners wanted Republican leaders in Congress, who were following a consistently conservative path, to move in a more conservative direction.[82] In perhaps the most extreme expression of this orientation, four months later the Utah Republican Party denied long-time conservative Senator Robert Bennett its nomination for re-election. The previous month, Republican governor Charlie Crist had to leave his party and run for the Senate as an Independent in Florida because he was unlikely to win the Republican nomination against conservative Marco Rubio. A year earlier, Republican Senator Arlen Specter of Pennsylvania switched parties, believing there was little chance he could win a Republican primary against conservative Pat Toomey.

Similarly, House Republicans with any moderate leanings were more concerned about the pressures from their right than about potential fallout from opposing a popular president. The conservative Republican Study Committee – which included more than 100 of the 178 House Republicans – called for enforcing party unity on big issues and hinted at retribution against defectors. Conservatives also raised the prospect of primary challenges,[83] as they did in the 2009 race to fill the seat in New York state's 23rd congressional district. Led by Sarah Palin and Dick Armey, conservatives forced the Republican candidate to withdraw from the race shortly before Election Day.

Compounding the pressure has been the development of partisan communications networks – led by liberal blogs and conservative talk radio – that relentlessly incite each party's base against the other. These constant fusillades help explain why presidents now face lopsided disapproval from the opposition party's voters more quickly than ever – a trend that discourages that party's legislators from working with the White House.

These centrifugal forces affect most the Republican Party. The Right has more leverage to discipline legislators because, as we have seen, conservative voters constitute a larger share of the GOP coalition than liberals do of the Democratic Party. The Right's partisan communications network is also more ferocious than the Left's.

Given the broad influences of ideology and constituency, it is not surprising that scholars have shown that presidential leadership itself demarcates and deepens cleavages in Congress. The differences between the parties and the cohesion within them on floor votes are typically greater when the president takes a stand on issues. When the president adopts a position, members of his party have a stake in his success while opposition party members have a stake in the president losing. Moreover, both parties take cues from the president that help define their policy views, especially when the lines of party cleavage are not clearly at stake or already well established.[84] This dynamic of presidential leadership was likely to complicate further Obama's efforts to win Republican support.

Moving the public

The prediction that the president would fail to move the public was correct. With the exceptions of limits on executive pay, which was popular when George W. Bush occupied the White House, regulating the highly unpopular large financial institutions, food safety regulatory reform, which had always received public support, and repealing 'Don't ask, don't tell', which the public had backed for several years before Obama took office, there was no major Obama initiative that enjoyed widespread public support. Indeed, the president could not muster majority backing for his policies regarding the TARP programme and bank bailouts, the auto-maker bailouts, his overall handling of the economy and of the deficit, and health care reform and his handling of it. The public supported the 2010 tax bill, but it is a stretch to call it an Obama initiative. From the White House's perspective, the bill was clearly a compromise position that contained a number of important elements that the president opposed. The public did back the compromise, however, largely because it adopted its standard pose of opposing an increase in taxes. A bare majority of the public supported ratification of the START treaty. Although a mod-est majority supported the cap-and-trade proposal, opinion on the underlying premises of climate change legislation moved clearly and rapidly against the White House, as did views of the presi-dent's handling of the global warming issue. The public also clearly opposed closing the prison at Guantánamo Bay and transferring prisoners from there to the US, and it lost confidence in his handling of Afghanistan in particular and foreign policy in general.[85]

In addition, identification with the Democratic Party declined substantially, as did evalu-ations of the party's ability to handle issues relative to that of the Republicans. These party assessments provided the foundation for the Democratic losses in the 2010 midterm elec-tions.[86] These party assessments undermined the chances for Democratic success in the 2010 midterm elections, in which the Democrats lost 63 seats – and their majority – in the House and six seats in the Senate.

Shortly before the 2010 midterm elections, Gallup asked the public about its approval of some of the major legislation passed in the 111th Congress. As the results in Table 1.6 show, the public approved only of financial regulation. Majorities disapproved of the other legisla-tion about which Gallup inquired. Perhaps most troubling for the president, financial regula-tion was the only legislation receiving the majority approval of Independents (Table 1.7). No more than 40 per cent of Independents approved of any of the other legislation.

Table 1.6 Public approval of major legislation

Legislation	Approve (%)	Disapprove (%)	No opinion (%)
Financial regulation	61	37	3
Economic stimulus	43	52	5
Automaker bailout	43	56	2
Health care reform	39	56	5
Bank bailout	37	61	2

Question: 'Now, thinking back on some of the major pieces of legislation Congress has passed in the last two years, would you say you approve or disapprove of _____?'

Source: Gallup poll, 27–30 August 2010.

Table 1.7 Partisan approval of major legislation

Legislation	Approve		
	Republicans (%)	Independents (%)	Democrats (%)
Financial regulation	42	62	76
Economic stimulus	21	38	71
Automaker bailout	31	40	57
Health care reform	13	35	69
Bank bailout	27	32	51

Source: Gallup poll, 27–30 August 2010.

There is not much evidence that Barack Obama could depend on creating opportunities for change by obtaining public support and leveraging it to gain support for his proposals in Congress. In general, public opinion moved against the president over time. Andrew Kohut, president of the Pew Research Center, summarized these trends well when he declared at the end of 2009:

> What's really exceptional at this stage of Obama's presidency is the extent to which the public has moved in a conservative direction on a range of issues. These trends have emanated as much from the middle of the electorate as from the highly energized conservative right.[87]

Bipartisan support

Despite the president's efforts to reach across the aisle and his expectations of success in doing so, he could not obtain bipartisan support for his major proposals. House Republicans overwhelmingly opposed the most significant legislation the White House proposed in the 111th Congress (Table 1.8). Whether the issue was the economy, regulating the financial industry, health care reform, the budget, civil rights, immigration, campaign finance reform, student loans, climate change, or mortgage loan modifications, Republicans uniformly opposed Democratic initiatives. Even a modest bill on child nutrition championed by Michelle Obama garnered only 17 Republican votes.

Of course, even a few Republicans could make a difference between winning and losing. On only two bills did Republican support make a difference in the outcome, however. The eight Republican representatives who voted for the climate change mitigation bill made the difference in it passing, because 44 Democrats voted against it. Whether the president could have won this much Republican support on a conference report if the Senate had also passed a version of the bill is an open question. The opposition of many Democrats to the extension of the Bush-era tax cuts during the lame-duck session of Congress in 2010 necessitated obtaining Republican support for passage of the bill. Because Republicans were eager to continue the existing tax rates, this support was forthcoming.

A similar pattern of opposition existed in the Senate (Table 1.9). Not only did the Republicans overwhelmingly oppose White House initiatives when they came to a vote, but they

Table 1.8 House party support for Obama initiatives

Legislation	Democrats		Republicans	
	For	*Against*	*For*	*Against*
Block release of TARP funds	99	151	171	4
Stimulus bill conference report	246	6	0	177
Financial regulation reform conference report	234	19	3	173
Health care reform conference report	219	34	0	178
Health care reconciliation conference report	233	17	0	176
FY 2010 budget conference report	233	17	0	176
Increase debt limit, 2010	217	37	0	175
Extension of Bush-era tax cuts	139	112	138	36
Anti-discrimination on wages	244	4	3	167
Repeal 'Don't ask, don't tell'	235	15	15	160
DREAM Act	208	38	8	160
DISCLOSE Act campaign finance	217	36	2	170
Climate change mitigation	211	44	8	168

Table 1.9 Senate party support for Obama initiatives

Legislation	Democrats		Republicans	
	For	*Against*	*For*	*Against*
Block release of TARP funds	9	46	33	6
Stimulus bill conference report	60	0	2	38
Financial regulation reform conference report	57	1	3	38
Health care reform	60	0	0	39
FY 2010 budget resolution conference report	53	3	0	40
Increase debt limit, 2010	60	0	0	39
Extension of Bush-era tax cuts	44	14	37	5
Anti-discrimination on wages	56	0	5	36
Repeal 'Don't ask, don't tell'	57	0	8	31
Ratification of new START treaty	58	0	13	26
Sonia Sotomayor nomination	59	0	9	31
Elena Kagan nomination	58	1	5	36

also did their best to prevent final votes altogether. Their frequent resort to the filibuster succeeded in preventing action on climate change, immigration, and campaign finance reform.

There were only two bills on which Republican support made the difference in the outcome. The first was the effort to block release of the TARP funds, which six Republicans opposed and occurred before Obama took office. The other bill was the compromise plan to extend the Bush-era tax cuts passed near the end of the lame-duck Congress in 2010. In addition, the president required Republican support to reach the two-thirds margin for ratifying the new START treaty and for breaking filibusters on issues such as the repeal of 'Don't ask, don't tell'.

When the president was successful in winning congressional support for his legislation, which he often was, he exploited the opportunities the large Democratic majorities provided. Thus he mobilized those *predisposed* to support him and drove proposals through Congress on party-line votes. Success in exploiting opportunities requires the president have the commitment, resolution and adaptability to take full advantage of opportunities that arise. Obama had the energy, perseverance and resiliency to make the most of the Democrats' majorities.

Conclusion

It is critical that presidents carefully evaluate their opportunity structure. If they do not ask the right question, they certainly will not arrive at the right answer. To answer the question requires, first, not assuming success. Rejecting the assumption of success leads naturally to examining the nature of existing public and congressional opinion. It also leads to asking whether it is reasonable to rely on going public or bipartisan support to accomplish policy change.

Analysing the opportunity structure of the Obama presidency reveals that the nature of a president's opportunity structure is dynamic. The new administration quite reasonably felt it had to devote its initial attention to the crisis in the economy before moving to the issues, such as health care reform, energy, and environmental protection, on which Obama had campaigned for the previous two years. Doing so cost vast sums of money, however, and required unparalleled government intervention in the economy. The scope of the response to the recession discouraged rather than encouraged demand for government services.

Despite voting for a presidential candidate espousing change, the public had not changed its basic scepticism of government or its resistance to paying for it. For some, these policies triggered serious anxiety about the future and were a catalyst for mobilization into intense opposition that manifested itself in both mass protests and hostile confrontations at meetings in congressional constituencies. In sum, by taking dramatic and sweeping action to stem the economy's slide, the president narrowed the prospects for change in other areas of public policy. Political analyst Charlie Cook termed the effort to pass a large agenda rather than focusing on the economy 'a colossal miscalculation':[88]

> What Obama and Democrats failed to realize was that the escalation of spending under Bush, the bailouts and the implementation of TARP, created a political environment that made significant climate change and health care reform ring up 'no sale' in the minds of voters. It was too much for them to handle when all they [the public] wanted was a focus on job creation and the economy.[89]

It is not surprising that, after a year of Obama's tenure, Americans said they preferred smaller government and fewer services to larger government with more services by 58 per cent to 38 per cent.[90]

The White House anticipated that it could attract bipartisan support from Republicans. The foundations of this expectation were weak, however. Partisan polarization was at a historic high, and the Republican Party's locus in the economic and social conservatism of the South reinforced the disinclination of Republicans to offer support across the aisle. Indeed, the more homogeneous conservative ideology of Republican activists and the Right's strident and ever-expanding communications network meant that Obama would face a vigorous partisan opposition with strong incentives not to cooperate with the White House. There was no possibility that the president could win bipartisan support.

If we ask the right questions, we can explain – and predict – the likely success of strategies for governing. Once we understand that presidents are unlikely to create opportunities for change, we naturally focus on whether presidents recognize and exploit opportunities that do exist.

In a rational world, strategies for governing should match the opportunities to be exploited. Barack Obama is only the latest in a long line of presidents who have not been able to transform the political landscape through their efforts at persuasion. When he succeeded in achieving major change, it was by mobilizing those predisposed to support him and driving legislation through Congress on a party-line vote. In other words, he succeeded by exploiting the opportunities provided by the large Democratic majorities in Congress. The president's failure to understand the nature of presidential power contributed to the Democrats' substantial defeat in the midterm elections and diminished his ability to govern in 2011–12.

Notes

1 See George C. Edwards III, *The Strategic President: Persuasion and Opportunity in Presidential Leadership* (Princeton, NJ: Princeton University Press, 2009).
2 White House Transcript, 'Remarks by the President to the Business Roundtable', 12 March 2009.
3 Peter Baker, 'Obama Defends Agenda as More than Recession', *New York Times*, 13 March 2009.
4 Helene Cooper, 'Some Obama Enemies Are Made Totally of Straw', *New York Times*, 24 May 2009. See also Peter Baker, 'The Limits of Rahmism', *New York Times Magazine*, 14 March 2010.

5 Dan Balz, 'With New Priorities, Obama and Democrats Can Recover in 2010', *Washington Post*, 27 December 2009.
6 Baker, 'Limits of Rahmism'.
7 Michael D. Shear and Shailagh Murray, 'President Is Set to "Take the Baton": As Skepticism on Health Reform Mounts, He Will Intensify His Efforts', *Washington Post*, 20 July 2009. See also Baker, 'Limits of Rahmism'; and Scott Wilson, 'Bruised by Stimulus Battle, Obama Changed His Approach to Washington', *Washington Post*, 29 April 2009.
8 *Brian Friel, 'Democrats Face Daunting Legislative Agenda', National Journal Online, 9 May 2009.*
9 Jonathan Alter, *The Promise: President Obama, Year One* (New York: Simon & Schuster, 2010), 79.
10 Barack Obama, *Dreams from My Father* (New York: Crown Publishers, 1995), 106.
11 Quoted in Ken Auletta, 'Non-Stop News', *New Yorker*, 25 January 2010, p. 44.
12 George C. Edwards III, *On Deaf Ears: The Limits of the Bully Pulpit* (New Haven, CT: Yale University Press, 2003).
13 Edwards, *Strategic President*, 26–34; George C. Edwards III, *Governing by Campaigning: The Politics of the Bush Presidency*, 2nd edn (New York: Longman, 2007).
14 See Edwards, *Strategic President*, chaps 2–3, 6.
15 Edwards, *On Deaf Ears*.
16 Quoted in Dan Balz, 'He Promised Change, but Is This Too Much, Too Soon?', *Washington Post*, 26 July 2009.
17 Shailagh Murray and Paul Kane, 'Obama's Ambitious Agenda Will Test Congress', *Washington Post*, 26 February 2009.
18 Ronald Brownstein and Alexis Simendinger, 'The View for the West Wing', *National Journal*, 16 January 2010, p. 27.
19 Wilson, 'Bruised by Stimulus Battle, Obama Changed His Approach to Washington'.
20 For example, White House communications director Anita Dunn concluded that the administration failed at selling health care reform as a central part of its economic message. Dan Balz, 'For Obama, a Tough Year to Get the Message Out', *Washington Post*, 10 January 2010.
21 Barack Obama, State of the Union Address, 27 January 2010.
22 George C. Edwards III, *At the Margins: Presidential Leadership of Congress* (New Haven, CT: Yale University Press, 1989), chap. 8; Lawrence J. Grossback, David A. M. Peterson and James A. Stimson, *Mandate Politics* (New York: Cambridge University Press, 2006).
23 For more on the conditions that encourage perceptions of a mandate, see Edwards, *At the Margins*, chap. 8; and Grossback, Peterson and Stimson, *Mandate Politics*, chap. 2.
24 Transcript of press conference on 25 November 2008.
25 ABC News/*Washington Post* poll, 13–16 January 2009.
26 Barack Obama, Inaugural Address, 20 January 2009.
27 Gallup poll daily tracking polls, throughout 2009. The sample includes 291,152 US adults. The margin of sampling error for most states is ±2 percentage points, but is as high as ±5 percentage points for the District of Columbia.
28 Gallup poll surveys conducted January–September 2009.
29 Shawn Treier and D. Sunshine Hillygus, 'The Nature of Political Ideology in the Contemporary Electorate', *Public Opinion Quarterly*, 73 (Winter 2009), 679–703; Christopher Ellis and James A. Stimson, 'Symbolic Ideology in the American Electorate', *Electoral Studies*, 28 (September 2009), 388–402; William G. Jacoby, 'Policy Attitudes, Ideology, and Voting Behavior in the 2008 Election' (paper presented at the Annual Meeting of the American Political Science Association, 2009); James A. Stimson, *Tides of Consent: How Public Opinion Shapes American Politics* (New York: Cambridge University Press, 2004); Pamela J. Conover and Stanley Feldman, 'The Origins and Meaning of Liberal/Conservative Identifications', *American Journal of Political Science*, 25 (October 1981), 617–645; David O. Sears, Richard L. Lau, Tom R. Tyler and Harris M. Allen, 'Self-Interest vs. Symbolic Politics in Policy Attitudes and Presidential Voting', *American Political Science Review*, 74 (September 1980), 670–684.
30 Philip E. Converse, 'The Nature of Belief Systems in Mass Publics', in David E. Apter, ed., *Ideology and Discontent* (New York: Free Press, 1964), 206–261.
31 Teresa E. Levitin and Warren E. Miller, 'Ideological Interpretations of Presidential Elections', *American Political Science Review*, 73 (September 1979), 751–771.

32 Robert Huckfeldt, Jeffrey Levine, William Morgan and John Sprague, 'Accessibility and the Political Utility of Partisan and Ideological Orientations', *American Journal of Political Science*, 43 (July 1999), 888–911; Kathleen Knight, 'Ideology in the 1980 Election: Ideological Sophistication Does Matter', *Journal of Politics*, 47 (July 1985), 828–853; Levitin and Miller, 'Ideological Interpretations of Presidential Elections'; James A. Stimson, 'Belief Systems: Constraint, Complexity, and the 1972 Election', *American Journal of Political Science*, 19 (July 1975), 393–417.

33 Paul Goren, Christopher M. Federico and Miki Caul Kittilson, 'Source Cues, Partisan Identities, and Political Value Expression', *American Journal of Political Science*, 53 (October 2009), 805–820; Christopher M. Federico and Monica C. Schneider, 'Political Expertise and the Use of Ideology: Moderating the Effects of Evaluative Motivation', *Public Opinion Quarterly*, 71 (Summer 2007), 221–252; William G. Jacoby, 'Value Choices and American Public Opinion', *American Journal of Political Science*, 50 (July 2006), 706–723; Paul Goren, 'Political Sophistication and Policy Reasoning: A Reconsideration', *American Journal of Political Science*, 48 (July 2004), 462–478; Paul Goren, 'Core Principles and Policy Reasoning in Mass Publics: A Test of Two Theories', *British Journal of Political Science*, 31 (January 2001), 159–177; Huckfeldt, Levine, Morgan and Sprague, 'Accessibility and the Political Utility of Partisan and Ideological Orientations'; William G. Jacoby, 'The Structure of Ideological Thinking in the American Electorate', *American Journal of Political Science*, 39 (April 1995), 314–335; William G. Jacoby, 'Ideological Identification and Issue Attitudes', *American Journal of Political Science*, 35 (January 1991), 178–205; Stanley Feldman, 'Structure and Consistency in Public Opinion: The Role of Core Beliefs and Attitudes', *American Journal of Political Science*, 32 (May 1988), 416–440; Sears, Lau, Tyler and Allen, 'Self-Interest vs. Symbolic Politics'.

34 Thomas J. Rudolph and Jillian Evans, 'Political Trust, Ideology, and Public Support for Government Spending', *American Journal of Political Science*, 49 (July 2005), 660–671; William G. Jacoby, 'Issue Framing and Government Spending', *American Journal of Political Science*, 44 (October 2000), 750–767; William G. Jacoby, 'Public Attitudes toward Government Spending', *American Journal of Political Science*, 38 (April 1994), 336–361.

35 Andrew Kohut, 'Obama's 2010 Challenge: Wake Up Liberals, Calm Down Independents', Pew Research Center for the People and the Press, 17 December 2009.

36 The poll did not define the term 'traditional values'. Gallup found that, when it disaggregated the results by party and ideology, they suggested that respondents understood traditional values to be those generally favoured by the Republican Party.

37 Gallup poll, 31 August – 2 September 2009.

38 Gallup polls, 13–16 November 2008 and 5–8 November 2009.

39 Phil Mattingly, 'Debt Takes a Holiday', *CQ Weekly*, 28 December 2009, pp. 2934–2941.

40 *USA Today*/Gallup polls of 27–29 March 2009.

41 Gallup poll, 17–19 July 2009.

42 *Washington Post*/ABC News poll, 15–18 July 2009.

43 *New York Times*/CBS News poll, 5–10 February 2010.

44 Gallup poll, 6–9 August 2009.

45 Gallup poll, 31 August – 2 September 2009.

46 Robert S. Erikson, Michael B. MacKuen and James A. Stimson, *The Macro Polity* (New York: Cambridge University Press, 2002), chap. 9.

47 See Gary C. Jacobson, *A Divider, Not a Uniter: George W. Bush and the American Public*, 3rd edn (New York: Longman, 2010).

48 If independent leaners are included as partisans, the figure rises to 8.0 per cent; only John F. Kennedy attracted fewer (7.1 per cent). These figures are from Gary C. Jacobson, 'Legislative Success and Political Failure: The Public's Reaction to Barack Obama's Early Presidency', *Presidential Studies Quarterly*, 41 (June 2011), 221.

49 Ibid., 221–222.

50 Kate Kenski, Bruce W. Hardy and Kathleen Hall Jamieson, *The Obama Victory: How Media, Money, and Message Shaped the 2008 Election* (New York: Oxford University Press, 2010).

51 Spencer Piston, 'How Explicit Racial Prejudice Hurt Obama in the 2008 Election', *Political Behavior*, 32 (December 2010), 431–451; Michael Lewis-Back, Charles Tien and Richard Nadeau, 'Obama's Missed Landslide: A Racial Cost?', *PS: Political Science and Politics*, 43 (January 2010), 69–76.

52 Jay Cost, 'Electoral Polarization Continues under Obama', *RealClearPolitics*, HorseRaceBlog, 20 November 2008.

53 Alan I. Abramowitz, *The Disappearing Center* (New Haven, CT: Yale University Press, 2010).

54 Jeffrey M. Jones, 'Obama's Approval Most Polarized for First-Year President', Gallup poll, 25 January 2010; Jeffrey M. Jones, 'Bush Ratings Show Historical Levels of Polarization', *Gallup News Service*, 4 June 2004.
55 Charlie Cook, 'Intensity Matters', *National Journal*, 24 October 2009.
56 Democracy Corps poll, 19–22 June 2010.
57 CNN poll conducted by Opinion Research Corporation, 16–21 July 2010. See also *Adam J. Berinsky, Pollster.com, 13 September 2010*, www.pollster.com/blogs/poll_shows_false_obama_beliefs.php.
58 Pew Research Center for the People and the Press poll, 21 July – 5 August 2010.
59 *Newsweek* poll, 25–26 August 2010.
60 As Gary Jacobson points out, some of the mistaken views about Obama were probably driven by opinions about Obama more generally. See 'Legislative Success and Political Failure', 229–230.
61 Pew Research Media Attitudes Survey, 22–26 July 2009.
62 Gallup poll, 11–13 June 2010.
63 Gallup poll, 23–24 June 2009.
64 Gallup poll, 24–25 May 2010.
65 Edwards, *Strategic President*, chaps 4–5; Edwards, *At the Margins*, chaps 9–10; Jon R. Bond and Richard Fleisher, *The President in the Legislative Arena* (Chicago, IL: University of Chicago Press, 1990), chap. 8; Richard Fleisher, Jon R. Bond and B. Dan Wood, 'Which Presidents Are Uncommonly Successful in Congress?', in Bert Rockman and Richard W. Waterman, eds., *Presidential Leadership: The Vortex of Presidential Power* (New York: Oxford University Press, 2007); Keith Krehbiel, *Pivotal Politics: A Theory of U.S. Lawmaking* (Chicago, IL: University of Chicago Press, 1998), chaps 7–8.
66 Shailagh Murray, Michael D. Shear and Paul Kane, '2009 Democratic Agenda Severely Weakened by Republicans' United Opposition', *Washington Post*, 24 January 2010.
67 Transcript of press conference on 25 November 2008.
68 Wilson, 'Bruised by Stimulus Battle, Obama Changed His Approach to Washington'.
69 John Harwood, '"Partisan" Seeks a Prefix: Bi- or Post-', *New York Times*, 6 December 2008.
70 See George C. Edwards III, *Overreach: Strategic Assessments in the Obama Presidency* (Princeton, NJ: Princeton University Press, 2012), chap. 5.
71 Nolan McCarty, Keith T. Poole and Howard Rosenthal, *Polarized America: The Dance of Ideology and Unequal Riches* (Cambridge, MA: MIT Press, 2006).
72 Shawn Zeller, 'Party Unity – Parties Dig In Deep on a Fractured Hill', *CQ Weekly*, 15 December 2008, pp. 3332–3341.
73 John Cranford, 'This Change Isn't Very Hopeful', *CQ Weekly*, 17 February 2009, p. 335.
74 Richard Rubin, 'Party Unity: An Ever Thicker Dividing Line', *CQ Weekly*, 11 January 2010, p. 124.
75 Gary C. Jacobson, 'Barack Obama and the American Public: From Candidate to President', *Presidential Studies Quarterly*, 41 (June 2011), 220–243.
76 See, for example, Gallup polls, 4–7 December 2010 and 7–9 January 2011; and Pew Research Center for the People and the Press poll, 5–9 January 2011.
77 Ronald Brownstein, 'For GOP, a Southern Exposure', *National Journal*, 23 May 2009.
78 Nate Silver, 'Popularity of "Don't Ask" Repeal May Have Drawn Republican Votes', *New York Times*, 19 December 2010.
79 Bruce Smith, 'Graham Censured by Charleston County GOP', *The State*, 12 November 2009.
80 Lexington County Republican Party, 'Lexington County Party Passes Resolution of Censure for Lindsey Graham', accessed at www.lcrp-online.com/1.html.
81 Robert Draper, 'Lindsey Graham, This Year's Maverick', *New York Times*, 4 July 2010.
82 Pew Research Center for the People and the Press poll, 6–10 January 2010.
83 Alan K. Ota, 'GOP Moderates See Political Benefits in Opposing Obama's Economic Agenda', *CQ Today*, 6 February 2009.
84 Frances E. Lee, *Beyond Ideology: Politics, Principles, and Partisanship in the U.S. Senate* (Chicago, IL: University of Chicago Press, 2009), chap. 4.
85 See Edwards, *Overreach*, chap. 3.
86 Edwards, *Overreach*, chap. 3.
87 Kohut, 'Obama's 2010 Challenge'.
88 Charlie Cook, 'Colossal Miscalculation on Health Care', *National Journal*, 16 January 2010.
89 Charlie Cook, 'Too Much All at Once', *Off to the Races*, 2 February 2010.
90 *Washington Post*/ABC News poll, 12–15 January 2010.

2 The problem of presidential strategy

Jon Herbert

Introduction

As President Obama neared the end of his first term, claims that he had failed as president were plentiful. The accusation came not just from Republicans eager to evict him from office, but from disappointed Democrats and a public frustrated with a recalcitrant economy. Explanations of the apparent failure included poor leadership skills, poor policy choices and misplaced priorities. In the preceding chapter, George Edwards raises a more considered explanation, that of strategic incompetence. He portrays an administration adopting flawed strategies derived both from misreadings of governing context and from misplaced faith in their chosen leadership strategies. He argues that the administration believed that the public, including some Republicans, would support Obama's legislative proposals because of the crises of 2008 and the president's rhetoric. Edwards proves that this support was not forthcoming. He also argues that the administration pursued bipartisanship believing that some Republican members of Congress would be persuaded to support Obama's proposals. Edwards shows that those legislators remained loyal to their party and explains why. He argues that the administration believed in an 'advancing tide' (or momentum) theory of presidential success, by which one legislative success would create more favourable contexts for further proposals. Edwards outlines good reasons to doubt such a theory. Finally, he argues that the administration, labouring under these delusions, adopted a comprehensive legislative agenda which, if strategic reality had been acknowledged, would have been recognized as impractical. This strategic naïveté is seen to have contributed to legislative failures, the 2010 midterm results and weakening of the administration's governing position. For Edwards, the lesson to draw from Obama's first two years is that presidencies cannot create their own possibilities, but must facilitate change within relatively narrow boundaries set by election results, public sentiment and both partisanship and ideology within Congress.

Edwards nearly generates an 'impossible presidency' argument, by which presidents cannot lead. He argues that the success of 'going public' and bipartisan strategies depends upon the fulfilment of unlikely conditions: a president requires public tolerance of governmental activism, support from opposition party identifiers among the public and support from moderate opposition party legislators. Edwards also argues elsewhere that presidents can do little to change public or congressional sentiment.[1] Research on increasing partisanship reinforces his message: as government institutions and the US public have become more partisan, there are fewer independents or weakly identifying partisans to win to a president's cause. Partisans seem more resistant to persuasion from an opposition party president, while opposition legislators are increasingly unlikely to support their opponents' proposals.[2] Such difficulties are exaggerated by the increasingly super-majoritarian character of the Senate, where it is difficult to garner the 60 votes required to invoke cloture and overcome the filibuster.[3] Effectively, Edwards portrays a constrained presidency, where leadership, presented as facilitation, is virtually reduced to ratification of public and congressional sentiment.

This approach does both the Obama administration and the leadership potential of the presidency a disservice. First, Edwards's characterization of Obama's strategy, and its failure, is open to challenge. Obama's legislative failings are overstated. Of the major legislative proposals that the administration supported with significant resources in 2009 and 2010, most reached the statute books. Once these successes are noted, a paradox results: why should a presidency marked by significant legislative achievement be considered strategically incompetent? This paradox derives from our limited understanding of presidential strategizing, which allows misinterpretation of presidential actions and so misreading of presidential strategy. Focusing on the 111th Congress, this chapter offers a different conception of Obama's presidential strategy rooted in recent scholarship on the partisan presidency and pivotal voters, plus a rethinking of presidential 'going public'.

The Obama agenda and legislative failure

To condemn the Obama administration as a failure on legislative grounds seems perverse. Equally, the evidence does not suggest that the administration pursued an overwhelming agenda. The administration passed a $787 billion stimulus package, the American Recovery and Reinvestment Act (ARRA). This package included $288 million worth of tax cuts, and substantial investments. Infrastructure was improved through investment in the electricity grid, transport modernization and enhanced broadband and wireless internet access. Education spending was boosted by $4.35 billion, presented through the 'Race to the Top' initiative designed to encourage state-level innovations. Tax credits for college tuition, energy conservation and renewable energy production also featured. Unemployment assistance was extended, and scientific and medical research investment made. The stimulus package could have constituted many separate, major achievements for Obama. Noting other achievements, such as tobacco regulation, a credit cardholders' bill of rights, defence procurement reform and expanded children's health insurance provision, Norman Ornstein of the American Enterprise Institute labelled Obama's first year as a period of 'record accomplishment'.[4] The following year, the administration passed its momentous health care reform and added the Dodd–Frank Wall Street Reform and Consumer Protection Act, designed to re-regulate the financial system. Unambiguously, the administration's first two years were marked by substantial legislative achievements.

Suggesting that faith in their strategic choices allowed the administration to adopt an overwhelming agenda is also overstating. It is notable how few measures received extensive White House backing during the 111th Congress and were then rejected. Clearly, some dreamed of a twenty-first-century New Deal, and Obama's campaign promises did not disabuse them of this fantasy. The incoming administration confronted an extraordinary range of demands, whether from their own partisans' stratospheric expectations or public concern over pressing issues. However, the administration did not begin with a Jimmy Carter-esque stream of legislative proposals, each declared a priority and inducing confusion and consternation in Congress. Rather, Obama's team clearly recognized the need to act on few legislative items at any one time, delivering a measured process which allowed presidential resources to be concentrated on the highest priorities, sometimes despite extraordinary distractions. Indeed, the administration fought to keep issues off the agenda to avoid clogging committees or distracting from core concerns, even when such priorities incurred political costs. Most notably, in early 2010, congressional Democrats pushed the administration to soft-pedal health care reform and refocus on the economy. Instead, the administration pushed for its extraordinary health care victory.

Only one proposal received extensive administration attention, including public declarations of support and considerable congressional liaison efforts, but then failed. Administration pursuit of energy and climate change policy reform can be considered an outright legislative failure. Administration efforts were sabotaged by the Deepwater Horizon oil spill. The administration indicated a willingness to permit exploratory drilling in new areas that included the Gulf of Mexico, to capture conservative support for reform, but the spill reinforced liberal resistance to compromise, rendering difficult negotiations impossible. Many administration decisions may have been poor politics or policy in other respects, but suggesting that the administration actively chose an inappropriately large and therefore strategically unrealistic agenda is not sustained by the evidence. The administration failed to push, for example, immigration reform, but this reflected tough, necessary choices, not strategic incompetence.

Thus a paradox is established. An administration with legislative successes is alleged to have adopted a flawed strategy. Addressing this paradox demands a re-examination of the Obama administration's strategy. Edwards argues that the administration placed its faith in bipartisanship and 'going public'. Substantial evidence suggests that these strategies were widely misunderstood.

Obama's bipartisanship?

As US politics became more partisan, the presidency's strategic options narrowed.[5] The forces shaping presidential conduct channel presidents into more partisan behaviour. Confronting a more partisan Congress, presidents have less opportunity to win waverers from the other party to support legislation. Therefore presidents pursue bipartisan legislative strategies less often. Partisan media push presidents toward outlets which report favourably on them. Presidents attempt to mobilize the party base among the public, often best achieved by taking positions close to one's own base and demonizing the other party. Structural incentives push presidents towards their partisan base to underpin governing strategy. Rather than wooing opposing party members who lean towards the president's ideology, the president works to retain support from his own-party legislators. The party, now more ideologically aligned than in previous decades, must be roused by the president. Effectively, as growing partisanship weakens potential for bipartisanship, it has, under appropriate conditions and handling, created opportunities for presidential leadership in Congress. If the president faces a Congress controlled by his own party's majorities, he can legislate, because his own party is more likely to rally in support. As George W. Bush proved, enormous benefits can be gleaned from such a strategy, as shown by then-extraordinary levels of support for his legislative proposals.[6] Obama's main strategic advantage was neither rhetorical talent nor the malleability of independent or Republican support, but his own party's majorities in Congress. Democrats held a 257–178 majority in the House and a near filibuster-proof 58–40 majority in the Senate. For Obama, then, substantial structural incentives pushed him towards a partisan strategy.

Yet candidate Obama had presented himself as a bipartisan, even post-partisan, leader. In *The Audacity of Hope*, Obama condemned the havoc wrought by partisanship in Washington and the broader US.[7] In his election night speech, he revisited the theme:

Americans who sent a message to the world that we have never been just a collection of individuals or a collection of red states and blue states. We are, and always will be, the United States of America. . . . In this country, we rise or fall as one nation, as one people. Let's resist the temptation to fall back on the same partisanship and pettiness and immaturity that has poisoned our politics for so long. . . . As Lincoln said to a nation far more divided than ours, 'We are not enemies but friends. Though passion may have strained, it must not break our bonds of affection.'[8]

Obama continued his bipartisan rhetoric in office, right through to the midterm campaign of 2010.[9] The administration also made substantial efforts to communicate with Republicans. Symbolic events were staged to demonstrate Obama's openness to cooperation. A public conference with Republicans over economic policy was organized in January 2009, and Obama visited congressional Republicans to discuss the stimulus package. A bipartisan health care summit took place in February 2010. The administration supported the development of bipartisan legislation on key issues. Particularly in the Senate, the administration encouraged centrist groups operating across party boundaries to negotiate reform proposals. On health care, a 'Gang of Six' senators from the Senate Finance Committee, including Republicans Charles Grassley, Olympia Snowe and Michael Enzi, were given months to develop a proposal. On energy and environment issues, the administration encouraged Senator John Kerry to work with Republican Senator Lindsey Graham to develop reforms with bipartisan appeal. Even when these initiatives failed, the administration pursued Republican votes for its reforms. For example, the administration conducted an extended and sometimes undignified courting of Snowe, all in the hope of earning a single Republican vote for health care reform.

Bipartisanship appeared fundamental to Obama's approach. One author described him as 'wedded to a naïve and platonic ideal of bipartisanship'.[10] Another offered psychological explanations of his 'obsessive bipartisan disorder'.[11] Many considered him strategically inept. According to Eugene Robinson, 'in a number of specific instances, especially early on, Obama erred by offering self-defeating concessions to Republicans who had no good-faith intention of seeking compromise'. It therefore 'took the administration far too long to realize that the overall Republican strategy was not to negotiate but simply to say no – even to the point of rejecting ideas the party had supported in the past'.[12]

Despite evidence that Obama talked bipartisan, organized bipartisan gatherings, encouraged bipartisan policy planning and appealed for Republican support of his proposals, he also used partisan leadership techniques. First, his White House staff featured many committed partisans. Most notably, Rahm Emanuel, notorious for partisan endeavours during his congressional service, was appointed Chief of Staff and the administration's 'field general' for policy planning and congressional dealings over the stimulus.[13] Second, policy was often planned in a partisan manner. The administration and the Democratic congressional leadership met to plan the stimulus package on an almost daily basis during Obama's transition to office. Repeatedly, Obama did not propose legislative specifics initially, allowing congressional Democrats to draw together proposals. For example, despite the health care 'Gang of Six' discussions, Hacker notes that health care reform was the product of Democrats' intra-party concessions.[14] Republicans resented their exclusion, vocally. Third, Obama relied heavily on Democratic congressional leadership, his work with Speaker Nancy Pelosi and Senate Majority Leader Harry Reid tying him to his own-party delegations. The administration may have preached bipartisanship, but it developed relationships and policy proposals that would later allow a switch to partisanship.

Most significantly, many of Obama's legislative triumphs relied upon partisan votes. The stimulus bill passed the House without a single Republican vote, and won over only three Republicans in the Senate. Health care did not win a floor vote from a Republican in the Senate and only one House Republican vote. Not every achievement was quite as partisan. Re-regulating the financial markets won bipartisan support, as did a handful of agreements made during the winter 2010 lame-duck session. However, overall party unity scores from the 111th Congress reflect very high levels of partisan voting. In the House, the proportion of each party voting with the majority of their party in partisan votes topped 90 per cent for both Democrats and Republicans. The same was nearly true of the supposedly less partisan Senate, Democrats voting with their party on partisan votes on 89.3 per cent of occasions and Democrats doing so 93.2 per cent of the time. The preponderance of partisan roll call votes in the Senate, that is, the number of times that at least half of each party lined up against the other, leapt to a figure unmatched for a century of 75.1 per cent.[15]

Debates raged over the responsibility for bipartisanship's absence. Republicans, both Tea Party and establishment, alleged that Obama's bipartisan front masked a traditional Democrat hell-bent upon a high-spending, budget-breaking, secular, big (or 'socialist') government. Meanwhile, Democrats highlighted Republican intransigence in policy negotiations and the stridency of Republican opposition. For example, by July 2009, the Republican National Committee was running advertisements in 33 states casting Obama's health care plans as a 'dangerous experiment'. Observers noted the advantages that outright Republican opposition to a Democratic president had gleaned in 1993 and 1994, suggesting that Republicans were exploiting the potential for history to repeat itself, to their benefit.[16]

Whoever was to blame, the Obama administration had retained the capacity to switch to a partisan strategy and relied upon partisan votes in Congress, so labelling his strategy as 'bipartisan' seems simplistic. Whether the administration used 'going public', as presidential scholars would normally understand it, is also questionable.

Obama goes public?

Coe and Reitzes argue that Obama's 'formidable rhetorical skills have been a central component of his public persona and his political success'.[17] Bligh and Kohles suggest that his charismatic appeal, expressed through rhetoric, shaped the 2008 election result.[18] Many journalists share this view. Obama's campaign also won attention for innovative use of social media, some crediting the campaign with an inspired innovation that influenced the election result.[19] Some eagerly anticipated these techniques' translation to the challenges of governing: the internet seemed to offer opportunities to extend the permanent campaign through new means to persuade the public.

Kernell's classic model of 'going public' suggests that presidents court public opinion to influence legislators' votes in Congress. Broad public appeals are propagated to make the president popular.[20] Edwards's analysis additionally considers whether the administration made its chosen policies popular, concluding that it did not.

Much press ink and many bytes have been consumed in explaining the administration's failure to win such support. Some blamed the administration, particularly David Axelrod as Obama's senior adviser and primary architect of his communications strategy.[21] Others detected broader problems in the administration's lack of message.[22] Allegedly, an incompetent communications operation allowed Republicans to control the administration's narrative, portraying Obama as a budget-busting liberal remote from the American people.

Others argued that the administration never tried to win public support. Hacker suggests that no intense campaign to win public support for health care reform took place.[23] Few noted any 'Facebook model' of governing, employing the successful social media techniques of 2008 to garner public support. David Plouffe, key to the social media innovations, disengaged himself from the business of governing, only taking an external advisory role in 2009. It is legitimate to ask whether the administration even attempted to 'go public' and, if it did, what role public liaison efforts played within the administration's overall strategy.

Obama deployed many formats to project messages: interviews with journalists, town hall meetings, news conferences, major televised addresses and informal remarks, both in Washington, DC and across the nation. While establishing the intended audience for a particular event can be difficult, certain types of event are usually directed to reach the broader US public. The following discussion considers Obama's use of major addresses, interviews, town hall meetings and remarks delivered to publics outside Washington.

Obama delivered very few major addresses on domestic policy. Beyond his inaugural and State of the Union addresses, he delivered four main addresses during his first two years in office. Two addressed Afghanistan and Iraq, leaving only two on domestic issues, on health care reform in September 2009 and on the oil spill in the Gulf of Mexico during June 2010.

Administration use of town hall meetings was limited. Excepting a period between May and August 2009, the administration rarely exploited this format. Obama did travel, delivering remarks to audiences outside Washington, but they appear to have been carefully rationed. In 13 of 24 months studied, Obama delivered public remarks outside Washington fewer than ten times. This was not a president trying to lead purely through public rhetoric.

The timing of Obama's remarks outside Washington raises a further question. Did the presidency 'go public' to persuade Congress to support legislation? If he had been following Kernell's characterization of 'going public', Obama would have issued relevant rhetoric shortly preceding key congressional votes.

Examining the relevant timing closely reveals that the greatest efforts to go public did not coincide with key votes. Figure 2.1 represents Obama's attempts to go public during the

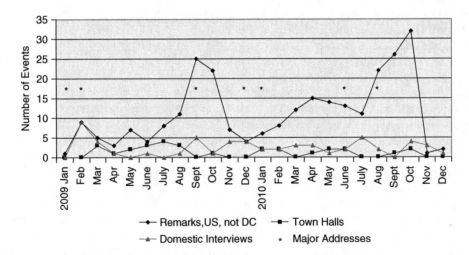

Figure 2.1   Obama goes public: presidential remarks outside Washington, town hall meetings, interviews to domestic outlets and major televised addresses

Source: Data compiled by the author, derived from Gerhard Peters and John T. Woolley, *The American Presidency Project*, http://www.presidency.ucsb.edu.

111th Congress through the means listed. Clearly, the administration chose certain periods to emphasize public engagement. The data suggest three such periods. First, Obama spoke more in September and October 2009. The number of presidential remarks outside Washington is high, Obama gave an unusual number of interviews to domestic news sources, and the major address was delivered on health care. Most notably, on 20 September, Obama appeared on an unprecedented five Sunday morning news shows to advocate health care reform. The second period of peak activity occurred in June, July and August 2010. Obama delivered a relatively high level of public remarks, while offering a high number of interviews and two major addresses. Both peak periods were preceded by an uptick in the number of town hall meetings. The third period of more intense communication over August, September and October 2010, marked particularly by remarks from Obama outside Washington, related to the looming November 2010 midterm elections.

The peak periods do not correlate with any classic understanding of 'going public'. In September and October 2009, no major reform was close to passage. The health care reform was under consideration by the Senate Finance Committee, while Dodd–Frank and the energy bill had made little progress. The deployment of Obama in public was not timed to sway key votes on the floors of Congress.

The second peak period, between June and August 2010, is more complicated. Major Obama proposals were receiving attention in Congress. Key votes on Dodd–Frank took place in the House in June and the Senate in July. Obama launched energy and environmental policy reform just weeks before the oil spill which would provide the focus of his major address on 15 June. However, closer examination reveals that these legislative proposals were not the primary subjects of Obama's communication. Obama delivered 13 sets of remarks outside Washington during June 2010. Eight were delivered in Southern locations and directly addressed the impact of, and government response to, the Gulf of Mexico oil spill. Proposed energy and climate change reform barely featured. His major address on the oil spill, only mentioned, without much detail, energy and climate change reform at the end. Four sets of remarks discussed the US economy, with particular emphasis on help provided for small businesses and the virtues of ARRA. Re-regulating the financial markets received little attention. A high school commencement address outlined the virtues of Obama's education initiatives. One of the two town hall meetings specifically highlighted the virtues of health care reform, while the other emphasized the economy.[24] In the first half of July, Obama delivered remarks in Maryland, Missouri and Nevada, each focusing on the economy.[25] Dodd–Frank received passing mention, as did ARRA efforts to develop green technologies, but only in the context of broader arguments about the role of government and the economic crisis. Obama was not using the bully pulpit to promote the major reforms under consideration in Congress. Rather, Obama's rhetoric suggests early campaigning before the midterms, with attendant partisanship and defence of his record. By mid-July, the fate of Obama's policy proposals was sealed. Dodd–Frank was cleared for presidential signature on 15 July, while the energy and climate reform was shelved by congressional leaders.

The Obama administration did not follow the 'going public' model. Its conduct did not suggest any assumption of a straightforward relationship by which presidential attempts to influence the public registered in increased issue salience or greater public support for the specific reform proposal. While Obama did employ public travel and rhetoric, he did not go public in a classic manner, nor was he unambiguously bipartisan. The Obama strategy requires more detailed explanation to explain presidential behaviour and successes.

A framework for studying strategy

Much has been written on presidential strategy. Various scholars have stressed the strategic context each president confronts, considering the balance of partisan power in Congress, election results, public support and budgetary resources. The term 'strategy' is used to refer to a myriad of concepts, including congressional strategies, communication strategies, strategic use of executive power and many further behaviours.[26] Confusion reigns over the purposes of presidential strategy and which behaviours should be considered strategic. Obama's first two years suggest the value of an approach based on the concept of 'pivotal voters' and the calculus underlying their voting decisions in Congress. Following this approach reveals that power lies in the presidency's capacity to influence the context in which pivotal voters make decisions.

The first assumption employed is that the Obama administration targeted legislative achievements during its first 18 months in office. Legislative success would be crucial to Obama's ability to be re-elected, given the promises of 2008. This assumption turns the focus of any account of presidential strategy to head counts in Congress. To achieve success, Obama needed a majority in the House and a super-majority in the Senate.

Studies of presidential–congressional relations highlight the importance of 'pivotal voters' in Congress. Brady and Volden, and Krehbiel develop spatial theories of voting, arguing that the key target for presidents trying to push policy proposals through Congress is the 'pivotal', or marginal, voter.[27] Legislators are ordered along a single ideological scale from conservative to liberal, allowing identification of those whose ideological position is closer to any potential reform proposal than the status quo. Theoretically, a strategically sophisticated presidency can design a reform proposal with an ideology to just glean a passing vote, thus bringing policy as close as possible to the presidency's preferred position. The key legislative player in this process is the 'pivotal voter' at the margin: in the House, with its simple majority rules, the legislator who takes reform support above 50 per cent, and, in the Senate, the 60th voter needed to overcome filibusters. Naturally, presidents will concentrate their lobbying on those at the pivots.[28] Strategy, considered here as a series of decisions on how to employ presidential tools and resources, therefore, becomes a process of winning over the pivotal voter. The Obama case demonstrates that pivotal voters were the hub of strategic planning, but, by considering the decision-making calculus of pivotal voters, it identifies how the presidency used its influence to exploit that calculus.

If pivotal voters are assumed to be strategy's primary focus, any 'going public' is subservient to this goal. This requires a rethinking of how the success of public appeals should be assessed. When Kernell identified 'going public', he recorded the increasing tendency for presidents to speak publicly, particularly through minor addresses. The core of his work was an observation of presidential behaviour. He also promoted these behaviours to a leadership 'strategy', by which presidents levered a recalcitrant Congress into action through the power of personal popularity. However, Kernell's 'strategy' label is often over-interpreted, as though offering an independent form of presidential leadership. In its crudest usage, 'going public' conjures up images of Teddy Roosevelt's bully pulpit as the means to convert a nation's opinion. Presidential leadership thrives or founders according to the ability to make an appeal as judged by the public opinion numbers that follow. Edwards has done much to dismiss this naïve conception of a simple connection between presidency and public as an effective form of leadership.[29]

However, 'going public' is more complex than the naïve conception of a presidential–public connection can accommodate. As Kernell first defined it, 'going public' was a leadership strategy intended to induce results in Congress: as a key vote approaches, the presidency goes to the public, becomes popular, and induces a fear of electoral defeat among legislators that changes congressional votes. The penultimate clause is crucial here: the presidency influences legislators' decision-making calculus by shaping their perception of the route to re-election. Deploying presidential rhetoric was part of a broader strategy to muster votes in the legislature.

While this re-attachment of the presidency's public liaison efforts to congressional strategy is useful, it still oversimplifies Congress and its legislators. The idea that 'going public' can only be used to target key floor votes is questionable. For example, Eshbaugh-Soha and Miles highlight presidential efforts to influence committee proceedings, recognizing Congress's institutional complexity as offering other opportunities to go public productively.[30] Canes-Wrone recognizes that presidents may not need to change public opinion, but merely to activate existing public sentiment so that legislators must take it into account. She suggests that, through 'conditional pandering', presidents use appeals to move policy in the direction of majority opinion. Her work demonstrates the presidency's capacity to influence legislators' decision making.[31]

Re-attaching 'going public' to congressional strategy and allowing for more complexity in legislators' calculus offer more fruitful understandings of its possibilities and a means to address the conundrum posed by scholarship in the field: if, as alleged, 'going public' doesn't work, why do presidents still do it?

Obama's congressional context: Barack and the Blue Dogs

Undoubtedly, Obama would have welcomed Republican support for his proposals, had it been forthcoming. However, the 111th Congress that confronted Obama in 2009 did not, prima facie, dictate the need for a bipartisan approach. Assuming that Obama built legislative coalitions from his own party, Democratic majorities could serve him well. In the House, Obama needed 218 votes, with a caucus of 257 Democrats. The pivotal voter was in his own party. While the Senate picture was more complicated, once Arlen Specter (Republican, then Democrat, Pennsylvania) had defected, Al Franken (Democrat, Minnesota) had been seated and assuming that Joe Lieberman (Independent, Connecticut) retained a residual loyalty to his former party, no Republican support was required to overcome a filibuster. Obama did not need Republican votes. The real constraint was not his inability to persuade wavering Republicans or independents among the public. His primary strategic challenge was derived from his partisan support in Congress: to keep his party sufficiently together by winning over the pivotal voters within it.

The idea of a single, crucial, pivotal voter is unrealistically clear cut. The generation of useful theory demands a little more precision than reality can strictly support. If a president persuades the marginal voter to support a proposal, one might assume that he has moved the legislator towards the president's ideological position.[32] If so, the pivotal legislator may sacrifice his or her pivotal position to another legislator. Therefore the presidency may have to woo a handful of legislators. The legislative tendency to act in groups also suggests that the single pivotal voter idea is too precise. Pivotal voters often identify themselves as part of caucuses, rely upon cues from colleagues when time and energy for information gathering are scarce, and sometimes appreciate the political cover of group support. Rather than one voter, Obama required support from a number of Democrats.

The Democratic caucus in the 111th Congress presented a problem traditional to Democratic presidents. While the party maintained a liberal core, the congressional Democrats were not ideologically homogeneous.[33] The liberal core were too few to pass legislation alone, needing support from more conservative Democrats. Particularly, one group of moderates occupied pivotal ground in the House, the 'Blue Dogs'. This caucus consisted of centrist Democrats, usually elected from mid-West and Southern districts. After the party's electoral successes of 2006 and 2008, the caucus had grown by 19 new 'Blue Pups', creating a substantial body of 54 members. The very electoral triumphs that helped Obama's party increase its majority in Congress also defined the key problem for governing, by generating a strained party majority.

The Blue Dogs were not only, as pivotal voters, key to Obama generating congressional majorities in House floor votes. They also held significant committee positions, giving them disproportionate influence over Obama's proposals. Notably, eight Blue Dogs served on the House Energy and Commerce Committee, allowing them to bottle up Obama's health care reform if they so chose. Also, many interests in the health industry had aligned themselves with these conservative Democrats, making them particularly important in negotiating health care reform.[34]

While the Blue Dogs did not subscribe to one consistent ideology, their power was tied to a broadly similar set of values. Blue Dogs were concerned about the budget deficit and especially controlling federal spending, which they worried could undermine economic growth. Many evinced a strong concern for the well-being of small businesses. Most also subscribed to some social conservative positions, notably mid-Westerners supporting gun rights and many taking a pro-life position. Many were also intensely aware of their electoral vulnerability. Democrats had won many Republican-leaning districts by small margins. They worried about their re-election prospects, looking nervously at districts with career-threatening proportions of conservative voters. Forty-nine House Democrats won in 2008 despite majorities in their districts voting John McCain for president. This electoral vulnerability shaped the decision making of many Blue Dogs when they cast votes in Congress, as they considered how each decision might impact upon their re-election.

The administration's strategy to win their pivotal votes was based in understanding the Blue Dogs' incentives, as derived from the legislators' strategic situations. By grasping the calculus applied by pivotal voters when making voting decisions, the administration could then work to adjust that calculus in its favour by influencing the legislators' strategic circumstances. 'Going public' and images of bipartisanship both contributed to this re-shaping.

The Blue Dog calculus I: ideology and partisanship

Many Blue Dogs worried that they would be perceived in ideological terms as tax-and-spend liberals and in partisan terms as traditional Democrats. In competitive districts, such perceptions could cost them re-election. Instead, they presented themselves as ideologically moderate and weak partisans. Representative Bart Gordon (Democrat, Tennessee) explained: 'People in my district want me to be independent.'[35] Blue Dogs feared that the White House would 'force Blue Dogs "off into that swamp" of supporting bills that would be unpopular with voters back home'.[36]

When confronting Obama-sponsored proposals, Blue Dog Democrats could see each decision in both partisan and ideological terms. Voting with the president held the potential to make the Blue Dog look partisan and ideologically liberal. Voting against the president offered the opportunity to appear centrist and independent. Considering these dimensions, the incentives seemed to indicate the need to vote against the president. Therefore the administration's challenge, if Blue Dog votes were to be won, was to counterbalance these incentives. The administration needed to provide opportunities for legislators to present themselves as moderate and independent without voting against Obama proposals.

Allowing Blue Dogs to appear less partisan could be achieved in many ways. First, if Obama maintained his post-partisan image, those associated with his legislation would appear less as though they were voting with a partisan president. As detailed above, the administration worked to achieve this goal. Ironically, using a partisan strategy to pass legislation demanded that the administration appeared bipartisan. Second, achieving bipartisan support for legislation by finding Republican votes would provide cover for Democrat moderates supporting Obama's reforms. The administration also pursued this goal, although most notably in the Senate and largely unsuccessfully. Extended negotiations with moderate Republicans on the stimulus and with Snowe over health care were notable. The latter was particularly significant given that, at the time, the administration did not necessarily need Snowe's vote to pass legislation. The single Republican vote would have enabled administration claims of bipartisan support, providing at least a fig leaf of political cover for conservative Democrats supporting reform. Negotiation over legislative substance could also suggest independence from the party yoke. Without opposing the whole, moderate Democrats could demonstrate independence, and effectiveness as legislators, by defeating symbolic, radical elements of a proposal. The administration could collaborate in this process by guiding moderates to attackable targets.

Some of these approaches also fed into Blue Dog efforts to look moderate on the ideological dimension. Policy proposals had to be presented as moderate. Blue Dogs looked less extreme if they won concessions to make the legislation less radical. Unsurprisingly, these needs led to extensive and sometimes very public bargaining over legislative substance. The administration made an extensive insider effort to win Blue Dog support, employing direct discussion by organizing meetings between White House staff and legislators, and indirect leadership, encouraging party and committee leaders to lobby House colleagues.[37] The result was a series of negotiations reminiscent of traditional Neustadtian – 'power to persuade' – forms of presidential leadership, sometimes occurring behind the scenes and on other occasions performed as public theatre.

While the stimulus package consisted of spending levels to make a Blue Dog blanch, the moderates won concessions on greater transparency in federal spending and an administration commitment to the 'PayGo' principle, so that future spending programmes would be budget neutral. They also won funding for a commission to study Medicare and Medicaid's cost-effectiveness. Rhetoric surrounding the package reflected the bargaining, *Time* labelling the package an 'uneasy compromise between Western populist rhetoric about getting the economy going again but budget busting spending'.[38] Blue Dogs also negotiated gains in the drafting of financial regulation proposals, gutting provisions intended to address the problem of 'too-big-to-fail' businesses.[39]

Blue Dogs feared many elements of the proposed health care reform. They resisted the mandate on individuals to purchase coverage, fearing the impact on small businesses that would have to cover employees. Many disliked the proposed surtax on high incomes and feared the 'public option' of providing a widely available federal insurance programme. Blue Dogs also demanded clearer cost controls to attack long-term medical inflation before federal budgets were wrecked by the programme. Not all concerns featured lower spending, though, as some worried over the effect that low levels of Medicare compensation might have on rural doctors and hospitals. Negotiations were intense, particularly during July 2009, and Blue Dogs eked out numerous concessions, including adjustments to plans for the surtax on high-earners and so-called 'Cadillac plans' with extensive benefits. They also engineered protection from Medicare cuts for rural hospitals. Most notably, they weakened the public option, before moderates in the Senate forced its complete elimination.

Oversimplifying this bargaining process as purely a function of ideological differences would be convenient, but naïve. Blue Dogs were intensely aware of how they were perceived, along both partisan and ideological dimensions. The administration, needing Blue Dog votes and reading the strategic context, recognized the need to burnish its bipartisan credentials, to woo Republican support and to offer public concessions to pivotal voters. Frustrated liberals could only fulminate and hope for an outcome as close as possible to their ideological goals, or withdraw support and sacrifice any potential gains from reforms.[40]

The Blue Dog calculus II: the party label and 'effectiveness'

A further element of the Blue Dog calculus was crucial to administration appeals. Cox and McCubbins recognize that legislators' ability to be re-elected in part depends upon the reputation, including the effectiveness, of a legislator's party.[41] Legislators carry the party label into elections and trade on its marketability. A party perceived as ineffective in addressing national problems will struggle, particularly shaping elections in marginal districts. The incumbent presidency influences voters' judgement of party effectiveness: do president and party appear capable of responding to national problems? When they share a party label, this dynamic gives legislators a vested interest in their president's success. Hence perceptions of party effectiveness feature in the legislator's decision-making calculus. A legislator may disagree with a proposal on ideological grounds, but still support it because it will enhance the party's image. Strengthening a partisan ally in the presidency may also assist the legislator in achieving goals in future.[42]

This vested interest offers the presidency power, because the presidency can, through agenda setting, influence the grounds on which its effectiveness is judged. The Obama administration exploited this power, shaping the issues by which it, and by extension all Democrats, would be judged. Obama presented Blue Dogs with a choice. They could destroy the president's programme, potentially fatally weakening the presidency, their party and their own electability, or they could support his reforms.

Delivering this strategy involved two strands, one public and one congressional. The public strand demanded that the administration give very high profile to an issue, keeping public attention focused and establishing the key association between Obama's reputation and the success, or otherwise, of his proposals. The stakes had to be made clear very publicly, as in the intense period of going public over health care reform during September 2009. Media coverage that summer had featured dramatic demonstrations against administration proposals, and Democrats had faced hostile town hall meetings. Meanwhile, economic concerns pressed as recovery remained elusive; congressional Democrats toyed with dropping health care to make space for further economic measures. The administration's response was robust, re-asserting health care as the priority and effectively daring congressional Democrats to drop it from the agenda and wreck his image as an effective leader. Health care remained on the agenda. In early 2010, confronting Republican Scott Brown's shock victory in the Massachusetts Senate race and a similar wobble in Democratic resolve, the administration unleashed a comparable effort. Commentators described the administration as 'doubling down' on health care, recognizing the gambling with its reputation.[43] Was the party willing to look incompetent, as rejection of health care reform would imply, and sustain the consequent electoral damage? The aim was less to focus public attention on health care but more to emphasize Obama's personal involvement, so that Democrats uncomfortable with liberal-looking health care policy had less excuse to retreat from the Obama project. The administration heightened the stakes for wavering Democrats, providing a countervailing force to the desire to use the administration as contrast for their own moderation. The administration created this high-stakes environment for moderate Democrats, proving very willing to drive them 'off into that swamp'.

The second strand of this strategy was to articulate this framing of voting choices directly to the relevant legislators.[44] As Sinclair writes, the administration argued 'vigorously and incessantly to their members, and persuaded most that failing once again on health care reform would have electoral consequences worse than any resulting from passing a less than universally popular bill'.[45] Particularly, the administration cited the Clinton administration's experience, when the failure of Democratic majorities to pass a health care proposal was widely understood to have contributed to the party's catastrophic 1994 midterm performance. Historical precedent suggested that Democrats could not afford to fail. At worst, Obama presented Blue Dogs with a no-win situation; if they voted for reform they would be labelled tax-and-spend liberals, while, if they voted against, their party label would incur such damage as to lose them re-election.

The administration went public to generate desired effects in Congress, but not by making the presidency or policy more popular, or even by simply giving profile to an issue to encourage public response. Each was desirable, but a key purpose of the communication was to tie the fate of Obama's presidency to legislative success. Presidential activity changed the Blue Dogs' calculus for making voting decisions, by raising stakes on the 'effectiveness' dimension and trying to reduce the stakes on party and ideological dimensions. In this high-stakes environment, some moderate Democrats voted for health care. The presidency's focus on the electoral calculations of pivotal voters shaped administration bipartisanship and its use of going public, and resulted in significant legislative successes.

Conclusion

Studying presidential strategy is problematic. The Obama case suggests that labels of particular strategies, such as 'going public' or 'bipartisanship', are deceptively simple and potentially confuse, not aid, our understanding of presidential behaviour.

This chapter has raised questions about how to judge whether an administration is pursuing a 'bipartisan' strategy. No doubt, the administration would have delighted in bipartisan victories if they had been forthcoming. Clearly, bipartisanship was a leading theme in Obama's communication. However, given the voting patterns during the 111th Congress, 'bipartisanship' seems a strange label for the administration's congressional strategy. Instead, the administration approach is best described as contingent bipartisanship: Obama's team did much to generate opportunities for bipartisanship, but, from transition on, the administration retained the capacity to move to a partisan strategy. Simple labels for strategies are inadequate, because sophisticated strategic design can be multi-layered and conditional. The Obama presidency operated amid uncertainty and planned to maintain strategic flexibility.

The Obama example also highlights the complexity of 'going public' as a strategy. The administration commitment to Kernell's broad version of going public was distinctly limited. However, Kernell's initial model, oversimplifying legislators' decision making, captures little of the complexity reflected in administration attempts to trade on the Democratic party label and perceptions of the party's effectiveness. The targets of going public, rather than just making the presidency or policy proposals popular, can be varied and strategically sophisticated. 'Going public' remains part of the presidential armoury to be used selectively, targeting particular legislators within a broader strategy for legislative achievement.

Use of the labels 'bipartisanship' and 'going public' are also awkward because it is not clear how they interrelate and fit with other elements of strategy. Most commentary uses these terms to describe fragments of strategy, rather than a coherent whole. Administrations are not afforded such luxury. They attempt to address the political system as a whole, applying a series of leadership techniques concurrently within a complex strategic context. The Obama case offers a more holistic approach to explaining presidential strategy. The focus on the pursuit of legislative success is rather traditional: presidential behaviour is understood as a function of circumstances in Congress. Those circumstances are seen through the lens of the pivotal voting scholarship: in Obama's case, the positioning of pivotal voters suggested the opportunity for a partisan strategy and the question became how to influence those voters. This chapter has demonstrated how the administration engaged with the decision-making calculus of these pivotal legislators, along dimensions of ideology, partisanship and the party's effectiveness. Presidential conduct is understood as a series of attempts to adjust pivotal voters' judgements along these dimensions.

This approach allows bipartisanship and 'going public' to be understood as elements in the broad strategy, rather than as dissociated fragments, and their purposes are clearer once they are appreciated for their influence on pivotal voters' calculus. The approach also moves towards a better understanding of one facet of presidential power, the capacity to shape key legislators' decision making to induce preferred results in Congress.

There are, of course, limitations to this approach. For example, focusing only on pivotal voters at the centre marginalizes administration calculations on the need to keep support from Democratic liberals. Although the Senate, which receives little attention here, could be integrated into a longer analysis, other institutional players such as interest groups are omitted. Other presidential techniques, such as executive orders, do not feature. Equally, this approach discounts most of the administration's electoral calculations, which surely contributed to the desire to maintain a moderate, bipartisan image. However, this approach does offer the chance to develop a baseline prediction of how the presidency will conduct strategy, which may allow us better to understand divergence from that baseline.

The approach also gives the Obama administration credit for its achievements. Clearly, the two years were not an unmitigated triumph. The administration lost battles to define itself and its policies to the public. The 2010 midterm elections were a disaster for Democrats and particularly the Blue Dogs, who witnessed a halving of their caucus. However, Obama's critics depend on counterfactual versions of history, wherein Obama could, through an alternative strategy, have overcome the presidency's traditional midterm reversals (or 'shellacking'). Obama won a series of major legislative accomplishments. Credit for those achievements lies with the administration's strategic sense. Obama recognized the challenge of conducting a post-partisan presidency in an era of structural partisanship. The administration generated a flexible strategy that allowed projection of a bipartisan impression to the public and generated an opportunity for inter-party cooperation in Congress, while preserving the option of pivoting back to achieving legislation by partisan means. The administration proved strategically light-footed in the face of Republican resistance, switching to a partisan strategy to develop a record of significant legislative accomplishment.

Notes

1 George C. Edwards III, *At the Margins: Presidential Leadership of Congress* (New Haven, CT: Yale University Press, 1990); George C. Edwards III, *On Deaf Ears: The Limits of the Bully Pulpit* (New Haven, CT: Yale University Press, 2003).

2 Sarah A. Binder, 'The Dynamics of Legislative Gridlock, 1947–96', *American Political Science Review*, 93(3) (1999), 519–533; Jon R. Bond and Richard Fleisher, eds, *Polarized Politics: Congress and the President in a Partisan Era* (Washington, DC: CQ Press, 2001); Gary C. Jacobson, *A Divider, Not a Uniter: George W. Bush and the American People* (London: Pearson Longman, 2008).

3 Gregory J. Wawro and Eric Schickler, *Filibuster: Obstruction and Lawmaking in the US Senate* (Princeton, NJ: Princeton University Press, 2006); Sarah A. Binder and Steven S. Smith, *Politics or Principle? Filibustering in the United States Senate* (Washington, DC: Brookings Institution, 1997).

4 Norman J. Ornstein, 'A Very Productive Congress, Despite What the Approval Ratings Say', *Washington Post*, 31 January 2010.

5 Pietro S. Nivola and David W. Brady, eds, *Red and Blue Nation?*, Vol. 1: *Characteristics and Causes of American Polarized Politics* (Palo Alto, CA and Washington, DC: Brookings Institution, 2006); Markus Prior, 'News vs. Entertainment: How Increasing Media Choice Widens Gaps in Political Knowledge and Turnout', *American Journal of Political Science*, 49(3) (2005), 577–592.

6 Robert Singh, 'George W. Bush and the US Congress', in Andrew Wroe and Jon Herbert, eds, *Assessing the George W. Bush Presidency: A Tale of Two Terms* (Edinburgh: Edinburgh University Press, 2009).

7 Barack Obama, *The Audacity of Hope* (New York: Crown Publishers, 2006), 13–43.

8 Barack Obama, Address delivered at Grant Park, Chicago, IL, 4 November 2008.

9 Peter Baker, 'Education of a President', *New York Times Magazine*, 12 October 2010.

10 David Remnick, *The Bridge: The Life and Rise of Barack Obama* (New York: Knopf, 2010).

11 Justin A. Frank, *Obama on the Couch: Inside the Mind of the President* (New York: Free Press, 2011).

12 Eugene Robinson, 'For President Obama, a Progressive Blitz Was Not an Option', *Washington Post*, 26 October 2010, p. A19.

13 John Heilemann, 'Obama Lost, Obama Found', *New York Magazine*, 29 November 2009.

14 Jacob S. Hacker, 'The Road to Somewhere: Why Health Reform Happened or Why Political Scientists Who Write about Public Policy Shouldn't Assume They Know How to Shape It', *Perspectives on Politics*, 8(3) (2011), 865–866.

15 'Party Unity Scores', accessed 14 August 2012 at http://pooleandrosenthal.com/party_unity.htm.

16 Christopher H. Foreman, 'Ambition, Necessity, and Polarization in the Obama Domestic Agenda', in Bert A. Rockman, Andrew Rudalevige and Colin Campbell, eds, *The Obama Presidency: Appraisals and Prospects* (Washington, DC: CQ Press, 2011), 247–248.

17 Kevin Coe and Michael Reitzes, 'Obama on the Stump: Features and Determinants of a Rhetorical Approach', *Presidential Studies Quarterly*, 40(3) (2010), 391.

18 Michelle C. Bligh and Jeffrey C. Kohles, 'The Enduring Allure of Charisma: How Barack Obama Won the Historic 2008 Presidential Election', *Leadership Quarterly*, 20(3) (2009), 483–492.

19 Michael Cornfield, 'Game Changers: New Technology and the 2008 Presidential Election', in Larry Sabato, ed., *The Year of Obama* (London: Longman, 2010).

20 Samuel Kernell, *Going Public: New Strategies of Presidential Leadership* (Washington, DC: CQ Press, 1997).

21 Mark Leibovich, 'Message Maven Finds Fingers Pointing at Him', *New York Times*, 6 March 2010.

22 William A. Galston, cited in Heilemann, 'Obama Lost, Obama Found'.

23 Hacker, 'The Road to Somewhere', 864.

24 Barack Obama, 'Commencement Address at Kalamazoo Central High School in Kalamazoo, Michigan', 7 June 2010; 'Remarks at a Town Hall Meeting and a Question-and-Answer Session on Health Care Reform in Wheaton, Maryland', 8 June 2010; 'Remarks at a Town Hall Meeting and a Question-and-Answer Session in Racine, Wisconsin', 30 June 2010. All online by Gerhard Peters and John T. Woolley, *The American Presidency Project*, http://www.presidency.ucsb.edu/ws/.

25 For example, Barack Obama, 'Remarks at the University of Nevada, Las Vegas, in Las Vegas, Nevada', 9 July 2010. Online by Peters and Woolley, *American Presidency Project*.

26 Charles O. Jones, *The Presidency in a Separated System* (Washington, DC: Brookings Institution, 2005); John B. Gilmour, *Strategic Disagreement: Stalemate in American Politics* (Pittsburgh, PA: University of Pittsburgh Press, 1995); George C. Edwards III, *The Strategic President: Persuasion and Opportunity in Presidential Leadership* (Princeton, NJ: Princeton University Press, 2009).

27 David W. Brady and Craig Volden, *Revolving Gridlock: Politics and Policy from Carter to Clinton* (Boulder, CO: Westview, 1998); Keith Krehbiel, *Pivotal Politics: A Theory of U.S. Lawmaking* (Chicago, IL: University of Chicago Press, 1998).

28 Matthew N. Beckmann, 'The President's Playbook: White House Strategies for Lobbying Congress', *Journal of Politics*, 70(2) (2008), 407–419.

29 Edwards, *On Deaf Ears*.

30 Matthew Eshbaugh-Soha and Tom Miles, 'Presidential Speeches and the Stages of the Legislative Process', *Congress and the Presidency*, 38 (2011), 301–321. See also Andrew W. Barrett and Matthew Eshbaugh-Soha, 'Presidential Success on the Substance of Legislation', *Political Research Quarterly*, 60(1) (2007), 100–112.

31 Brandice Canes-Wrone, *Who Leads Whom? Presidents, Policy, and the Public* (Chicago, IL: University of Chicago Press, 2006).

32 Beckmann, 'The President's Playbook'.

33 Democrats were more ideologically homogeneous than in many preceding decades, but were divided nevertheless.

34 Hacker, 'The Road to Somewhere', 865; Eric Alterman, 'The "Delusional Left" Wins', *thedailybeast.com*, 18 March 2010.

35 Perry Bacon, Jr., 'Reform Stance Puts Spotlight on Blue Dog Democrats', *Washington Post*, 23 July 2009.

36 Sean Trende, 'Obama's Unforced Error Poses Challenge for Dems', *realclearpolitics.blogs.time. com*, 17 August 2010.

37 Perry Bacon, Jr., Paul Kane and Ben Pershing, 'Liberal and Conservative Democrats Feud over Bill', *Washington Post*, 25 July 2009.

38 Jay Newton-Small, 'Can Obama Keep Moderate Dems in Line on His Budget?', *Time Magazine*, 11 March 2009. Later administration efforts to generate further stimulus often foundered upon Blue Dog opposition.

39 Joe Klein, 'Blue Dogs Dumped', *Time: Swampland*, 4 November 2010.

40 Ari Berman, 'Op-Ed: Boot the Blue Dogs', *New York Times*, 23 October 2010.

41 Gary W. Cox and Mathew D. McCubbins, *Setting the Agenda: Responsible Party Government in the US House of Representatives* (Cambridge: Cambridge University Press, 2005), 21–24.

42 Barbara Sinclair, 'Doing Big Things: Obama and the 111th Congress', in Bert A. Rockman, Andrew Rudalevige and Colin Campbell, eds, *The Obama Presidency: Appraisals and Prospects* (Washington, DC: CQ Press, 2011), 199.

43 Howard Kurtz, 'Dr. Obama's Prescription', *Washington Post*, 23 February 2010.

44 Ruth Marcus, 'Obama's Continued Audaciousness on Health Reform Could Backfire', *Washington Post*, 24 February 2010, p. A13.

45 Sinclair, 'Doing Big Things', p. 213.

3 Health politics and the Patient Protection and Affordable Care Act

Daniel Béland and Alex Waddan

Introduction

Health care reform is one of the defining elements of Barack Obama's presidential record. Likely to appear as the most central aspect of his domestic legacy, the Patient Protection and Affordable Care Act (PPACA) is a controversial piece of legislation that proved extremely hard to enact, as it generated strong opposition from Republicans and their Tea Party supporters. Although the legislation was passed in March 2010, it is being implemented gradually, over nearly a decade and there is much uncertainty about the long-term fiscal and policy effects of key PPACA provisions. Finally, the very implementation of major aspects of the legislation is problematic, as suggested by the decision in autumn 2011 to cancel its long-term care programme because of cost-related issues.

This chapter explores the politics leading to the enactment of the PPACA before discussing the implementation and political challenges stemming from this ambitious legislation. The chapter first describes the institutional context of health insurance reform in the United States before illustrating that context through brief remarks about the 1993–94 failed reform attempt of the Clinton administration. The chapter next focuses on the Obama administration and its efforts to push for health insurance before turning briefly to the convoluted enactment process that led to the signing of the PPACA. The chapter then analyses the content of this complex legislation and the challenges to its implementation. After that, the chapter deals with the ongoing political controversy over the PPACA, especially the constant Republican attacks on it and the various court challenges that could endanger its long-term survival. The chapter concludes with some remarks about the role of health care reform in shaping the presidential legacy of Barack Obama.

The institutional and partisan obstacles to reform

In the United States, health care reform has been a contentious endeavour for decades. This is especially true of the idea of extending coverage to the entire population, in a country where, in the mid-2000s, more than 45 million people were excluded from health insurance coverage at any given time.[1] Although this absence of universal coverage has been debated for years, expanding coverage has proved difficult. This is largely due to the convergence between two crucial institutional factors. First, since the Second World War, the creation of a mostly private health care system has created powerful constituencies that oppose changes that may harm their interests.[2] This is true not only of health insurance companies but also of doctors and private hospitals, who all play a direct role in the politics of health care reform. Ironically, the creation of Medicaid and Medicare in 1965 consolidated the role of the private health sector by having government focus on 'bad risks', in this case the poor on social assistance (Medicaid) and the elderly and – starting in 1972 – the disabled (Medicare). The creation of these two programmes did increase the role of government in health policy but yet, simultaneously, they explicitly confirmed the role of the private sector as the legitimate provider of health insurance coverage for the working population. Although Medicare and, especially, Medicaid expanded in recent decades, they remained targeted programmes focusing on vulnerable populations facing problems with getting private coverage. Overall insurance coverage remained incomplete, owing to the absence of compulsory insurance and, more recently, to growing health care costs that made it more expensive for businesses, especially smaller ones, to purchase coverage for their workers. As businesses attempted to continue providing insurance yet also to control their outlays, they increasingly passed costs on to workers through lower wages and, more directly, higher health contributions. In periods of economic downturn like the early 1990s and the post-2008 recession, the percentage of Americans excluded from coverage increases, a situation that creates stronger demands for health insurance reform.[3] Not surprisingly, since the Truman era it has been during Democratic presidencies that increasing health coverage has been pushed to the centre of the federal agenda.[4] The most recent examples are the Clinton and Obama presidencies, which both featured dramatic and highly contentious debates on health insurance reform that divided the nation and witnessed the direct involvement of powerful interest groups.

Second, the institutional features of the federal political system complicate the task of Democratic presidents and members of Congress who push for comprehensive health insurance reform. Partly because of the fragmentation of power in Washington, interest groups play a direct role in the policymaking process, a major problem in a field like health care reform, where the level of interest group mobilization is especially striking.[5] In order to pass, legislation must receive support from three actors possessing a 'veto point' over the legislative process: the House of Representatives, the Senate and the presidency. Even when the same party controls these three institutions, legislative success can remain elusive owing to the absence of party discipline in the two chambers of Congress. Over the last decade, only Republicans succeeded in creating something like party discipline in Congress.[6] In the aftermath of the 2010 midterm elections, this was especially the case in the House of Representatives, where Republican members, especially those tied to the Tea Party, formed an ideologically cohesive group opposed to Democratic reform proposals. As for Democrats, they are more divided over the issue of health care reform than Republicans, as became clear during both the Clinton and the Obama years. Although Democrats generally support a greater role for government in health policy, they are sometimes divided over the extent of this role. Considering such institutional and partisan logics, one can understand why health care reform became such a risky business for recent Democratic presidents.

Another complicating factor, especially for Obama, was that the push for greater health coverage was now tied to the complicated task of controlling spending in what had become the most expensive health care system in the world. As a proportion of GDP, the United States is the OECD (Organisation for Economic Co-operation and Development) country that spends most on health care. For instance, in 2008, the United States spent 16 per cent of GDP on health care, compared with only 8.7 per cent in the United Kingdom.[7] As if the challenge of increasing coverage was not already daunting in a context of institutional fragmentation, interest group mobilization and cohesive Republican opposition, health insurance reform was simultaneously centred on two distinct policy objectives: increasing coverage and reducing costs in a context of budgetary constraints. A few remarks about the experience of the Clinton administration in health insurance reform will illustrate the scale of such challenges, which remained just as relevant more than 15 years later, during the Obama presidency.

In the 1992 presidential campaign, Democratic candidate Bill Clinton promised to reform a health care system that 'leaves 60 million Americans without adequate health insurance and bankrupts our families, our businesses, and our federal budget'. Aware of the anxieties of people who had good private coverage and were afraid that reform could endanger it, Clinton vowed to 'preserve what's best in our system: your family's right to choose who provides care and coverage, American innovation and technology, and the world's best private doctors and hospitals'.[8] In the name of what became known as 'managed competition', Clinton promised to maintain the central role of the private health sector, while regulating it in such a way that universal coverage could be brought about without threatening too directly the perceived interests of various health care interest groups. Instead of boldly advocating national health insurance on the earlier Democratic model, Bill Clinton attempted to create universal health coverage through extended private coverage and regulatory mechanisms.[9]

Because of the sheer complexity of this endeavour and the decision to develop a detailed legislative proposal within the White House, it took more than nine months for the proposed Health Security Act to take shape, at first through the work of the Task Force on National Health Care Reform created immediately after Clinton became president in January 1993. When the Health Security Act finally became public in the autumn, interest groups and Republicans in Congress began mobilizing against it. Even more worrying for President Clinton, influential Democratic figures in Congress like Senator Daniel Patrick Moynihan publicly criticized the proposed legislation. In such a context, it became increasingly difficult for President Clinton to defend a complex piece of legislation that few Americans fully understood. Paradoxically related to the desire to accommodate private health care interests by regulating the market rather than displacing it through the creation of a national health insurance system, this complexity provided ammunition to opponents of the reform plan. In the end, as President Clinton faced attacks on the plan, public support for reform began to fall, as people started to fear the alleged negative effects of the new regulations. This led to the humiliating defeat of the proposal, which helped turn voters against 'big government' while paving the way to the stunning victory of the Republicans at the 1994 midterms.[10] This episode and the perceived mistakes of the Clinton administration in handling health reform (for example, the formulation of a detailed legislative proposal within the White House and lack of coordination with Democrats in Congress) directly influenced the way the Obama administration dealt with the issue.

The sinuous road to reform

During the 2008 presidential campaign, Democratic candidate Obama made a case for health insurance reform. During the campaign, however, he refused to formulate a detailed plan or even to pledge that his administration would bring about universal coverage. His rhetoric about health insurance remained vague largely because, in the field of health care, the devil is in the detail. Difficulties are exacerbated not only because of vested interests, but also because of the fears of insured Americans that further governmental intervention, aimed at extending coverage, could lead to a degeneration of those health services they currently accessed. In this context, the financial crisis that hit the country in September 2008 both helped Obama get elected and made the health care situation even more dramatic, as the recession increased the number of uninsured.[11]

After entering the White House, despite strong opposition from Republicans who claimed he should focus exclusively on the economy, Obama decided to pursue health insurance reform immediately. In retrospect, this choice made sense because, in 2009, Democrats controlled both the House of Representatives and the Senate.[12] Moreover, in the Senate, the Democratic caucus had enough members (60) to break potential filibusters.[13] Although particularly favourable, this institutional context remained problematic in the absence of formal party discipline, especially in the Senate. Additionally, the powerful interest groups likely to be affected by health care reform still maintained their access to the White House and to members of Congress, creating both opportunities and challenges for reformers. Finally, in both chambers of Congress, Republicans generally adopted a confrontational stance; the president found a shrinking number of Republican lawmakers interested in discussing a potential bipartisan deal over health care. In the end, the debate on health care coverage became purely partisan, further complicating the task of President Obama, who had campaigned in 2008 to end 'politics as usual' in Washington through genuine bipartisan dialogue. Ultimately, this approach to reform did not materialize, at least in the field of health insurance.

In order to counter Republican arguments that the recession and the increasing federal deficits it triggered necessitated the postponement of health care reform altogether, Obama asserted that fixing health care was necessary to economic recovery and the long-term future of the country, since increasing health costs represented a direct threat to US competitiveness. The president also stressed that citizens increasingly felt the burden of rapidly increasing health costs, as employers were transferring the burden of paying for health insurance to their workers. Simultaneously, the federal government faced a growing fiscal burden because of its inability to control Medicaid and Medicare spending, a situation that reflected structural problems with the health care system as a whole.[14] Thus, according to President Obama, a close relationship existed between the push for health insurance reform, on the one hand, and the quest for economic recovery and fiscal sustainability, on the other.[15] Most Republicans rejected this line of argument from the start, arguing that President Obama should postpone reform until the return to economic prosperity. Democrats rejected this Republican call, which they saw as a blatant excuse to kill reform altogether.

Yet, if bipartisan talks in Congress proved futile, the same did not apply to the White House campaign to bring some of the most powerful interest groups on board. Aware of what happened during the Clinton years, the Obama administration reached out to these constituencies to pre-empt future large-scale interest group mobilization against reform.[16] For instance, long before a bill was produced, an agreement was reached with the pharmaceutical industry, which included a list of cost-saving measures the industry agreed to embrace. The administration also struck a deal with the hospital industry to prevent it from opposing reform. Although a number of Democrats complained about the compromises made to accommodate these industries, the White House saw these as necessary steps to weaken potential opposition to reform. Interestingly, while the insurance industry did not strike a deal, it was the insurance industry that was left relatively isolated as a consequence. Eventually, although insurers were unhappy about some of the provisions that ended up in legislation, the industry did not directly attack reform with the same intensity with which it had rebuked Clinton's reform plan. Instead, insurers simply channelled money to the US Chamber of Commerce, which had launched a crusade against the proposed legislation.[17]

In all likelihood, resistance from the insurance industry would have been much stronger if both chambers of Congress had passed the so-called 'public option', an idea Obama supported during the 2008 presidential campaign. The creation of a 'public option' would have allowed the federal government to sell health insurance coverage directly to individuals, a move that, according to its proponents, would have increased competition within health insurance markets, thus forcing insurance companies to lower their prices and, ultimately, help control health costs. Popular among the Democratic base, the 'public option' provision was adopted by the House of Representatives but rejected by the Senate, which ended up killing the idea, to the frustration of the left.[18] Importantly, although the White House claimed to support the 'public option', it gradually became clear that it was willing to let it die in order to secure the enactment of reform in the Senate, where conservative Democrats disliked the idea.[19]

This discussion about the fate of the 'public option' points to the autonomy of Congress in the development of health insurance reform. This was the case partly because, as opposed to the situation prevailing during the Clinton years, the Obama administration decided not to advance a detailed legislative proposal. Instead, the White House granted significant autonomy to Democrats in Congress to craft the health insurance legislation. This was especially important in the Senate, where the Democrats needed to get all the members of their caucus on board to avoid a potentially disruptive Republican filibuster. As always, the institutional logic of separated institutions and, especially, the weakness of formal party discipline in Congress complicated the reform process. The delays this institutional situation created and the blatant and sometimes unpopular trade-offs among Democrats in the Senate helped turn part of the population against reform, as it seemed tainted by the apparent self-interest of influential members of Congress who seemed willing to exchange their support for the legislation against advantages for their state, among other considerations. From this perspective, the decision to grant considerable autonomy to Congress in designing reform created delays and exacerbated existing popular anxieties – a situation that Republicans like Sarah Palin exploited, with the help of the emerging Tea Party movement. Palin in particular filled the policy blanks with false claims about 'death panels' (in fact, nothing more than end-of-life counselling), which helped generate a climate of hysteria among the conservative base. In August 2009, opponents of reform voiced their rage in the context of the traditional town hall meetings organized by members of Congress during the summer recess.[20]

Enacting the PPACA

In September 2009, afraid that the reform process could stall as a consequence of the August protests and the endless discussion taking place in the Senate, President Obama gave a major health care speech in front of Congress.[21] This passionate discourse about the fate of the uninsured and the need to enact reform increased pressure on the Senate Finance Committee, the last of the relevant committees to report its health insurance bill.[22] In the end, it was the House of Representatives that enacted the first health care bill, which included the 'public option'. The enactment process in the House was complicated by the mobilization of the anti-abortion members of the Democratic caucus. As a response, House Speaker Nancy Pelosi struck a deal on abortion funding that generated much frustration among pro-choice Democrats. The Democratic caucus in the Senate took even longer to agree a legislative compromise, which did not include the 'public option' and was adopted as late as 24 December, just before elected officials left Washington for the holiday.[23]

At that stage it was anticipated that the next step was for the leadership of House and Senate to agree common legislation to reconcile the important differences between the bills enacted by the two chambers. Unfortunately for the Democrats, on 19 January 2010, an unexpected turn of events further complicated the legislative process, threatening the proposed reform. A special Senate election in Massachusetts to replace the late Edward Kennedy, who had died the previous August, saw Republican Scott Brown triumph. Brown's election altered power relations in Washington, as it gave 41 votes to Republicans in the Senate, allowing them to sustain a filibuster. Soon after Brown's surprise election, in his State of the Union address President Obama stated that he remained fully committed to health reform.[24] Yet for weeks the fate of the reform remained highly uncertain.

In February and March 2010, the White House and Democratic leaders in Congress engaged in long discussions about how to enact legislation without having to send a new version of the law to the Senate, where the fresh threat of a Republican filibuster was too serious to ignore. In this more constraining institutional environment, it was finally decided that the best way forward was for the House to pass the Senate version of the bill. With the bill passed in the same form in both House and Senate, the president could sign it into law. This plan created discontent among left-wing House Democrats, who had to accept the final demise of the 'public option'. As for pro-life Democrats in the House, they took issue with the lack of strong language restricting the use of public money for abortions in the Senate bill; this ultimately forced President Obama to issue an executive order to stress that federal money would not be used for abortions. Ultimately the House did enact the Senate version of the bill by a slight majority, as House Republicans united against what officially became the Patient Protection and Affordable Care Act. Moreover, the House and the Senate enacted 'fixes' to the initial Senate bill through the reconciliation process, which does not allow for a filibuster on the Senate floor. Finally, on 30 March, President Obama signed this second piece of legislation, marking the end of a long and tumultuous legislative process, during which a growing number of Americans became sceptical about reform. This situation weakened support for the Obama administration and may have helped Republicans to take over the House in the 2010 midterm election.[25] This outcome shares some similarities with the aftermath of the defeat of Clinton's health proposal, when Republicans won the 1994 midterms, taking over both House and Senate and with House Speaker Newt Gingrich using strong anti-government rhetoric.[26] In contrast to Clinton, Obama had won the policy battle and signed a major health insurance reform into law. Yet, as suggested above, factors stemming from the nature of the federal policymaking process complicated the enactment process, even as Democrats controlled both the executive and legislative branches of government. The slow pace of the reform process and the multiple deals necessary for the enactment of the final legislation tainted the law while providing ammunition to Republicans, who scored political points against the White House simply by opposing change.[27]

Understanding the PPACA

As outlined above, the PPACA was designed to accomplish two distinct objectives. First, it aimed significantly to reduce the number of Americans lacking health insurance. In 2010, 16.3 per cent of Americans remained uninsured, with many others underinsured. Second, PPACA aimed to restrain health care inflation and so to limit the growing burden of health care costs on federal and state governments, as well as on American business. It is in fact not surprising that the US spends more of its GDP on health care than other nations, since there is a correlation between a country's wealth and its expenditure on health. The dilemma is the level of excess spending. A McKinsey Global Institute study found that in 2006 the US spent $2.1 trillion on health care, amounting to 'nearly $650 billion more . . . than peer OECD countries, even after adjusting for wealth'.[28] Hence the PPACA was intended to resolve the contradiction that the country with the highest price tag for its health care arrangements was the only one in the industrialized world to leave a significant part of its population without institutionalized health coverage.

The methodology adopted in the PPACA to bring about change mirrored the complex legislative process in its multi-faceted approach, as it built upon elements of the existing system, created new institutions and aimed at adjusting incentives for some health care providers. Fundamentally, the PPACA did not challenge the assumption that most Americans should get their health insurance as part of their terms of employment, but there were changes providing more formal incentives and encouragement to employers to offer insurance to their employees. Large firms will face penalties if they do not provide insurance, while smaller businesses will be able to draw upon subsidies to help them pay for insurance.[29] In this way the PPACA bolstered the existing employer-based insurance system. The main innovations aimed at reducing the number of uninsured were the major expansion of the Medicaid programme and the creation of health insurance exchanges. In the years through to 2019, Medicaid eligibility will be extended to everyone with an income at or below 133 per cent of the poverty line, regardless of family or household status. It is estimated that this will result in an extra 16 million Americans having access to health cover.[30] As explained below, the Supreme Court ruling in June 2012 made this figure less certain. The health insurance exchanges, to be established from 2014, will be state-monitored, regulated insurance markets with a variety of private health plans (but, as noted, no 'public option') available to low-income households. The federal government will provide subsidies to people getting their insurance through an exchange on a sliding scale up to 400 per cent of the poverty level. According to the Congressional Budget Office (CBO), by 2019, 24 million Americans will be insured in these exchanges.[31]

One way of reducing the number of uninsured that could be more swiftly implemented was to instruct insurance companies that they had to allow children to remain covered by their parents' insurance up to age 26. In addition, the PPACA imposed new regulations on insurance companies. Insurers will no longer be allowed to refuse insurance to people with pre-existing illnesses, nor will they be able to impose annual or lifetime caps on insurance plans. One aspect of the law that will compensate insurers for these new rules, which effectively reduces their commercial autonomy, is that, beginning in 2014, everyone will have to buy available insurance or face fines. By coercing those healthy people who might otherwise be tempted to gamble on their health well-being (people sometimes referred to as 'invincibles'), this measure helps collectivize the insurance risk pool. This so-called 'individual mandate' proved to be highly controversial and became the subject of constitutional challenge. However, it was one element of the law that the health insurance industry supported.[32]

In addition to reducing the number of Americans without health insurance the other key goal of the PPACA was to slow the growth of US health spending. This meant that throughout the legislative process there was a constant focus on how the CBO scored the likely impact of the reforms. If the reform was to gain the votes of uncertain Democrats it was critical for the administration that the CBO estimated that the law would save the federal government money. As it was, in its initial projections at the time of the final vote on the PPACA the CBO did predict that the law would result in a net saving of $143 billion for the federal budget through to 2019.[33] This meant that the extra spending that would be incurred through the expansion of Medicaid and the subsidies provided to people buying insurance through the health exchanges would be more than offset by savings and new revenues generated elsewhere. The CBO's predictions were that through to 2019 the expansion of Medicaid would cost $434 billion and the subsidies for the exchanges a further $358 billion.[34] To pay for these and other measures extra revenues will come from an increased Medicare payroll tax on people earning over $200,000 a year, a new tax on unearned income of over $200,000, and various taxes and fees on medical providers, notably branded drug manufacturers and hospitals.

The introduction of these last arrangements reflected the outcomes of the negotiations that the administration conducted with these powerful health care stakeholders.[35] But if the large drug companies ('Big PhRMa') and the hospitals were relatively quiescent about these new costs imposed on them, the savings written into the PPACA were a source of greater political controversy, since they included reductions in projected spending on Medicare. The reduced growth in the rate of Medicare spending was primarily to be driven by cuts in the annual updates of Medicare's fees for service payments and in reductions to the payments to private insurers who operated in the Medicare Advantage programme. The PPACA also created a new institution to be known as the Independent Payment Advisory Board (IPAB), which will be an autonomous board with the power to recommend limits to Medicare spending. Importantly, Congress will not be able simply to ignore recommendations made by IPAB. Lawmakers will have either to act on IPAB's suggestions or enact alternative measures that cut costs to a similar degree. The political consequences of these changes to Medicare, at least in the short term, reflect the complex, and at times counter-intuitive, politics of health care. Medicare has traditionally been seen as a programme 'owned' by the Democrats.[36] That is, the Democrats are seen as the party most trusted by the public to protect this particular programme. In the mid-1990s, for example, Bill Clinton revitalized his presidency following the 1994 midterm elections by standing against proposed Republican cuts to Medicare spending.[37] This established pattern, however, was at least temporarily suspended in 2010 as Republicans complained that the PPACA threatened the future of Medicare,[38] and turned this to their advantage in the midterm elections.[39] This episode illustrates well the intense difficulty policymakers face when trying to introduce measures that are designed to control costs in US public health programmes. Even when there appears to be consensus that these programmes represent the biggest challenge to the federal government's long-term fiscal credibility,[40] political actors will likely attempt to gain advantage from initiatives by their political opponents that put cost containment rhetoric into practice.

In addition to slowing health care inflation for government, the PPACA also aimed to reduce the burden of health costs on the private sector. The measures to be introduced in this respect were in fact even less explicit than those to reduce public spending. One controversial measure, which angered the labour unions that were generally allied to the reformers, was the so-called 'Cadillac tax'. Starting in 2018, insurance plans where the premium, however shared between employer and employee, is more than $10,200 for an individual and $27,500 for a family will become subject to a new tax.[41] This tax, to be paid by the insurance companies, will be 40 per cent of the additional cost. These numbers should be viewed in the context of an average premium of $5,429 for individual coverage and $15,073 for family coverage in 2011, although there is wide variation around these figures owing to factors such as the benefits covered, the level of cost sharing in the plan and geographical differentiation.[42] The rationale for the tax is that these high-value insurance packages encourage unnecessary treatments and thus add to wasteful spending. The PPACA also stipulated that government officials had the power to review increases in an insurer's annual premiums if that increase was deemed 'unreasonable'. In May 2011 that was more precisely defined by Kathleen Sebelius, Secretary of Health and Human Services, as meaning that from September 2011 a premium increase of 10 per cent or more would need to be reviewed by state or federal government experts. From September 2012 each state should have been allocated its own threshold rather than that blanket national figure. Sebelius justified the intervention by saying: 'Insurers are seeing lower medical costs as people put off care and treatment in a recovering economy, but many insurance companies continue to raise their rates. Often these increases come without any explanation or justification.'[43]

In addition to these controversial initiatives, the PPACA lays out plans to modernize medical care delivery through encouraging greater efficiency and integration. The aim is to accelerate the introduction of evidence-based medicine so that health care providers can make better recommendations to their patients in order to reduce unnecessary and potentially harmful treatments. To this end the bill calls for improved communication flows and changing incentives so that hospitals are rewarded for lowering short-term readmission rates. In fact the stimulus bill, enacted in 2009, already contained subsidies to encourage health providers to adopt new information technologies in their work. One aspect of the reorganization of the practice of health care is that the PPACA aims to promote the establishment of accountable care organizations that will bring together primary and secondary care doctors as well as hospitals to look after a group of patients to improve the coordination and hence efficiency of care. Evaluation of the likely impact of these ideas and the efficacy of the projected cost savings for both government and the private sector was, not surprisingly, contested in a highly, and sometimes ideologically, charged fashion. A dramatic sense of this can be gained from comparing analyses from the conservative Heritage Foundation with that of the liberal Center for American Progress.[44]

Implementing the PPACA

As reflected in the description above, many elements of the PPACA are only scheduled to come into effect over a period of years. Some aspects of the bill were introduced almost immediately, but in other cases final details of implementation were still to be worked out almost two years after the bill was enacted. One example of a provision enacted quickly was that allowing children to stay on their parents' insurance until age 26. The Obama administration claimed some vindication for the reform when, in December 2011, the Centers for Disease Control and Prevention released figures suggesting that this had led to 2.5 million extra people aged between 19 and 25 having access to insurance. This led Kathleen Sebelius to claim: 'Moms and dads around the country can breathe a little easier knowing their children are covered.'[45] In other areas, the specifics were slow to emerge. So, for example, the PPACA stipulated that from January 2014 all small group and individual insurance plans, including those due to be part of the health insurance networks, would have to cover an array of essential benefits. Yet, while the bill did identify ten areas that would be covered by these 'essential health benefit' (EHB) packages, it did not fully spell out what would be the minimum cover required in each area. In mid-December 2011 the Department of Health and Human Services did issue a bulletin providing some guidance on its thinking, but since that bulletin indicated that the final decisions defining an EHB package would be taken at state level, following a federally defined benchmark within each state, it could not offer a definitive answer as to what exactly would be covered.[46]

Other aspects of the PPACA that will unfold over time include the role of the IPAB designed to contain Medicare costs. On the surface, establishing this body involved a significant relinquishing of power by Congress in an area where legislators have traditionally been active. Interestingly IPAB was not included in the House version of health care legislation and may well have been a source of contention had the initial Senate and House bills gone to a conference committee. In this context it is simply uncertain whether IPAB will turn out to be a major innovation wielding worthwhile powers or whether it will be a marginal player merely tinkering with Medicare spending.[47] Further concerns surround the establishment of the health insurance exchanges. The PPACA requires that these should be operational in January 2014, but a number of states were slow in preparing the ground for the exchanges.

In some cases this sluggishness reflected a lack of political will to follow through on the PPACA, especially in anticipation of the Supreme Court ruling, while in other cases states found it difficult to gather and collate the necessary data.[48] The overall uncertainty surrounding the implementation of the PPACA is illustrated by the number of waivers that were already granted across the US even by the summer of 2011; for example, over 1,400 waivers had been issued by June 2011, allowing health plans to provide maximum levels of coverage which fell below the federally mandated minimum in the PPACA.[49]

Political and judicial challenges

In addition to the 'devil in the detail' of policy implementation, the PPACA faced an ongoing series of political challenges. One of the first acts of the new Republican majority in the House of Representatives in 2011 was to vote to repeal the law. With the Senate still in Democratic hands and Obama in the White House, this was in itself a symbolic rather than a practical piece of politics. Speaker John Boehner of Ohio explained Republican objections to the PPACA: 'Repeal means paving the way for better solutions that will lower the cost without destroying jobs or bankrupting the government. . . . Repeal means keeping a promise. This is what we said we would do.'[50]

Potentially of more practical importance were the legal challenges launched against the PPACA's constitutionality. In particular, opponents claimed that the individual mandate was an attempt to regulate individual activity that overstepped acceptable limits. Twenty-six states challenged elements of the law, and in November 2011 the Supreme Court agreed to rule on the contested issues, with oral arguments held in March 2012. In late June 2012, in a 5-to-4 decision, the Supreme Court upheld the constitutionality of the individual mandate. To some surprise, Chief Justice John Roberts sided with the four putatively liberal justices to uphold the law. In a complex ruling, he argued that the mandate could not be justified on the grounds laid out by the Obama administration, but could be legitimated as a tax.[51] While the ruling angered many conservatives, some immediately renewed their attacks on what they derided as 'Obamacare' for containing a massive tax increase.[52] Another aspect of the legal challenge, which had received less publicity, questioned whether the Medicaid expansion contained in the PPACA, which stipulated that states must expand coverage or be excluded from Medicaid, violated the rules of that joint federal–state administered programme. In this case, the Court partially ruled against the administration. The Court determined that the federal government could only deny the proposed new monies to states that did not expand Medicaid coverage to 133 per cent of the poverty line, rather than removing all existing Medicaid funding to those states. This made it more credible that some states might decide to refuse the extra funding and therefore not expand their Medicaid coverage.[53]

The ongoing conservative opposition to 'Obamacare' was also reflected in the battle for the Republican presidential nomination of 2012, as well as in the presidential election campaign itself. One line of attack against Mitt Romney, during the nomination stage, was that he had overseen the introduction of a health care reform similar to the PPACA while Governor of Massachusetts. Romney vigorously denied that the reform plans were the same.[54] He promised to take action to repeal the law if elected president. Republican public opposition to the PPACA thus continued long after the bill's passage. Among the wider public, polls provided a mixed picture. Detailed polling by the Kaiser Family Foundation showed the public to be reasonably evenly divided in their attitudes towards the reform and indeed positive about many aspects of it.[55] However, other polls suggested that the Republican opposition did chime with the public mood; for example, a Rasmussen poll conducted at the start of 2012 showed 54 per cent of voters in favour of repealing the law, with 42 per cent opposed.[56] Obama's signature legislative achievement clearly had not gained clear and widespread acceptance. Yet, the reelection of President Obama for a second term in November 2012 makes it virtually impossible for Republicans to repeal the legislation, for the time being.

Conclusion

Proponents of the PPACA have sometimes drawn an analogy between this reform and other landmarks of US social policy such as Social Security and Medicare.[57] These are now both hugely popular government programmes but, in the case of Social Security at least, it took many years before the programme became widely popular and strongly institutionally embedded. So, if the PPACA follows a similar political and policy trajectory, it will gain in popularity as Americans come to understand the benefits of the law, which in turn will reinforce the legitimacy of the reform and so create a virtuous loop. This 'positive' scenario for the PPACA and the Obama administration's domestic policy legacy, however, is far from certain. First, given the continuing intensity of opposition, it is likely that the Republicans will keep opposing the legislation possibly also disrupting PPACA through administrative decisions such as denying funding for agencies to implement the different aspects of the law.[58] Second, even if the PPACA is more likely to survive its many challenges as a consequence of Obamas reelection, it is not fully clear whether it will meet its own objectives. In part this is because the law took an incremental approach to reform. Even with significant Democratic majorities in both chambers of Congress, powerful institutional constraints affected the measure. Reformers looked to adjust rather than replace the highly fragmented mix of public and private elements of American health care arrangements. In this context the measures to reduce the numbers of Americans denied access to health insurance have some clarity, but the assumptions about how costs will be controlled in the future appear more nebulous.[59]

It still remains difficult to know quite where PPACA will stand as part of the Obama legacy; and predicting future developments is a risky business. Some elements of the reform look likely to become permanent features of the health care landscape. For instance, from a political standpoint, it would be extremely difficult for even the most hostile Republicans to repeal aspects of the law that protect people from being discriminated against by insurers because of pre-existing conditions or to roll back the provisions allowing children to stay longer on parents' insurance. But while these are not negligible changes, if 'Obamacare' were to be reduced to an array of measures of this sort, it would not constitute an enduring policy legacy. On the other hand, if fully implemented, for all its limitations, it would, in dramatically reducing uninsurance and tackling inequality, constitute the most significant US social policy reform in a generation.[60]

Notes

1 Debra Street, 'Balancing Act: The Public–Private Mix in Health Care Systems', in Daniel Béland and Brian Gran, eds, *Public and Private Social Policy: Health and Pension Policies in a New Era* (Basingstoke: Palgrave Macmillan, 2008), 15–44.
2 Jacob S. Hacker, *The Divided Welfare State: The Battle over Public and Private Social Benefits in the United States* (New York: Cambridge University Press, 2002); Jill Quadagno, *One Nation Uninsured: Why the US Has No National Health Insurance* (New York: Oxford University Press, 2005).
3 Mark Peterson, 'It Was a Different Time: Obama and the Unique Opportunity for Health Care Reform', *Journal of Health Politics, Policy and Law*, 36(3) (2011), 429–436.
4 Quadagno, *One Nation Uninsured*.

5 Sven Steinmo and Jon Watts, 'It's the Institutions, Stupid! Why the United States Can't Pass Comprehensive National Health Insurance', *Journal of Health Politics, Policy and Law*, 20(2) (1995), 329–372.

6 Jacob S. Hacker and Paul Pierson, *Off Center: The Republican Revolution and the Erosion of American Democracy* (New Haven, CT: Yale University Press, 2005).

7 Organisation for Economic Co-operation and Development, Directorate for Employment, Labour and Social Affairs, *OECD Health Data for 2010*.

8 William J. Clinton and Al Gore, *Putting People First: A Strategy for Change* (New York: Times Books, 1992), 107.

9 Jacob S. Hacker, *The Road to Nowhere: The Genesis of President Clinton's Plan for Health Security* (Princeton, NJ: Princeton University Press, 1997).

10 Theda Skocpol, *Boomerang: Health Care Reform and the Turn against Government* (New York: W. W. Norton, 1996).

11 Paul Fronstin, *The Impact of the 2007–2009 Recession on Workers' Health Coverage*, EBRI Issue Brief No. 356 (Washington, DC: Employee Benefit Research Institute, April 2011).

12 Jacob S. Hacker, 'Why Reform Happened', *Journal of Health Politics, Policy and Law*, 36(3) (2011), 437–441.

13 For a historical perspective on filibusters, see Gregory Koger, *Filibustering: A Political History of Obstruction in the House and Senate* (Chicago, IL: University of Chicago Press, 2010).

14 See Daniel Béland and Alex Waddan, 'The Obama Presidency and Health Insurance Reform: Assessing Continuity and Change', *Social Policy and Society*, 11(3) (2012), 319–330.

15 *Remarks of President Barack Obama – As Prepared for Delivery: Address to Joint Session of Congress* (Washington, DC: White House, Office of the Press Secretary, 24 February 2009).

16 Lawrence R. Jacobs and Theda Skocpol, *Health Care Reform and American Politics: What Everyone Needs to Know* (New York: Oxford University Press, 2012).

17 Jacob S. Hacker, 'The Road to Somewhere: Why Health Reform Happened', *Perspectives on Politics*, 8(3) (2010), 861–876, 865.

18 Béland and Waddan, 'Obama Presidency and Health Insurance Reform'.

19 Personal interview with congressional staffer, Washington, DC, August 2010.

20 Jacobs and Skocpol, *Health Care Reform and American Politics*, 76–78.

21 *Remarks by the President to a Joint Session of Congress on Health Care* (Washington, DC: White House, Office of the Press Secretary, 9 September 2009).

22 Béland and Waddan, 'Obama Presidency and Health Insurance Reform'.

23 Ceci Connolly, 'How We Got There', in The Staff of the *Washington Post, Landmark: The Inside Story of America's New Health-Care Law and What It Means for Us All* (New York: PublicAffairs, 2010).

24 *Remarks by the President in State of the Union Address* (Washington, DC: White House, Office of the Press Secretary, 27 January 2010).

25 Robert Saldin, 'Healthcare Reform: A Prescription for the 2010 Republican Landslide?', *The Forum*, 8(4) (2010).

26 Skocpol, *Boomerang*.

27 Béland and Waddan, 'Obama Presidency and Health Insurance Reform'.

28 McKinsey Global Institute, *Accounting for the Cost of US Health Care* (December 2008); US Census Bureau, *Health Insurance Coverage Status and Type of Coverage by Selected Characteristics*, http://www.census.gov/hhes/www/cpstables/032011/health/h01_001.htm.

29 Kosali Simon, *Implications of Health Care Reform for Employers* (Washington, DC: Center for American Progress, 2011).

30 Congressional Budget Office (CBO), 'HR 4872: Reconciliation Act of 2010' (18 March 2010), http://www.cbo.gov/ftpdocs/113xx/doc11355/hr4872.pdf.

31 Ibid.

32 Paul Starr, 'The Mandate Miscalculation', *New Republic*, 29 November 2011, p. 11.

33 CBO, 'HR 4872'.

34 Ibid.

35 Connolly, 'How We Got There', 169–178.

36 Béland and Waddan, 'Obama Presidency and Health Insurance Reform'.

37 Alex Waddan, *Clinton's Legacy? A New Democrat in Governance* (Basingstoke: Palgrave Macmillan, 2007), 104–106.

38 Daniel Gitterman and John Scott, '"Obama Lies, Grandma Dies": The Uncertain Politics of Medicare and the Patient Protection and Affordable Care Act', *Journal of Health Politics, Policy and Law*, 36(3) (2011), 555–563, 556.

39 Saldin, 'Healthcare Reform'.

40 Congressional Budget Office, *The Budget and Economic Outlook: Fiscal Years 2010 to 2020* (Washington, DC: US Congress, 2010), http://www.cbo.gov/ftpdocs/108xx/doc10871/01-26-Outlook.pdf, 21.

41 The premiums at which the Cadillac tax kicked in were in fact finalized in the reconciliation bill. The original Senate bill had contained a more punitive regime, since it defined a high-cost plan as one at $8,500 for an individual and $23,000 for a family, with that due to come into effect in 2013. For workers in some high-risk jobs, such as fire-fighters, the thresholds at which the tax will come into effect are significantly higher. See Jenny Gold, '"Cadillac" Insurance Plans Explained', *Kaiser Health News*, 18 March 2010, http://www.kaiserhealthnews.org/Stories/2010/March/18/Cadillac-Tax-Explainer-Update.aspx.

42 Kaiser Family Foundation and Health Research and Educational Trust, *Employer Health Benefits: 2011 Summary of Findings*, http://ehbs.kff.org/pdf/8226.pdf, 1.

43 Quoted in Robert Pear, 'Insurers Told to Justify Rate Increases over 10 per cent', *New York Times*, 19 May 2011.

44 Kathryn Nix, 'Top Ten Disasters of Obamacare', Heritage Foundation web memo (2010), http://thf_media.s3.amazonaws.com/2010/pdf/wm_2848.pdf; David Cutler, Karen Davis and Kristoff Stremikis, *The Impact of Health Reform on Health System Spending* (Washington, DC: Commonwealth Fund and the Center for American Progress, 2010), http://www.americanprogress.org/issues/2010/05/pdf/system_spending.pdf.

45 Quoted in Tim Langmaid, 'Health Reform Extends Coverage to Young Americans', CNN, 14 December 2011, http://edition.cnn.com/2011/12/14/health/health-insurance/index.html?hpt=hp_t1.

46 Jennifer Hakerborn, Jason Millman and J. Lester Feder, 'Theory to Practice: Health Care Reform', *Politico*, 31 July 2011.

47 Julie Appleby, 'Concern Growing over Deadlines for Health-Care Exchanges', *Washington Post*, 19 December 2011.

48 Robert Pear, 'Program Offering Waivers for Health Law Is Ending', *New York Times*, 17 June 2011.

49 David Herszenhorn and Robert Pear, 'House Votes for Repeal of Health Law in Symbolic Act', *New York Times*, 19 January 2011.

50 Adam Liptak, 'Justices to Hear Health Case as Race Heats Up', *New York Times*, 14 November 2011.

51 Jeremy Peters, 'Roberts, in a Switch, says Health Care Mandate Is a Tax', *New York Times*, 4 July 2012.

52 See, for example, the stance of Texas Governor Rick Perry in Manny Fernandez, 'Perry Declares Texas' Rejection of Health Care Law "Intrusions"', *New York Times*, 9 July 2012.

53 Jim Rutenberg and Jeff Zeleny, 'Perry and Romney Come Out Swinging at Each Other in GOP Debate', *New York Times*, 22 September 2011.

54 Saldin, 'Healthcare Reform'.

55 Kaiser Family Foundation, *Kaiser Health Tracking Poll*, December 2011, http://www.kff.org/kaiserpolls/upload/8265-F.pdf.

56 Rasmussen Reports, 'Health Care Law', 9 January 2012, http://www.rasmussenreports.com/public_content/politics/current_events/healthcare/health_care_law.

57 Lawrence Jacobs, 'America's Critical Juncture: The Affordable Care Act and Its Reverberations', *Journal of Health Politics, Policy and Law*, 36(3) (2011), 625–631.

58 Jacobs and Skocpol, *Health Care Reform and American Politics*; Rogan Kersh, 'Health Reform: The Politics of Implementation', *Journal of Health Politics, Policy and Law*, 36(3) (2011), 613–623.

59 Michael Gusmano, 'Do We Really Want to Control Health Care Spending?', *Journal of Health Politics, Policy and Law*, 36(3) (2011), 437–441; Jonathan Oberlander, 'Throwing Darts: Americans' Elusive Search for Health Care Cost Control', *Journal of Health Politics, Policy and Law*, 36(3) (2011), 477–484.

60 David Leonhardt, 'In Health Bill, Obama Attacks Wealth Inequality', *New York Times*, 23 March 2010.

4 The Obama administration, the promise of reform and the role of business interests

Edward Ashbee

I

The celebrations that met Barack Obama's election as president in November 2008 extended beyond the ranks of established left-leaning periodicals such as *The Nation* and *The American Prospect*. Even those on the far left who stressed the logic of the capitalist order and the inability of reformism to ameliorate economic crises seemed to be caught up in the emotions of the moment. Although doubts were raised about Obama's embrace of 'post-partisanship' during the campaign, his opposition to the Iraq war, his defeat of Senator Hillary Clinton in the primaries, and repeated insistence upon 'change' appeared to mark a repudiation of both George W. Bush's presidency and the Clinton administration that preceded it.

There were hopes that the new Obama administration would, together with the Democratic majorities in Congress, enact far-reaching economic reform and challenge the entrenched financial interests that had, it was said, brought about the 'Great Recession'. So far as foreign policy was concerned, there would be a profound change of tone on at least some core issues. The military presence in Iraq would be brought to an end. There would be international cooperation and a renewed focus on alliances, particularly those with the countries of Western Europe. As Spencer Ackerman recorded in *The American Prospect* during Obama's primary battle with Hillary Clinton, 'Obama is offering the most sweeping liberal foreign-policy critique we've heard from a serious presidential contender in decades. It cuts to the heart of traditional Democratic timidity.'[1]

The economic context added a further layer to these hopes and expectations. Although the scale of the financial crisis and the likely fallout for the 'real' economy were not fully evident until the final stages of the campaign, they coloured the accounts of the 2008 presidential election that were published in its immediate aftermath. Comparisons with the Great Depression and the 1932 election abounded. The front cover of the 24 November edition of *Time* magazine, which transposed a picture of Obama with an image of a triumphant Franklin Roosevelt, captured the sentiments of many on the left and broader opinion. Both elections had taken place in the midst of recession, had been tied to promises of reform, and constituted significant political and economic turning points.

Accounts of the 2008 election also drew upon demographic variables. The election had, it was said, brought forth a coalitional bloc based upon a grassroots mobilization and structured around minorities and young people. Obama's status as the nation's first African-American president was not only significant in itself but a potent symbol of long-term demographic shifts and the changing character of the American nation: 'The election of Barack Obama is just the most startling manifestation of a larger trend: the gradual erosion of "whiteness" as the touchstone of what it means to be American.'[2]

Against this background, 2008 was said to be, like 1932, a 'realigning' or 'critical' election. Although often used simply to denote a significant political shift, the concept of 'realignment' has a long and established history. It suggests that the history of the parties can be divided between distinct systems or eras. Walter Dean Burnham talked about 30- to 36-year periods. Within each of these periods there is a dominant and a subordinate party. In a celebrated metaphor that captures the concept in its least nuanced form, Samuel Lubell talked about one party as the sun and the other as the moon. The 'sun party' is electorally predominant and largely sets the political and ideological agenda. Although the 'moon party' will periodically win national contests in 'deviating elections', it is on the terms defined by the 'sun party'. While theorists concede that there can be a drawn-out process of 'secular realignment' such as the change in voting patterns among white southerners as they shifted from the Democrats to the Republicans, there is an emphasis on 'critical' elections at which the relationship between the major parties shifts in a fundamental way. The 1932 election had, it was said, ushered in a long era of Democratic Party hegemony based upon a broad coalition incorporating industrial workers, ethnic groupings, and the white south.

The claim that realignment was taking place had to some extent been anticipated before the 2008 election. In their 2002 book *The Emerging Democratic Majority*, John Judis and Ruy Teixeira cited the demographic shifts noted above, changes in attitude among the younger age cohorts, the break-up of the traditional family, and changes within professional groupings in the high-tech metropolises (which because of their associations with the knowledge economy Judis and Teixeira dubbed 'ideopolises').[3] From this perspective, the 2000 and 2004 presidential elections were aberrations. Had it not been for the mathematics of the Electoral College, it was argued, Vice President Al Gore would have won the White House in 2000. President George W. Bush secured only a narrow victory over Senator John Kerry in 2004. In 2006, the Democrats secured majorities in both chambers of Congress.

The 'critical' election of 2008 was said to have built upon these trends. Although some were more cautious, Harold Meyerson of the *Washington Post* wrote amidst the post-election euphoria: 'Even though Obama's victory was nowhere near as numerically lopsided as Franklin Roosevelt's in 1932, his margins among decisive and growing constituencies make clear that this was a genuinely realigning election.'[4] Meyerson was not an isolated voice. James Carville, who served as Bill Clinton's campaign manager in 1992, published a book entitled *40 More Years: How the Democrats Will Rule the Next Generation.*[5]

II

Given these hopes and expectations, disillusionment with the new administration inevitably set in at an early stage amongst many on the left.[6] Drew Westen, professor in the Departments of Psychology and Psychiatry at Emory University and author of the 2007 book *The Political Brain*, reviewed the progress of an administration which from its earliest days had failed to provide a coherent story or narrative to oppose 'Wall Street gamblers'.[7] Disappointment came quickly. Many of the new administration's appointees, particularly those who would direct economic policy, had close ties with the banking sector and, despite the pre-election pledges of 'change', the Clinton administration. Some saw the American Recovery and Reinvestment Act (ARRA), the $787 billion fiscal stimulus that Congress passed just four weeks after Inauguration Day, as a turning point. Although the *Wall Street Journal* described the measure as a Democratic 'wish list' because it included spending commitments that were close to the party's collective heart, many on the left echoed Paul Krugman's critique of the

Act.[8] Krugman used his columns in the *New York Times* to argue that, given the magnitude of the crisis, the stimulus was too limited in size.

While the administration could cite significant legislative victories during its first two years, the list of disappointments then grew rapidly. Health care reform was finally signed by the president in March 2010. Yet the public option (by which the federal government would itself offer health insurance) was abandoned. The administration, furthermore, did not expend political capital to ensure the passage of other measures that were core to many on the left such as the Employee Free Choice Act (which would have bolstered the labour unions) or the American Clean Energy and Security Act of 2009. Indeed, at times, the administration sought to weaken legislation. At the end of 2010, Obama agreed to extend the Bush-era tax cuts, thereby aiding those in the highest income groupings and adding further to the federal government budget deficit.[9] The compromise was according to Robert Reich, President Clinton's Labor Secretary, an 'abomination': 'The deal further concentrates income and wealth in America – when it's already more concentrated than at any time in the last 80 years. The bits and pieces the President got in return . . . are peanuts.'[10] Then, in July 2011, the debt ceiling crisis was resolved only when the administration committed itself to expenditure cuts. Despite talk of 'resetting' US foreign policy as the new administration took office and the withdrawal of forces from Iraq at the end of 2011, the 'war on terror' was maintained. The Guantanamo detention camp remained open, while Predator drone attacks on targeted individuals in Afghanistan and Pakistan intensified. As the veteran Pakistani-British leftist author Tariq Ali observed, 'There was no fundamental break in foreign policy between the Bush and Obama regimes. The strategic goals and imperatives of the US imperium remain the same, as do its principal theatres and means of operation.'[11]

All of this, it was said, was not only mistaken in itself. The administration and the congressional Democrats were abandoning the core constituencies that had secured election victories in 2006 and 2008. Their concessions enabled the right to win the ideological argument, bolstered the conservative narrative, lent credence to the Tea Party movement, which grew up among and energized grassroots conservative constituencies during 2009 and 2010, demoralized Democrats, and drew independents towards the Republicans. Michael Moore, the radical filmmaker who supported the Occupy Wall Street protests that sprang up in late 2011, emphasized the importance of 18- to 29-year-olds who had voted for Obama in significant numbers in 2008. If they were to vote again, Moore argued, young people would insist upon the fulfilment of election pledges: 'You promise them something, you better do it or they're gonna call you on it.'[12] From this perspective, the Republicans' victories in the Virginia and New Jersey gubernatorial contests at the beginning of November 2009, the Democrats' loss of Edward Kennedy's Massachusetts Senate seat, and the defeats in the November 2010 midterm elections were a direct consequence of the administration's failure to deliver on its commitments.

III

In a relatively early analysis of the administration, Lawrence Jacobs and Desmond King have argued that many critiques of the Obama White House have been guilty of overemphasizing agency-based variables. In other words, they have exaggerated the degree of discretion open to the administration and underplayed the solidity, resilience and 'stickiness' of institutional arrangements. As they note, 'much popular commentary has attributed Obama's accomplishments and setbacks to his personality and that of his senior advisors'.[13]

In place of this, Jacobs and King argue the case for a more balanced approach. They consider the Obama presidency in terms of the president's goals and skills and the structural circumstances which circumscribe the room that political actors have for manoeuvre. In a rebuke to agency-based narratives (which they describe as 'personalism'), Jacobs and King argue that accounts should instead be informed by the concept of 'structured agency'. Structures, write Jacobs and King, create 'significant barriers to dramatic policy change'. Some, most notably the ability of the Senate (which is in itself undemocratically apportioned) to filibuster legislation, are very familiar. However, Jacobs and King also point to 'a political environment in which . . . independent regulatory bodies, and officials in his administration . . . can reject, stymie, or sabotage policies that threaten key relationships'. Furthermore, the structural barriers that obstruct reform go beyond 'Beltway' politics. There is also 'an economic environment in which private firms and their customers could respond to policy proposals by taking actions that drive down profitability or by shifting capital out of the US'.[14] In other words, capital and market processes have significant structural leverage: 'the dominant political economic relationships shape government policy by determining the conditions and structures that define what seems rational and feasible to government officials'.[15]

Beyond the structural weight of capital, Jacobs and King particularly emphasize the porousness of the state apparatus. Such porousness provides business interests (through financial contributions and access as well as mechanisms such as the 'revolving door' between corporations, most notably Wall Street firms, and government service) further opportunities to constrain reform opportunities. Citing a commentary by Simon Johnson, a former International Monetary Fund economist, in *The Atlantic*, Jacobs and King refer to a 'quiet coup' by 'America's oligarchs' engineered through a 'confluence of campaign finance, personal connections, and ideology'. They acknowledge countervailing forces, in particular geographic and sectoral cleavages within capital. Nonetheless, they add with particular reference to finance capital: 'The most visible forms of corruption – such as bribes – are not necessary in Washington because the industry is literally represented within government.'[16]

All this has consequences. First, although reform opportunities are very limited, there have been windows of opportunity. These are the moments when agency seemingly has the potential to trump structure. Second, in these moments, the strategic abilities and personalities of significant political actors (within this context, presidents) come to the fore. Their capacity to frame issues, construct coalitions and develop narratives is pivotal. Jacobs and King use terms that seem to echo Niccolò Machiavelli's *Il Principe*: 'Presidents have opportunities to lead, but not under the circumstances they choose or control. These circumstances both restrict the parameters of presidential impact and highlight the significance of presidential skill in accurately identifying and exploiting opportunities.'[17]

IV

Jacobs and King's account is a valuable corrective to narratives that edge towards notions of personal failure or even 'betrayal'. Nonetheless, some issues arise. The emphasis on 'seizing opportunities' seems to suggest that agency (in other words the discretionary actions of President Obama and the reforming 'wing' of his administration) comes into play at particular points in time. In other words, there were what might be dubbed 'moments of agency and choice'.[18] From this perspective, the shock of the financial crisis and the realization of its implications for the 'real economy' significantly weakened existing structural arrangements and thus offered an opening that would allow actors with sufficient skill to secure progressive reforms: 'The profound disruption of the economy and of political/economic

relationships jarred received wisdom and eroded the position of financial and corporate interests and relationships, opening up space for economic and social welfare reform.'[19]

But to what extent was there 'space' in early 2009 after Obama took office? There was a
rapid counter-mobilization by the conservative right through the Tea Party movement, and
the peak organizations representing business interests quickly regained their footing. More
significantly, methodological questions should be asked about the character of 'space' itself.
Does it open up only when the structural logic of markets is weakened in some way? Does
it also require countervailing forces to make an impact? Or is there 'space' only when those
holding structural power themselves seek or facilitate reform?

The discussion could be taken further. 'Space' suggests an opening within which agents
have relative freedom. Agency is unleashed. Arguably, however, 'space' is textured, layered
and contested. In other words, there is less freedom of action than the term implies. Studies of
'structure' and 'agency' should pay some conceptual heed to 'structuration'. Political actors
are always subject to structural processes but at the same time consciously and unconsciously
remould those structures. To some degree at least, in the celebrated words of 'Red' Blaik, the
American football coach, 'the champion makes his own luck'.

It might furthermore be argued that representations based upon the opening up of political
opportunity at particular moments are informed to a disproportionate degree by the notion
of critical junctures. Such junctures are usually said to arise as a consequence of exogenous
shocks that periodically disturb and disrupt structural arrangements that would otherwise
remain locked in. However, although critical junctures can be decisive, political actors (as
well as endogenous strains within structures) continually adjust and modify the character of
particular structural arrangements.

V

Beyond this, the role of capital and the market requires further consideration. In Jacobs and
King's account, as in some others, capital and 'America's oligarchs' only seem to constrain
political actors and radically curtail the degree of discretion open to them. In other words,
they are a deadweight constraint upon agency.

Certainly, given the history of the Obama administration, business elites can easily be
represented in this way. The structural weight of capital, the logic of the market, and the
lobbying processes undertaken by individual firms and sectors have all been pivotal in shaping policy outcomes. Business organizations, most notably the US Chamber of Commerce
(which claims to represent more than 3 million firms through its affiliates), backed Republican candidates (as well as 'a pro-growth agenda') in the November 2010 midterm elections.
They campaigned against health care reform, regulatory reform, corporate tax rates and the
'uncertainty' which they said had been generated by administration policies. However, capital
also had its representatives within the administration itself. Figures such as Larry Summers
(Director of the National Economic Council) and Tim Geithner (the Treasury Secretary) had
close Wall Street associations. They reined in economic policy. For example, reports suggested that Geithner had sought to weaken and dilute key provisions in the Dodd–Frank Wall
Street Reform and Consumer Protection Act.[20]

Nonetheless, there should be greater nuance. First, firms and those within them are themselves also agents engaged in a process of dynamic interaction with each other (through
both markets and non-market relationships), the institutional landscape and, in particular,
the state, state structures and state processes. Second, although that process of interaction
may lead firms and business organizations to resist political reform, it can also (within

parameters) empower and facilitate, rather than constrain, processes of path-departing change. Institutions themselves provide the tools, principles and repertoires that enable actors, including firms, to modify institutional structures.[21]

As a consequence, although contemporary perspectives regard business organizations as a close ally of Republicans and the conservative movement, business interests and attitudes are not static. There are shifts. These fluctuations in business attitudes are evident if the historical record is considered. Although President Franklin Roosevelt was at times subject to intense criticism by business leaders, there was a degree of business backing for the New Deal and the mid-century social reforms that built upon it through the 'Great Society'.[22] 'Corporate liberalism' and (less assertively) 'welfare capitalism' are established, if contested, concepts. If patterns across nations are considered, employers' organizations have, as Jill Quadagno has noted, sometimes taken the initiative in creating social programmes.[23] Such reforms can reinforce the competitive position of larger businesses which can, unlike smaller firms, absorb the sizeable costs that may be imposed. It could also be argued that such reforms serve collective business interests even if there were anxiety and uncertainty amongst some individual firms. As Fred Block has recently noted:

> many types of government programs were, in fact, productive – including the entitlement programs so detested by market fundamentalists. . . . Rather than eroding their economic position, well-financed public programs have made Nordic nations more competitive. Substantial investments in higher education have resulted in a highly skilled labor force, and income supports have nurtured, not undermined, a risk-taking culture of entrepreneurialism and innovation.[24]

Alternatively, there have been claims that there are significant sectoral cleavages between business interests. Social reform, 'welfare capitalism' and the policies broadly associated with the Democratic Party are backed by some sectors but not others. Thomas Ferguson has drawn upon the 'investment theory' of party competition to argue that the New Deal (and the later reforms) secured particular support from capital-intensive industries that looked towards international markets and were less 'labour-sensitive' than more traditional labour-intensive firms. They were thus in more of a position to endorse progressive reforms that might add to their costs and had a direct interest in the adoption of reflationary policies.[25]

The shifts, ambiguities and tensions in business opinion are also evident if contemporary attitudes towards the Obama White House and the congressional Democrats are charted from January 2009 onwards. Less than a month after Inauguration Day, peak business organizations and many individual firms parted company with the Republicans and backed passage of the American Recovery and Reinvestment Act, the $787 billion fiscal stimulus package. They joined together with sub-national governments, the labour unions and other Democratic Party constituencies both to press Congress to pass the Act and in some instances to seek funding under its provisions. The National Association of Manufacturers (NAM) wrote to its member companies urging them to back the measure and stating that NAM might use the roll call a 'key vote' when constructing its 'ratings'.[26] Indeed, its support was held to be critical to the passage of the bill through Congress. Labor Secretary Hilda Solis publicly thanked NAM and said that its backing 'was key to its passage on Capitol Hill'.[27]

What explains these different business strategies? In part, as perhaps in the 1930s, the answer lies in cleavages between sectors. The new technology sector, which has ever-growing weight within business elites, has identified itself with the Democratic Party and, in particular, the Obama presidency. In the 2008 election, influential new technology entrepreneurs backed the Obama campaign. Indeed, Mike Davis, author of studies such as *City of Quartz*, cites Ferguson's 'investment theory' of party competition and invokes images of a marriage:

> The near constant presence of Google CEO Eric Schmidt at Obama's side (and inside his transition team) has been a carefully chosen symbol of the knot that has been tied between Silicon Valley and the presidency. The dowry included the overwhelming majority of presidential campaign contributions from executives and employees of Cisco, Apple, Oracle, Hewlett-Packard, Yahoo and Ebay.[28]

It should be added that the new technology sector expected to secure significant gains from the fiscal stimulus. There was, from an early stage, a commitment to include expenditure on broadband expansion and a high-tech infrastructure.

Nonetheless, this line of argument should not be pursued too far. All the indications are that the 'marriage' was under severe strain by late 2010. There was little difference between political action committee contributions to federal candidates in the new and the old technology sector. In both, donations were correlated with incumbency and expected election outcomes. In the 2010 election cycle, there was evidence of a pull towards the Republicans. And individuals also seemed to be shifting. In his biography of Steve Jobs, Walter Isaacson recalls a meeting between Jobs and Obama. Jobs told Obama: 'you're headed for a one-term presidency'. He urged the administration to become more business-friendly: 'He described how easy it was to build a factory in China and said that it was almost impossible to do so these days in America, largely because of regulations and unnecessary costs.'[29]

Other explanations should therefore be sought for the shifts and changes in business opinion. Arguably, economic pressures and the institutional architecture within which many business sectors operated pulled in different and competing directions. Firms were at times drawn towards 'corporate liberalism' or, at the least, away from the issue positions promoted by, and within, the Republican Party.

The reasons for this are readily evident. For many firms, opportunity cost ratios shifted during the 1990s and in the early years of the new century. In particular, there was a significant rise in the cost of health care provision borne by firms, and there were suggestions that this might lead companies to back an expansion of the federal government's role. Although the annual rise in costs spiked at the beginning of the new century (at over 14 per cent), the increase in employer-based health care costs was far above the rate of inflation.[30]

There were also concerns about the political character of the Republican grassroots and, at times, the congressional Republicans, particularly as the backlash against the Obama administration took off into self-sustained growth. These anxieties became pronounced as the Tea Party movement grew and at the time of the debt ceiling crisis. As Lisa Lerer and John McCormick suggested in *Bloomberg Businessweek*, 'The Tea Party's brand of political nitroglycerin, in short, is too unstable for businesses that look to government for predictability, moderation and the creation of a stable economic environment.'[31]

More significantly, a variant on the 'fiscal illusion' has played a part in pulling firms towards 'corporate liberalism'. The 'fiscal illusion' suggests that individuals will be ready to accept fiscal expansion because it is not immediately evident that the additional government expenditure that is required will later have to be recouped through increased tax revenue. In other words, it is a 'systematic misperception by individuals of both the public revenue burden borne by them and the amount of benefit they derive from public expenditures'.[32] Yet, for many US firms (and arguably individuals in the higher income and wealth brackets), the 'illusion' is only partly illusory. At first sight, firms pay substantial taxes. The top statutory rate imposed on corporate income at federal level is 35 per cent (payable on a company's entire taxable income once it exceeds $18.33 million [2008]). There are also state corporate taxes.[33] As Table 4.1 indicates, such rates put the US almost at the top among the OECD countries and far above the OECD average. Indeed, only Japan has a higher corporate tax rate.

However, as scholars increasingly note, the US state has a fragmented and often open character. For their part, Jacobs and King refer to 'the administrative state's generally porous, easily penetrated boundaries'.[34] That porosity encourages those particularistic interests with political resources to seek and secure exemptions and concessions, all of which taken together substantially reduce the tax base. For the most part, these are secured by congressmen and senators responding to pressures in either the district or the state that they represent from lobbying by organizations that have a national presence. They will tend to be larger firms or sectors that can exercise political influence. Smaller or less influential firms or business organizations may well face a proportionately higher tax bill.[35] As a consequence, there are: 'thousands of exemptions, deductions, credits, minimum taxes, and special rules that litter the tax code. Indeed, these tax expenditures are so significant to the system that they profoundly shape its very structure.'[36]

The effects can be seen if a comparison is drawn between the corporate tax rate (which was noted earlier) and the *revenue* that is secured from the levying of the tax. Corporate tax revenue is, as a proportion of GDP, substantially lower than in many other nations. A study for PricewaterhouseCoopers concluded:

> Although the United States has the second highest statutory corporate tax . . . U.S. corporate income tax revenue (federal and state) as a percentage of GDP paradoxically is much lower than the OECD average – 2.2 percent in the United States versus an OECD average of 3.4 percent – over the 2000–2005 period. In short . . . the United States has the second highest combined statutory corporate tax rate among OECD countries, yet is tied with Hungary in raising the fourth lowest amount of combined corporate income tax revenue relative to GDP in 2004.[37]

Table 4.1 Combined corporate income tax rate, 2009

Country	Combined corporate income tax rate, 2009 %
Japan	39.54
United States	39.1
France	34.43
Canada	31.32
Germany	30.18
United Kingdom	28
Denmark	25
Ireland	12.5
OECD average	26.29

Source: Adapted from Tax Foundation, *OECD Nations Continue Cutting Corporate Tax Rates while U.S. Stands Still (Federal plus Provincial/State Corporate Tax Rates for OECD Countries, 2008–2009)*, 3 August 2009, http://www.taxfoundation.org/taxdata/show/23473. html.

In sum, the many US business interests that have secured particularistic exemptions or concessions can back fiscal expansion while only bearing a limited tax burden at a later stage.

At the same time, other features of the institutional landscape pull firms and business organizations in a very different direction towards political positions associated with conservatism and the Republican Party. Although, as noted above, the character of US state structures and processes allows firms to seek (through both lobbying and legal channels) particularistic advantages, it also imposes burdens on corporate interests. While the left has made much of 'under-regulation' in recent years (particularly of the financial sector), the degree of regulation on firms is only evident if the regulatory constraints imposed by federal, state and local governments are considered alongside those that arise out of the relationship between US state structures and civil society. In contrast with the situation in many European countries, many forms of regulation are enforced through civil litigation rather than through 'a bureaucracy-centered enforcement regime . . . but they nonetheless impose significant costs upon firms'. Much de facto health and safety and recruitment policy is made in this way as firms seek to avoid the costs of compensation and litigation if cases are brought alleging negligence or discrimination.[38] As a consequence, the perception by firms that the Obama administration was adding yet further to the formal regulatory burden came within a context in which businesses already felt heavily restricted by the interaction of government and civil constraints.

Another factor was also of significance in drawing firms towards a coalitional bloc with the conservative movement and Republicans. Although corporate profits fell during 2007 and to a greater extent in 2008, they recovered comparatively quickly. Indeed, as Table 4.2 suggests, by 2010 the annual figures for US domestic industries more or less matched the 2006 pre-recession peak.[39]

Furthermore, following the dramatic rise in the federal government deficit as the 'Great Recession' took its toll, many firms had a direct interest in personal, corporate and government deleveraging, the restabilization of credit arrangements, and the maintenance in value of dollar-denominated holdings. Firms had such an interest because of the process of financialization and the inter-linkages between the financial sector and non-business firms that developed towards the end of the twentieth century. Many firms had begun to engage in financial and speculative activities. They purchased financial assets. It was reported that in 2004 General Motors earned $2.9 billion from its financing operations while making a loss on car production.[40]

Table 4.2 Corporate profits before tax – domestic industry, 2004–10

Year	Pre-tax corporate profits ($ million)
2004	1,229,403
2005	1,640,158
2006	1,822,720
2007	1,738,355
2008	1,359,934
2009	1,455,672
2010	1,819,468

Source: Adapted from Bureau of Economic Analysis, *National Income and Product Accounts Table* (2011), Table 6.17D: Corporate profits before tax by industry, http://www.bea.gov/national/nipaweb/TableView.asp?SelectedTable=243&ViewSeries=NO&Java=no&Request3Place=N&3Place=N&FromView=YES&Freq=Year&FirstYear=2004&LastYear=2010&3Place=N&Update=Update&JavaBox=no.

VI

Although some have explained the failure of the Obama White House to deliver upon its promises of 'change' as a personal lack of resolve, more balanced accounts consider the structural obstacles facing the administration. These include those that arise from not only the separation of powers but also the leverage exercised by business interests and the markets. Within this context, there is only limited 'space' for reformers to pursue their goals, and much depends upon the efficacy of the political skills that they deploy.

Accounts should however go further. Even when there is 'space', reform opportunities depend upon the interests and perceptions of those with disproportionate political influence, in particular business interests. Their structural location shapes those interests and perceptions. As in the New Deal era and the mid-century years, business is today pulled between 'welfare capitalism' (which offers social reforms) and a more individualist form of capitalism in which each firm seeks particularistic advantages within the market and from government. In these earlier periods, some significant firms made their peace with 'welfare capitalism'. In the economic crisis that took hold from 2007 onwards, business has for the most part been pulled backed towards individualist forms of capitalism. Within such a context, the reforms pursued and secured by the Obama administration were inevitably limited in both character and scope.

Notes

1   Spencer Ackerman, 'The Obama Doctrine', *American Prospect*, 19 March 2008, http://prospect.org/article/obama-doctrine.
2   Hua Hsu, 'End of White America?', *The Atlantic*, January/February 2009.
3   John B. Judis and Ruy Teixeira, *The Emerging Democratic Majority* (New York: Scribner, 2002).
4   Harold Meyerson, 'A Rapid Realignment', *Washington Post*, 7 November 2008, p. A19.
5   James Carville with Rebecca Buckwalter-Poza, *40 More Years: How the Democrats Will Rule the Next Generation* (New York: Simon & Schuster, 2009).
6   The right was as unremitting in its criticisms of the incoming administration as it had been of the Obama campaign. Glenn Beck's programmes on the Fox News Channel concentrated on the radical ties of some in the administration and claimed its first scalp in September 2009 when Van Jones was forced to leave his position as Special Advisor for Green Jobs. The rise of the Tea Party movement galvanized conservative opposition to increased federal government spending, health care reform and regulatory reform.
7   Drew Westen, 'What Happened to Obama?', *New York Times*, 6 August 2011.
8   'A 40-Year Wish List', *Wall Street Journal*, 28 January 2009, p. A14.
9   Brian Montopoli, 'Obama Signs Bill to Extend Bush Tax Cuts', *CBS News*, 17 December 2010, http:/onlinelibrary.Wiley.com/doi/10.1111/j.1467-6435.1978.tb00648.x/abstract.
10 Robert Reich, 'The President's Last Stand Is No Stand at All: Why the Tax Deal Is an Abomination', 7 December 2010, http://robertreich.org/post/2132901013.
11 Tariq Ali, 'New Face, Same Imperialism', *The Age*, 6 October 2010.
12 Quoted in Extreme Liberal's Blog, 'With Friends like Michael Moore, Who Needs Enemies?', 4 November 2011, http://extremeliberal.wordpress.com/2011/11/04/with-friends-like-michael-moore-who-needs-enemies/.
13 Lawrence R. Jacobs and Desmond S. King, 'Varieties of Obamaism: Structure, Agency, and the Obama Presidency', *Perspectives on Politics*, 8(3) (2010), 793–802, 794.
14 Ibid., 795.
15 Ibid., 797.
16 Ibid., 797.
17 Ibid., 794.
18 James Mahoney and Kathleen Thelen, 'A Theory of Institutional Change', in J. Mahoney and K. Thelen, eds, *Explaining Institutional Change: Ambiguity, Agency, and Power* (Cambridge: Cambridge University Press, 2010), 7.

19 Jacobs and King, 'Varieties of Obamaism', 796. White House Chief of Staff Rahm Emanuel's celebrated comment on the political exploitation of crises ('You never want a serious crisis to go to waste') also appears to represent the relationship between structure and agency in terms of a weakened structure bringing forth agency.

20 Robert Kuttner, 'So Long, So Long, and Thanks from All the Banks', *American Prospect*, 1 July 2011.

21 John L. Campbell, *Institutional Change and Globalization* (Princeton, NJ: Princeton University Press, 2004), 72.

22 As in other countries, many reforms were more restricted in character than it might initially appear. The 1935 Social Security Act restricted social insurance benefits to those in the labour force and devolved the administration of programmes to the individual states. See Jill S. Quadagno, 'Welfare Capitalism and the Social Security Act of 1935', *American Sociological Review*, 49(5) (1984), 632–647. It should be added that the degree of business backing for the New Deal should not be overstated and is subject to controversy. It has been argued that backing for the Democrats during the New Deal era owed much to sectional loyalties (most notably in the south) and ethnic group ties. See G. William Domhoff, 'Review: *Golden Rule: The Investment Theory of Party Competition and the Logic of Money-Driven Political Systems* by Thomas Ferguson', *Contemporary Sociology*, 25(2) (1996), 197–198.

23 Jill S. Quadagno, 'Theories of the Welfare State', *Annual Review of Sociology*, 13 (1987), 109–128.

24 Fred Block, 'Daniel Bell's Prophecy', *Breakthrough Journal*, Fall, 2011, http://breakthroughjournal. org/content/authors/fred-block/daniel-bells-prophecy.shtml. It might, however, be argued that the institutional complementarities associated both with market economies such as the US and with the coordinated market economies of continental Europe (which offer greater state social provision) militate against a shift from one 'variety of capitalism' to another.

25 Thomas Ferguson, *Golden Rule: The Investment Theory of Party Competition and the Logic of Money-Driven Political Systems* (Chicago, IL: University of Chicago Press, 1995), 121–129.

26 Paul M. Krawzak and Joseph J. Schatz, 'Senate Clears Stimulus Package without a Vote to Spare', *CQ Politics*, 15 February 2009, http:www.cqpolitics.com/wmspage.cfm?docID=news-000003046178&cpage=2.

27 The Hill's Blog Briefing Room, 'Solis Doesn't Mention Union Bill at Business Group Breakfast', 7 May 2009, http://thehill.com/blogs/blog-briefing-room/news/legislation/35962-solis-doesnt-mention-union-bill-at-business-group-breakfast.

28 Mike Davis, 'Obama at Manassas', *New Left Review* (2009), 5–40, 36.

29 Walter Isaacson, *Steve Jobs* (Boston, MA: Little, Brown, 2011), 544.

30 'Employers Accelerate Efforts to Bring Health Benefits Cost under Control', Mercer, 16 November 2011, http://www.mercer.com/press-releases/1434885.

31 Lisa Lerer and John McCormick, 'The Devil You Don't Know', *Bloomberg Businessweek*, 18–24 October 2010, p. 69.

32 Werner W. Pommerehne and Friedrich Schneider, 'Fiscal Illusion, Political Institutions, and Local Public Spending', *Kylos*, 31(3) (1978), 381–408.

33 State taxes are a deductible expense when federal taxes are paid. The total paid by a company will therefore be lower than the two tax rates added together.

34 Jacobs and King, 'Varieties of Obamaism', 798.

35 As Jennifer Rubin has noted in the *Washington Post*, this curtails the market pressures that larger and more influential firms face from smaller or less politically influential competitors. See Jennifer Rubin, 'Big Business vs. Conservatives on Tax Reform', *Washington Post*, 27 March 2011.

36 Sven Steinmo, 'Political Institutions and Tax Policy in the United States, Sweden and Britain', *World Politics*, 61(4) (1989), 500–535.

37 Peter R. Merrill, *The Corporate Tax Conundrum* (Washington, DC: PricewaterhouseCoopers, 2007), http://www.pwc.com/en_US/us/washington-national-tax/assets/corporate_tax_conundrum. pdf, 2. Furthermore, tax revenue has, as a share of GDP, fallen substantially over the past 50 years. See Kimberley A. Clausing, 'Corporate Tax Revenues in OECD Countries', *International Tax and Public Finance*, 14(2) (2007), 115–133.

38 Desmond King and Marc Stearns, 'How the US State Works: A Theory of Standardization', *Perspectives on Politics*, 9(3) (2011), 505–518.

39 Bureau of Economic Analysis, *National Income and Product Accounts Table* (2011), Table 6.17D: Corporate profits before tax by industry, http://www.bea.gov/national/nipaweb/TableView.asp?SelectedTable=243&ViewSeries=NO&Java=no&Request3Place=N&3Place=N&FromView=YES&Freq=Year&FirstYear=2004&LastYear=2010&3Place=N&Update=Update&JavaBox=no. The profits recovery was tied to a rebound after 2007 and 2008, productivity gains, the weakness of labour, the degree to which US companies had penetrated foreign markets, and a reluctance to invest in uncertain economic circumstances.
40 Fred Magdoff, 'The Explosion of Debt and Speculation', *Monthly Review*, 58(6) (2006), http://monthlyreview.org/2006/11/01/the-explosion-of-debt-and-speculation.

5 The quest for renewed economic prosperity

US economic policy in the twenty-first century

Iwan Morgan

In the second half of the twentieth century, the primary task of American economic policy was to manage prosperity. In the second decade of the twenty-first century, however, the economic challenge facing the United States is to renew prosperity in the wake of the deepest recession since the 1930s. The modern US economy had always rebounded from previous travails. The Great Depression gave way to post-war plenty, and 1970s stagflation was succeeded by economic revitalization in the late twentieth century. In contrast, the weak recovery that followed the Great Recession of 2007–09 engendered gloomy forecasts that the US would take years to regain economic vigour and was entering an era of relative economic decline in the face of the rise of new powers like Brazil, India and – most notably – China. This chapter offers an outline analysis of economic management during twentieth-century prosperity, considers the records of the George W. Bush and Barack Obama administrations in dealing with twenty-first-century economic challenges, and assesses US prospects of economic renewal in the wake of the Great Recession.

Managing prosperity, 1945–2000

America's prosperity in the quarter-century after the Second World War rested on broad foundations: the high productivity of its business enterprises; the purchasing power of its rapidly expanding middle class; the growth of defence-related industries thanks to public investment of some 10 per cent of national output annually in national security in the 1950s and nearly 9 per cent in the 1960s; and the reduced economic challenge of its foreign rivals while engaged in post-war reconstruction. When economic changes in the 1970s threatened to undermine prosperity, the United States found economic renewal through high-tech enterprise and financial service expansion. As a new century beckoned, the term 'new economy' was conventionally applied to signal this transformation that engendered widespread optimism about the continuation of America's economic power and prosperity.[1]

According to historian Robert Collins, pursuit of growth was both the defining feature of US economic policy and a vehicle for achieving ideological goals from 1945 to 2000.[2] There were three broad phases in its evolution: a liberal Keynesian period from 1945 to 1970, a transitional stage in the 1970s, and thereafter a conservative supply-side era. As historian Wyatt Wells observed, Keynesian-oriented policy aimed to 'smooth out the rough edges of American capitalism by limiting destructive competition, protecting workers, and stabilizing demand', while supply-side initiatives 'sought to hone the cutting edge of the capitalist system, encouraging innovation, investment and risk-taking'.[3]

In the Keynesian era, economic policy reflected the legacy of the Great Depression in prioritizing high employment and strong growth. Countercyclical policy sufficed to keep the economy on an expansionary track during the Truman–Eisenhower years. During recessions (habitually short and mild), fiscal deficits compensated for the decline of private demand, and interest-rate cuts eased the flow of credit. When creeping inflation was a concern (consumer price increases rarely exceeded 2 per cent annually), fiscal and monetary restraint dampened demand.[4] By 1960, however, there was consternation about an estimated $50 billion performance gap, equivalent to 10 per cent GDP, between actual and potential economic output. To close this, the Kennedy–Johnson Democratic administrations implemented a new economic policy to maximize growth rather than merely achieve countercyclical stabilization. The centrepiece of this strategy was the 1964 tax cut that marked the culmination of the fiscal revolution initiated in the 1930s to manage aggregate demand. However, the federal budget became an engine of inflation in the second half of the 1960s because economic production could not keep pace with the expanding consumer demand of a full-employment economy and the growth in public outlays occasioned by Great Society expenditure and, in particular, the Vietnam War.[5]

With the inflationary genie out of the bottle, new pressures sent consumer prices skyrocketing by 9 per cent yearly in 1973–80. Increasing dependency on imported energy exposed America to foreign oil-price hikes; the dollar's declining value following abandonment of post-war fixed-exchange rates in 1971–73 made imports dearer; and productivity fell sharply (mainly because of labour market changes, a shift of business investment to meet environmental regulation, and transfer of manufacturing to American subsidiaries abroad). The resultant economic uncertainty also precipitated recessions in 1969–70, 1974–75 and 1980. Seeking to restore good times, policymakers alternated between fighting inflation and boosting jobs, but, in addressing one side of the stagflation problem, they invariably aggravated the other.[6]

A new economic policy that continued to focus on growth but prioritized price stability over high employment finally conquered stagflation in the 1980s. Assuming principal responsibility for combating inflation, the Federal Reserve adopted a monetarist approach that suppressed inflation by slowing money-supply growth at the cost of the worst recession since the 1930s in 1981–82. Meanwhile the Reagan administration embarked on an anti-statist supply-side strategy to enhance individual incentive as the means of economic renewal. This elevated free-market principles over mixed-economy ones in featuring tax cuts, deregulation, and support for business over labour in industrial disputes.[7] Reaganomics, as it became known, assisted strong economic recovery from the recession, but also gave rise to new problems.

In the 1980s the US economy showed early signs of overreliance on debt-financed consumption that would culminate in the economic crisis of 2007–09. The root cause was the huge budget deficits that accrued from Reagan's 1981 tax cuts and massive defence build-up. By absorbing national saving, these imbalances compelled America to look abroad for new investment funds to sustain economic growth. As a consequence the US metamorphosed from the world's largest creditor with net foreign assets of $141 billion in 1980 to its largest debtor with net foreign liabilities of $111 billion in 1985. Although nominal interest rates came down after 1982, they remained higher in real (inflation-adjusted) terms than in other advanced nations to induce foreigners to hold American assets. This sent the dollar skyrocketing in value, which made imports cheaper and saddled exports with a price disadvantage, thereby creating a large trade deficit. The consequent hollowing out of traditional manufacturing industries resulted in the loss of blue-collar jobs, which in turn exacerbated income inequality in American society. Meanwhile, deregulation had somewhat inconsistent success. Its stimulation of competition in the airline, trucking and oil industries, in particular, forced down prices in these crucial sectors, but its effect on the financial sector offered a foretaste of future problems. By 1989, the savings-and-loans industry, the bedrock of home mortgage finance, verged on bankruptcy after deregulation enabled it to enter new investment markets that did not yield profits, necessitating an expensive public bailout that cost nearly $125 billion.[8]

Economic policymakers sought to build on the achievements of Reaganomics while correcting its deficit habit in the 1990s. President George H. W. Bush and leaders of the Democrat-controlled Congress agreed a $496 billion five-year deficit-reduction plan in 1990, but its inclusion of tax increases alienated many in the congressional GOP as a betrayal of the Reagan legacy. In 1993, President Bill Clinton promoted a $432 billion five-year deficit-reduction programme, whose tax increases further angered the Republican right. Despite this political fallout, the economic effects of deficit reduction were ultimately beneficial.[9]

As a 'New Democrat', Clinton adopted a middle-way supply-side strategy that sought to promote private investment by making loan capital more affordable. Fearful that large fiscal imbalances would reactivate inflation, the Federal Reserve had kept short-term interest rates at a high level, and the bond market, the main source of investment finance, did the same for its long-term lending. As the deficit shrank from 4.9 per cent GDP in fiscal year (FY) 1992 to 1.4 per cent GDP in FY 1995 and then gave way to four surplus budgets in FY 1998–2001 – the longest sequence since the 1920s – both sets of interest rates tumbled down. Meanwhile, productivity gains from new high-tech enterprises, whose emergence benefited from the supply of cheaper capital, drove the economy forward to produce the best figures for growth, unemployment and inflation since the 1960s in the last years of the twentieth century.[10]

Bust to bust 2001–08

The 1990s boom eventually turned into an unsustainable bubble, which burst with recessionary consequences shortly after George W. Bush became president. In seeking to mitigate the effects of this, economic policymakers created another bubble that burst with far more serious effects. The cyclical rollercoaster reflected structural economic weaknesses that had surfaced in the 1980s and grown worse over time.

Economic success in the 1990s exacerbated rather than eradicated reliance on debt to fuel economic growth, business investment, and consumption and failed to reduce income inequality. While GDP expanded from $5.8 trillion in 1990 to $9.8 trillion in 2000, total debt concurrently increased from $13.5 trillion to $26.3 trillion. In 2000, household debt amounted to $7 trillion ($3.6 trillion in 1990), financial firm debt was $8.1 trillion ($2.6 trillion), non-financial business debt was $6.6 trillion ($3.7 trillion), and local, state and federal government debt combined was $4.6 trillion ($3.5 trillion).[11] Factoring out home ownership, two out of five households had more debt than assets at the century's end. For Americans in the top half of the income distribution, borrowing facilitated participation in the consumer, real estate and stock market booms of the 1990s. For many in the bottom half it was a necessity of life because of income stagnation, the decline of blue-collar jobs, and lack of educational qualifications to participate in the buoyant employment sectors of the new economy. Further evidencing the limited distributional benefits of the boom, the poverty rate declined to only 11.8 per cent by 1999 compared with 12.8 per cent a decade earlier.[12]

Personal saving declined from 5 per cent GDP in 1990 to near zero by 1998 as Americans stocked up on cheap debt to finance consumer spending, real estate dealings and stock market speculation. In these circumstances, long-term investment – whether in private enterprise or US Treasury securities – again relied on capital from abroad. With foreigners increasingly enthusiastic about participation in the well-functioning American financial markets and seemingly assured of good returns, their increasing purchases of dollar assets did much to send the greenback's value into a new upward spiral from the mid-1990s onward. This followed a weak-dollar cycle after America and other G-5 nations in 1985 agreed to rebalance the international economy. The corollary effect was to widen America's trade deficit and its external imbalances, both of which had shrunk significantly as a result of international economic coordination.[13]

In contrast to the situation in the 1980s, high interest rates were no longer necessary to attract foreign capital. America could therefore act as the consumer of last resort to rescue the global economy from financial crisis as the twentieth century drew to a close. The strong dollar adversely affected a number of developing economies that had tied their currency to its value when relatively low in order to boost their global exports. This precipitated a current account crisis in a number of East Asian countries in 1997, with the contagion spreading thereafter to Russia and eventually Latin America. A renewed burst of Federal Reserve interest-rate cuts saved the day by stimulating a credit-driven US consumer boom that sucked in more cheap imports. The long-term effect, however, was to exacerbate global economic imbalance whereby high-saving, export-oriented nations, particularly in Asia, were reliant on America's propensity to borrow and consume.[14]

Cheap credit also turned the American stock market boom into an unsustainable bubble. The Dow Jones index, which stood at 5000 points in early 1996, more than doubled over the next five years. By 1999, almost half of American households owned stock, directly or through pension plans, compared to less than a third in 1990 and less than one in ten in the 1960s. However, much of the new money inflated the value of start-up dot.com companies to unsustainable levels. The bull market turned into a bear market when investors awoke to this reality. The resultant shakeout of dot.com stocks precipitated the onset of recession in early 2001. Signs of economic recovery in the second half of the year were then threatened by the shock from the 9/11 terrorist attacks on New York and Washington, DC.[15]

The Bush administration pinned its hopes for economic revitalization on massive tax reduction. The Economic Growth and Tax Relief Reconciliation Act (EGTRRA) of 2001 and the Jobs and Growth Tax Relief Reconciliation Act (JGTRRA) of 2003 were respectively the second and third largest tax cuts in American history after Reagan's Economic Recovery Tax Act of 1981. However, their impact on economic recovery was nowhere near as great as the administration claimed, because the distributional skew was heavily towards the affluent rather than towards broad-based stimulation of consumption. According to the non-partisan Citizens for Tax Justice, 40 per cent of EGTRRA's benefits flowed to the richest 1 per cent of the population, approximately the same share as the bottom 80 per cent on the income ladder received. JGTRRA was even more biased towards the wealthy, with three-quarters of its capital gains and dividend tax cuts flowing to the 3.1 per cent of households with an annual income in excess of $200,000. Bush spent much of his second term lobbying for these 'sunset' measures, which were due to expire in 2010, to be made permanent on grounds that they were vital to sustain economic growth. According to Treasury Department data, however, this would increase annual output by only 0.7 per cent over ten years, while the Congressional Budget Office estimated the cost in revenue lost to federal coffers at $1.5 trillion in FY 2011 to FY 2015.[16]

Making a limited contribution to economic growth, the Bush tax cuts along with the wars in Afghanistan and Iraq and an expansion of domestic spending combined to keep the budget in the red long after the 2001 recession had ended. The fiscal deterioration from a 2.4 per cent GDP surplus in FY 2000 to a 3.6 per cent GDP deficit in FY 2004 was unmatched in peacetime since the early 1930s. The deleterious effect of this on national saving, which turned negative in 2005 for the first time since 1933, meant that the United States increasingly had to look overseas to fund its private and public borrowing. However, foreigners aplenty found the opportunity to acquire dollar assets irresistible.

The United States became a magnet for capital investment from across the Atlantic because a then strong euro had considerable purchasing power. By 2006, some two-thirds of capital buying in America came from Europe. Meanwhile, East Asian banks lined up to buy US Treasury securities in part to build up dollar reserves as a hedge against the kind of financial crisis experienced in 1997 but more significantly to ensure that their countries' exports benefited from currency exchange rates favourable to their competitiveness in the giant American market. Foreigners held just over 50 per cent of the US public debt by the time Bush left office, with China's portion amounting to some $1.4 trillion. As a result of these parallel developments, America in 2006 absorbed an estimated 80 per cent of the savings that the rest of the world did not invest at home.[17]

One immediate consequence of this was to send America's trade deficit ballooning from $454 billion in 2000 to $847 billion in 2006. As a corollary to this, the US current account deficit (comprising the trade deficit, net interest payments to foreigners, and foreign transfers) mushroomed to $857 billion, equal to 6.5 per cent national GDP and 1.7 per cent world GDP in 2006. This level of external indebtedness was unsustainable and exposed the United States to the dangers of an eventual foreign retreat from the dollar. Since other nations had experienced financial crisis when their external imbalances approached 4 per cent GDP, many analysts warned that America was heading for a crash of epic proportions. Instead, it was domestic borrowing that precipitated the crisis, but America's foreign borrowing was intimately connected to this.[18]

When the US had needed foreign capital in the 1980s, it had operated high interest rates to attract overseas investors. Global enthusiasm for dollar assets made this unnecessary in the early twenty-first century. Accordingly the Federal Reserve under Alan Greenspan's leadership maintained interest rates at a historically low level from 2001 through 2004 to stimulate recovery from the recession of 2001 and counter the economic shock of 9/11. Low interest rates had fuelled a stock market boom in the 1990s; now their effect was to create a real estate boom, but with the same bubble consequences. By mid-2004, house-price inflation was at a 25-year high, and the aggregate value of single-family homes rose by $8 trillion in 2000–05. Many families with dubious credit histories or unstable income sources, particularly those living in economically declining, black, inner-city neighbourhoods, were tempted to enter the real estate market or refinance their homes through the availability of subprime mortgages. Of the nearly $3 trillion of home mortgage originations in 2006, a fifth fell into this category.[19]

By 2007 total private-sector debt was a massive $41 trillion (294 per cent GDP compared with 222 per cent GDP in 2000), with household, financial firm and non-financial business shares of this amounting to $13.8 trillion, $16 trillion and $10.6 trillion respectively.[20] As well as cheap credit, what made this debt binge possible was the laxity of lending institutions in over-extending their loan finance provision. This development was largely attributable to deregulatory initiatives undertaken in the past with a view to making US financial services more competitive in a globalized world. Most significant in this regard was the Financial Services Modernization Act of 1999, a bipartisan measure supported by the Clinton White House, the congressional GOP and the Greenspan Fed, which removed limitations imposed by the Glass–Steagall Act of 1933 on the ability of banks, investment firms and insurance companies to enter each other's markets. This paved the way for their engagement in the buying and selling of pooled securities known as derivatives for everything from mortgages to car loans to credit default swaps. The scale and complexity of debt repackaging increased enormously as a result of the housing boom. Having grown from a negligible level in the 1980s to $106 trillion in 2002, the market in derivatives spiralled to $531 trillion in 2006. In the words of Warren Buffett, America's most successful money manager, this form of loan finance became the 'financial weapons of mass destruction' that threatened to undermine the entire American economy.[21]

The real estate bubble was as unsustainable as the stock market bubble. Seeking to douse house-price inflation, the Federal Reserve incrementally raised interest rates from late 2004 to mid-2007. Many holders of subprime mortgages could not make their higher repayments, which led to a glut of foreclosures. Soon, many homeowners with stable incomes who had bought at the height of the boom in expectation of its continuation were in the same position. One in ten of all mortgage holders nationally were either delinquent or in foreclosure by autumn 2008. The consequent fall in house prices reverberated through the entire economy. Worst hit was the construction industry, the source of 15 per cent of all American jobs at the height of the real estate boom, but automobile manufacturing and selling, home appliance manufacturing, and financial services were not far behind. With many financial institutions holding mountains of bad debt, banks also grew reluctant to lend money to individuals, businesses and each other. This credit crunch had very serious consequences for an economy that had long depended on debt to fund growth.[22]

The Bush administration acted reactively rather than pre-emptively with regard to the escalating crisis. The collapse of Wall Street financial services giant Lehman Brothers on 15 September 2008 signalled that the entire financial system was on the verge of meltdown unless government intervened. The administration response was: to nationalize the government-created secondary mortgage giants Freddie Mac and Fannie Mae; effectively to nationalize the world's largest insurer, the AIG group; and, after an initial congressional veto, to enact the Troubled Assets Relief Program to take up to $700 billion of toxic private mortgages on to government books. In essence, over the course of a single month, the federal government expanded its gross liabilities by over $1 trillion, which was double the cost of the Iraq war to date.[23]

While these initiatives shored up the tottering financial system, government actions to boost demand proved ineffective, because debt overhang and job insecurity had undermined consumer confidence. In cooperation with congressional leaders of both parties, the Bush administration had promoted an economic stimulus in the form of a $100 billion tax rebate for 130 million households in the spring of 2008, but only a quarter of this money at most funded new consumer spending, while the rest was saved or used to pay down debts.[24] In late 2008, Bush also agreed a $17.4 billion bailout for automobile giants Ford, Chrysler and General Motors, but this was not enough to prevent the latter two applying for bankruptcy early in 2009. Poor management and business strategies in the good years had left the automotive industry highly vulnerable to the impact of recession.[25] In late 2008, meanwhile, the Federal Reserve embarked on a programme of quantitative easing to increase the supply of money and credit with the purchase of $600 billion of mortgage-backed securities, while the Treasury pumped $200 billion of loan funds into credit markets to encourage private-investor securities backed by student and auto loans, credit-card debt and small-business loans. However, financial institutions were more interested in building up their reserves, and households were reluctant to stock up on more borrowing in the economic circumstances.[26]

With George W. Bush's presidency ending amid financial crisis and worsening recession, liberal economist Joseph Stiglitz charged that Bush had been a worse steward of the US economy than even Herbert Hoover. This may appear a harsh judgement, since the banks were the principal authors of the economic mess and Federal Reserve easy credit had facilitated the real estate bubble. Nevertheless, Bush's policies had contributed fundamentally to the toxic mix of indebtedness, income inequality, and imbalance at the root of the crisis. Even factoring out the effects of recession, the economy in the Bush era was not the engine of growth of yore. GDP had risen by only 2.6 per cent annually in 24 quarters of consecutive expansion from 2001 to 2007, compared with 3.7 per cent in the 38-quarter expansion in 1991–2000. During this time, total civilian employment growth was just 6.6 per cent compared with 15 per cent during Bill Clinton's presidential tenure. Thus Stiglitz had some justification in asserting that the economic consequences were 'more insidious than those of Hoover, harder to reverse, and likely to be long-lasting'.[27]

The Great Recession and the fragile recovery, 2009–11

An outgrowth of the financial crisis, the Great Recession began in December 2007 and lasted until mid-2009. During this time, output declined by a cumulative 5.1 per cent (compared to 1.5 per cent and 0.6 per cent respectively in the 1990–91 and 2001 recessions) and employment fell by 6.3 per cent. Unemployment peaked at 10.1 per cent (just below the 10.8 per cent high in the 1981–82 recession), but it hovered around 9.0–9.5 per cent throughout the first two years of recovery (whereas it fell to 8.3 per cent within 12 months after the Reagan-era downturn ended). More jobs were lost in the 2007–09 recession (8.8 million) than in the four previous recessions combined, and only 900,000 of these were recovered in 2010, a monthly average of 75,000, which was far below the 130,000 figure needed just to accommodate new entries into the labour force. Employment recovery was slowest in the Sunbelt states of the South and South-West that had benefited most from the fruits of the Bush-era real estate boom. In early 2011, 13.8 million people were out of work nationwide, but, if another 8.4 million in 'involuntary' part-time employment were factored in, the actual household unemployment rate was nearly 17 per cent. Meanwhile a further 2.8 million were deemed to be 'marginally attached' to the labour force (about 1 million having given up job-seeking altogether, while the remainder were temporarily discouraged). In essence, therefore, 25 million Americans were either jobless or under-employed compared to 13 million at the depth of the Great Depression in 1933 (though this represented 25–30 per cent of a much smaller labour force).[28]

The slow pace of recovery is typical of downturns sparked by severe financial crashes, such as America experienced in the 1890s and the 1930s, because these destroy more wealth, and have longer-lasting effects on credit supply and confidence, and greater international consequences than conventional business cycle downturns.[29] Official projections suggest that the jobless rate will not fall back to pre-recession level until 2016. For some analysts, this signified that America was in a grip of depression rather than recession. If most economists would not make this semantic leap, there was widespread recognition that the recovery would be in effect a jobless one. After the dot.com recession of 2001, 62 per cent of jobs that had been lost in the downturn were recovered in the first six quarters of recovery with the aid of very little public stimulus. In the comparable period after the Great Recession, only 12 per cent had been recouped, despite the greatest burst of fiscal and monetary stimulus in US history.[30]

Less than a month after becoming president, Barack Obama had the American Recovery and Reinvestment Act (ARRA) enacted. This was the largest ever fiscal stimulus measure, with projected costs of $787 billion over three years. ARRA looked to save or create

3.6 million jobs through a combination of spending and taxation initiatives in a two-to-one funding ratio. Expenditure provisions included: the most expensive public works programme since the construction of the interstate highway system to rebuild the nation's crumbling road, bridge and flood control infrastructure; the upgrading of schools to modernize classrooms, libraries and laboratories; assistance to hard-pressed state governments; energy-efficiency improvements to public buildings; and a host of green initiatives that sought to double alternative energy sources. On the tax side, there were payroll tax credits, incentives for business, benefits for the working poor, and a temporary patch to prevent the alternative minimum tax (AMT) expanding its reach.[31]

Although interpretations as to its effect vary, the non-partisan Congressional Budget Office estimated that ARRA had created or prevented the loss of 3.3 million full-time jobs to September 2011, an assessment broadly supported by a Federal Reserve analysis.[32] Critics, by contrast, claimed that ARRA's spending provisions interfered with the operations of the free market and wasted money on unnecessary projects or ones that took too long to become operational.[33] Nevertheless, the plunge in the economy stopped in mid-2009 as the stimulus began to take effect and was followed by four respectable quarters of growth. Conversely, economic expansion slowed as stimulus provisions diminished in ARRA's final year of operation. This suggests that the main problem with the measure was that it was not large enough – as liberal economists like Paul Krugman claimed at the time of its enactment – and it was not left in place long enough.[34]

Despite ARRA's apparent largesse, the Obama administration had scaled back the initially projected $850 billion costs in hope of gaining some bipartisan support for its enactment. The inclusion of generous tax provisions – notably the AMT patch, which had little stimulus effect because the mainly affluent recipients were likely to save rather than spend the benefit – was motivated by the same concern. Nevertheless, the measure won only three Republican votes in the Senate and none in the House. The GOP attacked it as a Democratic initiative to renew big government and its pork-barrel benefits under cover of the economic crisis. ARRA's political effect, therefore, was to increase rather than diminish the already high degree of polarization in American politics. Henceforth the Obama administration found itself under sustained attack, not only from regular Republicans, but also from grassroots conservatives associated with the Tea Party movement, for engaging in a costly expansion of government that would ultimately require higher taxes to pay for the consequent growth of the public debt.[35]

Even without the economic downturn, America's public indebtedness was heading toward long-term unsustainability, mainly because of the costs of the three largest entitlement programmes. In 2007, the Government Accountability Office (GAO) had estimated that real GDP would grow by 71 per cent over the next 25 years, but Social Security, Medicaid and Medicare outlays would grow by 127 per cent, 224 per cent and 235 per cent respectively. Social Security expansion reflects the ageing of the population as the baby-boom generation, the cohort born between 1945 and 1965, reaches retirement age. Health care outlay growth was also driven by the increased longevity of senior citizens, but more fundamentally by the rising costs of constantly improving medical care.[36]

The Great Recession brought forward the day of reckoning when America must place its public finances on a sounder footing through painful adjustment of its expenditure and revenue programmes. In FY 2009 to FY 2011, the deficit annually averaged nearly 10 per cent GDP, by far the highest peacetime imbalances (the largest deficit in the Great Depression was 5.9 per cent GDP in FY 1934). This served to double the public debt from 36.2 per cent GDP in 2007 to 72 per cent GDP in 2011. On CBO projections, deficits will decline to

3–4 per cent GDP a year with full economic recovery, but their cumulative effect will likely increase the public debt–GDP ratio above its peak of 109 per cent (reached at the end of the Second World War) in 2023. With entitlement spending thereafter likely to accelerate fiscal deterioration, US public indebtedness is forecast to reach 190 per cent GDP by 2035. On this trajectory, outlays for the three largest entitlements and interest payment on the public debt will consume total budget revenues by 2030, leaving the rest of government to be funded from the deficit.[37]

Despite the mushrooming public debt, opinion polls consistently revealed that jobs constituted a greater concern for ordinary Americans by a more than two-to-one margin. Nevertheless, the deficit increasingly became the focus of debate among the Washington political community from mid-2009 to 2011. Linking it to out-of-control big government, Republicans insisted that the budget had to be balanced as soon as possible and entirely through expenditure retrenchment. Democrats, by contrast, contended that short-term deficits were necessary for economic recovery, which in turn would engender fiscal improvement. Seeking to defuse partisan conflict, the president appointed a bipartisan commission to explore ways of improving public finances, but this could not deliver the requisite supermajority in favour of its December 2010 report projecting achievement of primary balance by 2015 (operating a budget in which the deficit only funded interest repayments) and achieving aggregate deficit reduction of $3.9 trillion over ten years through a combination of entitlement reform, discretionary programme retrenchment and revenue enhancement.[38]

Liberals fulminated that Obama had not done enough to counter the Republican strategy of shifting political debate from the government's role in creating jobs to its responsibility for debt reduction. In their view, White House failure on this score had enabled the GOP to make the question of 'how much to cut' rather than 'when to cut' the dominant issue. Validating such concerns that the partisan battle was being lost, the Democrats' 30-point lead in the Ipsos-McClatchy poll as the party more trusted to deal with the deficit at the start of 2008 had given way to a Republican seven-point lead by the end of Obama's first year in office.[39]

With attention increasingly focused on the deficit, there was no post-ARRA fiscal stimulus of note until the end of 2010. In the meantime, the Federal Reserve's quantitative easing (QE) constituted the most significant expansionary initiative. Purchases of bank debt, mortgage-backed securities and Treasury notes, commenced in late 2008, reached a peak of $2.1 trillion in June 2010. Discontinued at this juncture, QE operations with a $600 billion target recommended in November 2010 in response to disappointing economic data and eventually stopped in mid-2011. This monetary strategy revived the confidence of the financial sector, evidenced by a stock market boom in the second half of 2010, but did little to boost aggregate demand, because consumers remained wary of stocking up on new debt.[40]

The fiscal dimension of stimulus came briefly to the fore once more in the wake of Democratic setbacks in the 2010 midterm elections. The Obama White House seized the opportunity to negotiate a bipartisan deal before the Tea Party-backed Republicans took control of the House of Representatives in the new Congress. The president agreed a plan with GOP leaders to preserve the Bush tax breaks for all income groups for two years, thereby compromising on his stated goal of letting them expire for the wealthiest 2 per cent of households, in return for the extension of emergency unemployment benefits and a 2 per cent reduction of payroll taxes for every worker, both to 2011, to boost economic recovery. Instead of being covered by pay-go obligations, the combined two-year cost of $900 billion would be financed through borrowing that would expand the public debt.[41]

This represented a brief interlude in the increasing polarization of deficit politics. Prolonged delay in agreeing where to make $33 billion cuts in the FY 2011 budget nearly resulted in a partial shutdown of government in April 2011. Even worse followed in the summer when the GOP House's refusal to agree a routine debt extension bill nearly resulted in a default on debt payments and led directly to Standard & Poor's downgrading America's AAA+ credit rating. The terms of the settlement that averted this outcome established a bipartisan congressional super-committee to agree a substantial deficit-reduction plan. However, this body failed in its task, mainly because Democratic members wanted to levy higher taxes on the rich while Republicans resisted increases of any kind. The legally mandated consequence of this deadlock was an automatic ten-year sequestration of $1.2 trillion cuts in defence and domestic spending that was scheduled to begin in 2013.[42]

The outcome of the deficit politics of 2011 was that America had prioritized medium- to long-term debt reduction at the cost of strengthening its economy, a trade-off likely to hinder rather than help attainment of fiscal sustainability. Cutting the deficit is not entirely a matter of austerity. If America's economy grew one-half of a percentage point faster than forecast each year from 2011 to 2030, this would diminish its deficit-reduction task by 40 to 50 per cent over that time frame. However, untimely anti-deficit initiatives undertaken while the economy is still not robust could have a serious effect on the strength and pace of its recovery. Exemplifying this danger, the expiry of stimulus measures contained in both the ARRA and the December 2010 package would have produced some $360 billion fiscal tightening, equal to 2.4 per cent GDP, in 2012, but the extension of the latter averted this danger. The combination of the Bush tax cuts expiring and the spending sequestration resulting from the super-committee's failure to agree a deficit-reduction plan raised concerns about America falling off the so-called 'fiscal cliff' in 2013. The combined effect of this retrenchment could have sucked the equivalent of 4.5 per cent GDP out of an economy barely growing at 2 per cent a year, thereby precipitating a new recession. Another short-term deal between the newly re-elected Obama and the House Republicans at the very end of 2012 preserved the Bush tax cuts for all but the top 1 per cent of income earners, but left spending-sequestration and entitlement-reform issues unresolved. This unsatisfactory outcome averted immediate economic decline but ensured continuing tensions between debt-reduction and recovery imperatives in Obama's second term.[43]

The prospects of renewed prosperity

For the United States, recovery from the Great Recession is not the same as renewing prosperity. Cyclical bounce-back will not resolve the structural weaknesses that had been eroding the foundations of America's economic strength for some time before the onset of the Great Recession. In essence, the United States relied too much on internal consumption and debt, both private and public, to drive growth from the 1980s through to the George W. Bush years. The real renewal of prosperity requires a rebalancing of the economy to focus more on saving, investment and exports, but this will be difficult to pull off. The early signs of improvement on this score are decidedly mixed. In the wake of the recession households have reduced their debt load and built up savings to the highest level in 20 years, but huge public deficits counterbalanced this to produce a negative rate of aggregate national saving in 2009–10. Meanwhile, the trade gap narrowed sharply from $696 billion in 2008 to $379 billion in 2009, but then widened again to $498 billion in 2010 as the economy picked up. The $273.1 billion bilateral trade deficit with China was America's largest ever with a single nation.[44]

Despite this, the United States has the potential to achieve export-led growth. It has evident strengths in key economic sectors, notably knowledge-intensive capital goods like microprocessors and health care technology, high-end services like engineering, environmentally friendly products, and business, financial and professional services. According to economist Matthew Slaughter, however, only 4 per cent of all American firms and 15 per cent of American manufacturers do any exporting at all, and just 1 per cent of firms account for 80 per cent of America's total trade. In line with this, US exports of goods and services made up just 10.9 per cent of GDP in 2009, far less than in Germany (40 per cent), China (28 per cent) and Britain (27 per cent). In his 2010 State of the Union address, President Obama set an ambitious target of doubling the dollar volume of exports in five years. Nevertheless some analysts contend that the US has to double the GDP share of exports within ten years to achieve economic rebalancing. For this to happen, many more American firms will have to become more export-oriented than was the case in 2010.[45]

The renewal of prosperity also requires the state to play a constructive role in this process. If premature deficit reduction is economically harmful, delayed action can be even more catastrophic. The most important task for national government in the medium to long term is to put its finances on a sustainable basis to pre-empt sovereign debt crisis. This arguably requires both entitlement reform to contain costs and revenue enhancement through taxation of those best able to pay. A fiscal course correction of this kind will also have beneficial effects for economic rebalancing. Firstly, twenty-first-century workers will carry a lesser burden of support for retired Americans. Secondly, a more equitable distribution of the tax burden will go some way to addressing the gross disparity of wealth in American society that has seen the top 1 per cent triple their share of national income to 23 per cent between 1979 and 2006. Tackling this inequality is a matter of good economics as well as ethics because, in the words of one analyst, it 'leaves the rich with so much money that they can binge on speculation, and leaves the middle class without enough money to buy the things they think they deserve, which leads them to borrow and go into debt'.[46] Finally, America will become less dependent on borrowing from foreign governments, thereby reducing the currency-value distortions that disadvantage its trade position.

While deficit reduction is ultimately essential, this cannot justify retrenchment on much-needed public programmes. A crumbling infrastructure, a school system that does not uplift pupils in the lower half of the income distribution, and a lack of green technology will damage America's future. The public universities have also been starved of funds as a result of state financial difficulties during the Great Recession and its aftermath. The effects of this could be a severe shortage of graduates – California's economy could face a shortfall of a million by 2025 – that threatens long-term economic growth.[47] Regardless of conservative fulminations about a drift to socialism, government spending on infrastructure, the environment and education represents an investment in America's future.

The United States also needs to promote a better balance of trade flows through its international economic policy. A low-value dollar would be the most effective agency of export growth, but a repeat of 1980s efforts to drive down the greenback's exchange value is unlikely. With the dollar not as obviously overvalued in the early twenty-first century as it was in the early 1980s, America's trade partners would oppose any such move. Nevertheless, the US could still look to promote acceptance of international exchange mechanisms limiting exchange rate deviations from their equilibrium values through close cooperation between economic policymakers in industrial and industrializing countries. It has to be recognized, however, that America has little leverage to induce emergent economic powers, most notably China, to participate in such a venture.[48]

In seeking renewed prosperity through a rebalanced economy, America faces a new and different challenge that is, in Bill Clinton's words, 'short-term, long-term, complicated'. The former president is convinced that his country is up to the task. 'People have been betting against the United States for 200 years', he commented, 'and they all wound up losing money.'[49] Such optimism does not preclude recognition that the road ahead will be long and hard, not least because of current political polarization over the role of the state. The United States took a long time to sink into the debt-laden condition that eventually precipitated the crisis of 2007–09. It will take time and lots of luck to restore economic wellbeing and renew the American Dream.

Notes

1   Robert Sobel, *The Great Boom, 1950–2000: How a Generation of Americans Created the World's Most Prosperous Society* (New York: Truman Talley, 2000); Samuel Rosenberg, *American Economic Development since 1945: Growth, Decline and Rejuvenation* (New York: Palgrave, 2003).
2   Robert M. Collins, *More: The Politics of Economic Growth in Postwar America* (New York: Oxford University Press, 2000), x–xi.
3   Wyatt Wells, *American Capitalism, 1945–2000: Continuity and Change from Mass Production of the Information Society* (Chicago, IL: Ivan Dee, 2003), 195.
4   John Sloan, *Eisenhower and the Management of Prosperity* (Lawrence: University Press of Kansas, 1991); Herbert Stein, *Presidential Economics: The Making of Economic Policy from Roosevelt to Clinton*, 3rd rev. edn (Washington, DC: AEI Press, 1994), 65–88.
5   Walter Heller, *New Dimensions of Political Economy* (New York: Norton, 1966); Herbert Stein, *The Fiscal Revolution: Policy in Pursuit of Reality*, 2nd rev. edn (Washington, DC: AEI Press, 1996); Irving Bernstein, *Guns or Butter: The Presidency of Lyndon Johnson* (New York: Oxford University Press, 1996), 27–42, 358–378.
6   Allen Matusow, *Nixon's Economy: Booms, Busts, Dollars, and Votes* (Lawrence: University Press of Kansas, 1999); Carl Biven, *Jimmy Carter's Economy: Policy in an Age of Limits* (Chapel Hill: University of North Carolina Press, 2002).
7   Paul Volcker, *Changing Fortunes: The World's Money and the Threat to American Leadership* (New York: Times Books, 1992); Martin Feldstein, ed., *American Economic Policy in the 1980s* (Chicago, IL: University of Chicago Press, 1994); Brian Domitrovic, *Econoclasts: The Rebels Who Sparked the Supply-Side Revolution and Restored American Prosperity* (San Francisco, CA: ICI Press, 2009).
8   Benjamin Friedman, *Day of Reckoning: The Consequences of American Economic Policy under Reagan and After* (New York: Random House, 1988); John Sloan, *The Reagan Effect: Economics and Presidential Leadership* (Lawrence: University Press of Kansas, 1999); Iwan Morgan, 'Reaganomics and Its Legacy', in Cheryl Hudson and Gareth Davies, eds, *Ronald Reagan in the 1980s: Perceptions, Policies, Legacies* (New York: Palgrave, 2008), 101–119.
9   Jeffrey Frankel and Peter Orszag, eds, *American Economic Policy in the 1990s* (Boston, MA: MIT Press, 2002), chaps 1–3; Iwan Morgan, *The Age of Deficits: Presidents and Unbalanced Budgets from Jimmy Carter to George W. Bush* (Lawrence: University Press of Kansas, 2009), chaps 5–6.
10 Bob Woodward, *Maestro: Greenspan's Fed and the American Boom* (New York: Simon & Schuster, 2000); Alan Blinder and Janet Yellen, *The Fabulous Decade: Macroeconomic Lessons from the 1990s* (New York: Century Foundation, 2001); Alan Greenspan, *The Age of Turbulence: Adventures in a New World* (New York: Penguin, 2007), 142–181.
11 See data reproduced in John Bellamy Foster and Fred Magdoff, *The Great Financial Crisis: Causes and Consequences* (New York: Monthly Review Press, 2009), 121.
12 Robert Frank, *Luxury Fever: Why Money Fails to Satisfy in an Age of Excess* (New York: Free Press, 1999); Lawrence Mishel, Jared Bernstein and John Schmitt, *The State of Working America, 2000–2001* (Ithaca, NY: Cornell University Press, 2001).
13 Robert Brenner, *The Boom and the Bubble: The US in the World Economy* (London: Verso, 2002), chaps 2–4; Iwan Morgan, 'The Indebted Empire: America's Current Account Deficit', *International Politics*, 45(1) (2008), 92–112.
14 Brenner, *Boom and the Bubble*, chaps 5–7; Joseph Stiglitz, *The Roaring Nineties: Seeds of Destruction* (London: Allen Lane, 2003), 3–28, 56–86.
15 Robert Shiller, *Irrational Exuberance* (Princeton, NJ: Princeton University Press, 2000); Greenspan, *Age of Turbulence*, 164–181.

16 Daniel Altman, *Neoconomy: George W. Bush's Revolutionary Gamble with America's Future* (New York: PublicAffairs, 2004), 74–88; Jacob Hacker and Paul Pierson, *Off Center: The Republican Revolution and the Erosion of Democracy* (New Haven, CT: Yale University Press, 2005), 55–62; Morgan, *Age of Deficits*, 216–217, 220–221.

17 Brad Sester and Nouriel Roubini, 'Our Money, Our Debt, Our Problem', *Foreign Affairs*, 84 (2005), 198–206; William Bonner and Addison Wiggin, *Empire of Debt: The Rise of an Epic Financial Crisis* (Hoboken, NJ: Wiley, 2006); Iwan Morgan, 'Bush's Political Economy: Deficits, Debt, and Depression', in Iwan Morgan and Philip Davies, eds, *Assessing George W. Bush's Legacy: The Right Man?* (New York: Palgrave, 2010), 192–195.

18 Larry Summers, 'America Overdrawn', *Foreign Policy* (July/August 2004), 47–49; Kenneth Rogoff, 'America's Current Account: A Deficit of Judgment' (2005), www.globalagendamagazine. com/2005/kennethrogoff.asp; Nouriel Roubini and Brad Sester, 'Will the Bretton Woods 2 Regime Unravel Soon? The Risk of a Hard Landing', www.stern.nyu.edu/globalmacro/.

19 Greenspan, *Age of Turbulence*, 229–233.

20 'Worse than Japan', *Economist*, 14 February 2009, pp. 83–84; Foster and Magdoff, *Great Financial Crisis*, 121–122.

21 'The Doctor's Bill', *Economist*, 27 September 2008, pp. 92–94; Buffett, quoted in Peter Goodman, 'Taking a Hard Look at the Greenspan Legacy', *New York Times*, 8 October 2008. For broader analysis of the financial system weakness, see: Charles Morris, *The Trillion-Dollar Meltdown: Easy Money, High Rollers, and the Great Credit Crash* (New York: PublicAffairs, 2008); and Robert Shiller, *The Subprime Solution: How Today's Global Financial Crisis Happened and What to Do about It* (Princeton, NJ: Princeton University Press, 2008).

22 Morgan, 'Bush's Political Economy', 195–196; Marc Zandi, *Financial Shock: A 360 Degree Look at the Subprime Mortgage Explosion, and How to Avoid the Next Financial Crisis* (Upper Saddle River, NJ: FT Press, 2009).

23 Clive Crook, 'Nationalization in All but Name', *Financial Times*, 8 September 2008; 'When Fortune Frowned: A Special Report on the World Economy', *Economist*, 11 October 2008, pp. 3–6.

24 Christian Broda and Jonathan Parker, 'The Impact of the 2008 Rebate', www.vocu.org/index. php/q=node/i541.

25 'Fortune – Detroit's Downfall', accessed 5 December 2011 at http://money.cnn.com/news/specials/ detroitcrisis/.

26 Ron Lieber and Tara Siegel Bernard, 'U.S. Consumer Loan Aid Will Trickle Only So Far', *New York Times*, 27 November 2008; Dan Milmo, 'U.S. Pumps Another $800 Billion into Mortgage and Credit Markets', *Guardian*, 26 November 2008.

27 Joseph Stiglitz, 'The Economic Consequences of Mr. Bush', *Vanity Fair* (December 2007), 228; Neil Irwin and Dan Eggen, 'Economy Made Few Gains in Bush Years', *Washington Post*, 12 January 2009; 'The Frat Boy Ships Out', *Economist*, 17 January 2009, pp. 26–28.

28 Federal Reserve Board of Minneapolis, *The Recession and Recovery in Perspective*, 22 November 2011, http://www.minneapolisfed.org; Dean Baker, 'The Path of Unemployment in the Great Recession', Centre for Economic Policy and Research Paper, 14 July 2010, http://www.cepr. net; Mortimer Zuckerman, 'The Great Jobs Recession Goes On', *US News and World Report*, 11 February 2001, http://www.usnews.com/opinion/mzuckerman/articles; Michael Cooper, 'Slump Alters Jobless Map in U.S., with South Hit Hard', *New York Times*, 26 September 2011.

29 Carmen Reinhard and Kenneth Rogoff, *This Time Is Different: Eight Centuries of Financial Folly* (Princeton, NJ: Princeton University Press, 2009).

30 David Rosenberg, 'It's Time to Start Calling This for What It Is: A Modern Day Depression', 14 September 2011, http://www.zerohedge.com/news/david-rose...depression; John B. Judis, 'You Say Recession, I Say Depression', *New Republic*, 7 September 2010, www.tnr.com.

31 For full details of ARRA's implementation, see the regularly updated website Track the Money at www.recovery.gov.

32 Congressional Budget Office, *Estimated Impact of the American Recovery and Reinvestment Act on Employment and Economic Output from July 2011 through September 2011* (Washington, DC: CBO, November 2011); Daniel J. Wilson, 'Fiscal Spending Job Multipliers: Evidence from the 2009 American Recovery and Reinvestment Act', Federal Reserve Bank of San Francisco Working Paper, October 2011, http://www.frbsf.org/publications/economics/papers/2010/wp-10-17bk.pdf.

33 The Cato Institute organized a petition of some 200 economists that appeared in a full-page advertisement in the *New York Times* and the *Wall Street Journal*. See 'Economists Say Stimulus Won't Work', *St. Louis Post-Dispatch*, 29 January 2009.

34 Paul Krugman, 'Failure to Rise', *New York Times*, 12 February 2009.

35 Mimi Hall and David Jackson, 'Stimulus Slammed as Democrats' Agenda', *USA Today*, 17 February 2009; 'The End of Innocence', *Economist*, 21 February 2009, p. 50; Lori Montgomery, 'America's Tax Burden near Historic Low: Despite Obama's Pledge, Some Fear Future Hikes as Debt Grows', *Washington Post*, 16 April 2009; 'GOP Slams Stimulus Plan with List of 100 Worst Projects', *CNN*, 3 August 2010, www.cnn.com.

36 *U.S. Financial Condition and Fiscal Future Briefing* (Washington, DC: GAO, January 2008). For discussion, see Dennis S. Ippolito, 'Fiscal Sustainability and Deficit Politics in the United States', in Diego Sanchez-Ancochea and Iwan Morgan, eds, *The Political Economy of the Public Budget in the Americas* (London: Institute for the Study of the Americas, 2008), 82–103.

37 *FY 2012 Budget of the United States Government: Historical Tables*, 25, 140. *The Congressional Budget Office's Long-Term Budget Outlook* (Washington, DC: CBO, 2011), x–xi.

38 Lori Montgomery and Brady Dennis, 'Obama Commission's Final Deficit Report Preserves Controversial Spending Cuts and Tax Increases', *Washington Post*, 1 December 2010; Richard Wolf, 'Obama Commission Backs Cuts but Lacks Supermajority', *USA Today*, 3 December 2010; 'The President's Deficit Commission: No Cigar', *Economist*, 11 December 2010, p. 56.

39 Michael McCarthy, 'Why Washington Has Given Up on the Unemployed', *Globalist*, 4 May 2011, www.theglobalist.com; 'Barack Obama's First Year: Reality Bites', *Economist*, 16 January 2010, pp. 24–26.

40 Jon Hilsenrath, 'Fed Fires $600 Billion Stimulus Shot', *Wall Street Journal*, 4 November 2010, http://online.wsj.com; James Mackintosh, 'Quantitative Easing Does It – Up to a Point', *Financial Times*, 24 June 2011, www.ft.com.

41 Lori Montgomery and Shailagh Murray, 'Obama, GOP Reach Deal to Extend Tax Breaks', *Washington Post*, 7 December 2010.

42 Paul Harris, 'US Budget Deal Avoids Government Shutdown, but Painful Cuts Ahead', *Observer*, 10 April 2011; John Detrixhe, 'U.S. Loses AAA Rating at S&P on Concern Debt Cuts Deficient', *Business Week*, 6 August 2011, www.businessweek.com; Jackie Calmes and Jennifer Steinhauer, 'As Sides Dig In, Panel on Deficit Has an Uphill Fight', *New York Times*, 25 September 2011.

43 Alan Auerbach and William Gale, 'Déjà Vu All Over Again: On the Dismal Prospects for the Federal Budget', Tax Policy Center, 29 April 2010, www.taxpolicycenter.org; David Leonhardt, 'One Way to Trim Deficit: Cultivate Growth', *New York Times*, 16 November 2010; 'The Last Best Hope: Why the Supercommittee Failed' and 'Finally, Some Good News: A Shame It Probably Won't Last', *Economist*, 26 November 2011, pp. 57–58; 'The Fiscal Cliff Deal: America's European Moment', *Economist*, 5 January 2013, pp. 7–8.

44 Martin Feldstein, 'America's Saving Surprise', 31 August 2010, http://www. project-syndicate. org; BBC News, 'US Trade Deficit Widened by 33% in 2010', www.bbc.co.uk.

45 Matthew Slaughter, *How US Multinational Companies Strengthen the Economy* (Washington, DC: Business Roundtable/United States Council Foundation, 2009), www.uscib.org; 'A Special Report on America's Economy: Export or Die', *Economist*, 3 April 2010, pp. 8–9; Fred Bergsten, 'The United States in the World Economy', Peterson Institute for International Economics Speeches and Papers, 12 August 2011, www.iie.com.

46 George Packer, 'The Broken Contract: Inequality and American Decline', *Foreign Affairs*, November/December 2011, www.foreignaffairs.com.

47 'Before the Fall: California Universities in Trouble', *Economist*, 6 August 2009, www.economist. com.

48 Fred Bergsten, 'Foreign Economic Policy for the Next President', *Foreign Affairs*, 83(2) (2004), 88–101; Stephen Cohen and Brad de Long, *The End of Influence: What Happens When Other Countries Have the Money* (New York: Basic Books, 2010).

49 'Bill Clinton Talks to Simon Schama', *FT Magazine*, 14 October 2011, www.ft.com.

6　The culture war

Is America polarizing?

Andrew Wroe

American society is at war with itself. Arrayed on one side of the battlefield are culturally orthodox conservatives, who view the world through a morally traditionalist and religious lens. On the other side are the culturally progressive, liberal in values and secular in spirit. On the day's most pressing cultural and social issues – abortion, contraception, stem-cell research, same-sex partnerships and marriage, the role and importance of family, drugs, immigration and even health care, the economy and the constitution – the two sides are engaged in a battle of ideas, unwilling, indeed unable, to compromise, each certain of the supreme rightness and morality of its own position. The fight is for the heart and soul of America. Or so the argument goes. The goal of this chapter is to strip away the hyperbolic, and frequently hysterical, language, to examine whether the United States has indeed polarized ideologically or is in a process of polarization.

The analysis is divided into two main parts. The first explores whether there could be said to be a culture war among America's elites. Are its politicians, office seekers, opinion formers, commentators and self-appointed guardians of the public interest at war with each other? The answer is a resounding 'yes'. On nearly every indicator, the divide between liberals and conservatives is wide and deep and getting more so. On this, nearly all academic observers are in agreement. However, there is much disagreement in the academy over the extent to which ordinary Americans could be said to be engaged in a culture war. The second part of this chapter explores the arguments of scholars who contend that the American public is polarized on cultural issues and of those who dismiss the idea that such a deep and fundamental divide exists among ordinary citizens. The chapter attempts to resolve the differences of the two sides by bringing new evidence to bear regarding the extent to which Americans feel strongly about cultural issues. In short, while there is little evidence to suggest that people's positions on the key culture war issues are changing and becoming more polarized, those same issues are becoming more important to Americans. They are increasingly at the forefront of people's minds, to be discussed, argued and fought over. This finding lends support to the argument that there exists a culture war at the mass level, even while other data demonstrate that issue polarization has not occurred. The chapter ends with a brief examination of the causes of polarization and what can be done about it.

Elite polarization

There is no absolute agreement about where one should look for evidence of a culture war, nor what type or level of evidence is necessary to establish its veracity or not, but nearly all scholars agree that the facts stack heavily in favour of the proposition that America's elites are very deeply divided and getting more so.

The most compelling evidence of elite polarization comes from the US Congress, the highest lawmaking body in the United States. In the middle of the twentieth century, bipartisanship – where members of both parties worked together to achieve common goals and voted together on the same side of an issue – was much more common than it is today. Ideologically, there was considerable overlap between the two main parties. The Republican caucus included many members of a liberal persuasion, especially on social issues, and the Democratic caucus many conservatives. Today, however, conservative Democrats and, especially, liberal Republicans are an endangered species. The 2010 midterm elections saw Tea Party candidates oust sitting liberal Republicans in several primary contests. The few remaining liberal/centrist Republicans faced hostile criticism from within their own party and were challenged by more conservative Republicans in the run-up to the 2012 elections. For example, Indiana's Richard Lugar, the joint longest-serving Republican in the Senate, was defeated in the GOP primary by Richard Mourdock; and Utah's Orrin Hatch, the other joint longest-serving Senate Republican, had to fight off a tough primary challenge from former state senator Dan Liljenquist. Hatch had in 2010 seen Bob Bennett, his fellow Republican Utah senator, defeated by Tea Party favourite Mike Lee. Moreover, the upper chamber's most liberal Republican member – three-term senator Olympia Snowe – said in February 2012 that she would not seek re-election in November, specifically blaming the decline in bipartisanship for her decision:

> I do find it frustrating that an atmosphere of polarization and 'my way or the highway' ideologies have become pervasive in campaigns and in our governing institutions. . . . I see a vital need for the political center in order for our democracy to flourish and to find solutions that unite rather than divide us. It is time for change in the way we govern.[1]

With Snowe's retirement, the number of Senate Republicans supporting abortion rights can be counted on one hand. On the other side, the Democratic Party's most conservative member, Senator Ben Nelson of Nebraska, also announced his retirement in 2012. Other prominent moderate senators – James Jeffords, Lincoln Chaffee, Arlen Specter, Blanche Lincoln and Evan Bayh – had already made their exits from the chamber, replaced by more radical members. The result is a 'dysfunctional and paralysed' Congress, divided by ideology and party.[2]

Figures 6.1 and 6.2 place the contemporary congressional polarization in its historical perspective. Constructed by Keith Poole and based on Poole and Rosenthal's influential DW-NOMINATE scores, the figures show the positions of the most moderate and conservative Republicans (at the 10th and 90th percentiles, respectively) and moderate and liberal Democrats (again at the 10th and 90th percentiles, respectively) over time.[3] While polarized parties were the norm in the pre-Second World War period, from the end of the war until the late 1960s there was a considerable ideological overlap between the parties in the House of Representatives (where 10 per cent of Democrats were actually more moderate than 10 per cent of Republicans). From the 1970s onwards, however, the parties began to diverge, a trend that accelerated in the 1980s and beyond. While the most liberal wing of the Democratic Party (measured at the 90th percentile) has not become especially more liberal, the most conservative wing of the Republican Party (90th percentile) has veered sharply to the right. Moreover, the moderate wing (measured at the 10th percentile) of the Democratic Party has grown noticeably more liberal, while the GOP's moderate wing (10th percentile) has become considerably more conservative. Today, there is no ideological overlap between the parties in the House. The gap between the parties' moderate wings is much larger than during the bipartisan post-war years and as large as it was at the start of the twentieth century. The gap between their

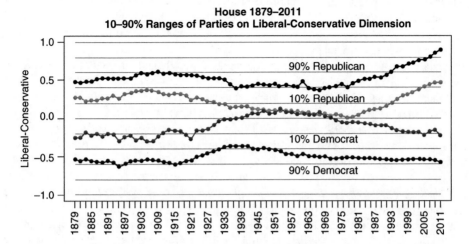

Figure 6.1 Poole–Rosenthal DW-NOMINATE House polarization score

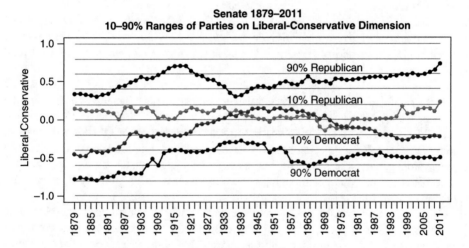

Figure 6.2 Poole–Rosenthal DW-NOMINATE Senate polarization score

more radical wings has never been as large. The trends in the Senate are not quite so stark, but they are in the same direction, especially in the centre of the ideological spectrum.

It is more difficult to uncover robust data on elite polarization outside the US Congress, but many academics argue that the phenomenon is nonetheless real. Buchanan's speech at the 1992 Republican Party convention is perhaps the best quoted and most notorious, in which he claimed that:

> there is a religious war going on in our country for the soul of America. It is a cultural war . . . [in which the Clintons are trying to impose] abortion on demand, . . . homosexual rights, discrimination against religious schools, women in combat . . . [which] is not the kind of change we can tolerate in a nation that we still call God's country.

There are many other examples. Newt Gingrich's career, from young congressman to Speaker and his 2012 attempt to win the GOP presidential nomination, was built on incendiary, polarized language. His claim on 10 February 2012 that the Obama 'administration is waging war on religion' is a notable example, which none of the other 2012 Republican presidential hopefuls disowned.

Polarization is also reflected in the many books of political commentators on both sides of the divide. The titles capture the contempt, anger and suspicion directed towards the other side. Liberal-leaning, pro-Democratic ones include: Al Franken's *Lies and the Lying Liars Who Tell Them: A Fair and Balanced Look at the Right*; James Carville's *We're Right, They're Wrong: A Handbook for Spirited Progressives*; Daniel Kurtzman's *How to Win a Fight with a Conservative*; Thomas Franks's *The Wrecking Crew: How Conservatives Rule*; Charles Pierce's *Idiot America: How Stupidity Became a Virtue in the Land of the Free*; Chris Hedges' *American Fascists: The Christian Right and the War on America*; Peter Beinart's *The Good Fight: Why Liberals – and Only Liberals – Can Win the War on Terror and Make America Great Again*; and so on ad infinitum.

On the conservative side, the list includes: Glenn Beck's *Arguing with Idiots: How to Stop Small Minds and Big Government*; Bill O'Reilly's *Pinheads and Patriots: Where You Stand in the Age of Obama*; Ann Coulter's *Demonic: How the Liberal Mob Is Endangering America* and her *How to Talk to a Liberal (If You Must)*; David Limbaugh's *Crimes against Liberty: An Indictment of President Barack Obama*; Jerome Corsi's *Where's the Birth Certificate? The Case That Barack Obama Is Not Eligible to Be President*; Aaron Klein's *Red Army: The Radical Network That Must Be Defeated to Save America*; and, perhaps most unpleasantly, David Freddoso's *Gangster Government: Barack Obama and the New Washington Thugocracy*.

What is remarkable about these tomes, apart from their hyperbolic titles, is the absolute belief in the rightness of their own side and the unwavering certainty in the wrongness of the other. Indeed, there can be no room for compromise, because the other side is not just wrong but actually evil and very likely involved in a grand conspiracy against the United States of America. The 'paranoid style', first noted by Richard Hofstadter in the 1960s, is particularly prominent among, but not restricted to, conservative commentators. Obama's presidency has generated a publishing boom on the right, with no argument as to his motives, objectives and lineage too outlandish to print.

The hysterical, compromise-free tone of the printed word is mirrored in the electronic sphere, where websites publish stories in which balance is an alien concept and conservative and liberal bloggers write in apocalyptic terms. The battle also rages on the airwaves after the Federal Communication Commission repealed its Fairness Doctrine in 1987, which had required balance in programming. Talk radio hosts such as Rush Limbaugh, Sean Hannity and Glenn Beck attract millions of listeners each week with their particular brands of anti-liberal rhetoric and baiting. Limbaugh, for example, felt obliged in March 2012 to call Sandra Fluke, a Georgetown University student and reproductive rights campaigner, a 'slut' and a 'prostitute' in response to her attempt to require her Jesuit university to provide contraception on its health care plan. Conservative viewers are also well served by cable television, particularly Fox News. While talk radio is dominated by conservative hosts and listeners, MSNBC views the world via a liberal lens and is an antidote to Fox News. Because conservatives and liberals tend to watch and listen to conservative and liberal shows, respectively, such programming has the effect of reinforcing Americans' ideological positions.

The evidence presented above, and the view of most observers and academics, is quite clear. There is a culture war raging among America's elites. There is, however, no similar agreement on whether the elite-level conflict is reflected at the level of ordinary Americans. In the following section, we present and critique the arguments of both sides, and bring new data to bear.

The mass public

As noted at the beginning of the chapter, academic opinion is divided on whether ordinary Americans are engaged in a culture war. To illuminate this debate, this section presents and critiques the work of two scholars, Morris Fiorina and Alan Abramowitz, who with their various co-authors have taken opposite positions. On the one hand, Abramowitz concludes that his 'evidence indicates that since the 1970s, ideological polarization has increased dramatically among the mass public'.[4] On the other, Fiorina argues:

> the simple truth is that no battle for the soul of America rages, at least none that most Americans are aware of. . . . The myth of the culture war rests on misinterpretation of election returns, lack of hard examination of polling data, systematic and self-serving misinterpretation by issue activists, and selective coverage by an uncritical media more concerned with news value than getting the story right.[5]

Abramowitz's and Fiorina's first dispute regards the issue of geographic polarization. The basic idea is that red (Republican) states are getting redder (more Republican) as native residents become increasingly conservative and/or liberals leave and are replaced by conservative newcomers. The process in blue (Democratic) states is said to be the same. Contrary to many media reports and popular stereotypes, Fiorina holds that America is not clearly and deeply divided into red and blue states. Inter-state differences – in party identification, ideology, religion, beliefs and attitudes – are frequently small and often statistically insignificant. For example, large and equal numbers of red state residents and blue state residents identify themselves as ideological moderates (about 30 per cent), while small and equal numbers identify themselves as extremely liberal (3–4 per cent) and extremely conservative (4–5 per cent). Moreover, the two parties were closely matched in half the states in the 2000 presidential election (defined by less than 55 per cent of the electorate voting for either one of the two parties). The evidence is clear, claims Fiorina: American political parties may occupy the ideological poles, but the voters and states do not.[6]

Abramowitz slices the data differently. While Fiorina's analysis is temporally static, offering only a snapshot at one point in time, Abramowitz examines geographic polarization over time, comparing the nationally competitive presidential elections of 1960 and 1976 with those in 2000 and 2004. He shows that the average margin of victory across states has risen from around 8 to 14 percentage points and that the number of states considered to be competitive has declined by around ten, confirming that 'red states have been getting redder while blue states have been getting bluer'.[7] As polarization is as much a trend as a state, Abramowitz's dynamic over-time analysis is most convincing than Fiorina's, even though Fiorina is right to point out that a plurality of states is not solidly Republican or Democratic but marginal.

Both scholars address the issue of religious polarization. The idea is that the Republican Party is increasingly the party of God-fearing Americans, particularly evangelicals, while the Democratic Party's constituency is increasingly secular. Fiorina points out that the correlation between partisanship and religious denomination has actually declined in recent years (mainline Protestants are less Republican and Catholics are less Democratic, for example), but agrees with Abramowitz that the correlation between partisanship and religiosity (one's religious commitment, usually measured by frequency of church attendance) has grown stronger. While more religious Americans are increasingly supportive of the Republican Party, this shift is counterbalanced by the movement of secular and less religious Americans towards the Democratic Party. Thus, while neither party has particularly benefited electorally from the changes, religiosity is nonetheless an increasingly powerful predictor of voting behaviour.

Where Abramowitz and Fiorina disagree is over the *relative* importance of religiosity. Fiorina argues, based on his analysis of presidential elections up to 2000, that religiosity is more important than it was but that it has not replaced the old New Deal cleavage of class. Indeed, income, as a proxy for class, seems to be growing in importance, with poor Americans increasingly voting for Democratic candidates and richer ones for Republicans. The exception to this trend, acknowledges Fiorina, was the 2000 presidential election, when income played a lesser role in determining vote choices, both absolutely and relative to religiosity. While Fiorina suggests that it would be premature to make any robust conclusions about trends based on the 2000 election alone, evidence from the 2004 presidential election suggests that 2000 was not an aberration, but the beginning of a trend away from class and towards religion. Abramowitz's data are persuasive. Controlling for other factors, religiosity is a considerably more powerful predictor of vote choice in 2004 among white voters than any other social characteristic, including income. Abramowitz predicted that the trend would deepen as secular voters increased as a proportion of the electorate and religiously committed voters aligned increasingly with the GOP.[8] While 2008 did not see a deepening of the trend, it certainly saw its consolidation.[9]

One of the most popular arguments levied in favour of the culture war thesis is a reworking of the argument presented above that political parties in Congress are more clearly divided along ideological lines. Similarly, at the mass level, social conservatives are increasingly likely to support and vote for Republican candidates and social liberals for Democratic ones. The evidence seems indisputable, and the phenomenon has been called party or partisan polarization. Fiorina does not challenge the conventional wisdom that this has occurred. Instead, he challenges its extent and what it means.[10] First, regarding its extent, Fiorina acknowledges the increasing importance of cultural and social concerns, but argues that ordinary Americans are less differentiated by culture than are party elites and points to a large body of research that emphasizes the increasing importance of class in structuring partisan affiliations. Second, and regardless of any evidence presented on the first point, Fiorina rejects its importance. The reason is that party affiliations and vote choices may have changed, but issue and ideological positions have not. Americans have sorted themselves more neatly by ideology and party, mirroring the elite-level sorting in Congress, with Republican liberals switching to the Democratic Party and Democratic conservatives switching to the GOP. For this reason, Fiorina prefers the term 'party sorting' to 'party polarization'.

While Fiorina engages Abramowitz and other culture war theorists on questions of party, religious and geographic polarization, he does not actually believe that these are relevant indicators of polarization. According to Fiorina, polarization is best defined and measured by the distribution of politically related attitudes: 'The most direct way to measure polarization of political positions is to measure political positions.'[11] Conservatives may be moving to red states and religious Americans may be increasingly lining up in support of the Republican Party, but these trends do not demonstrate that Americans are becoming more polarized. If Americans are polarizing, their opinions should be changing. Specifically, Americans' opinions should be moving towards the poles of the distribution and away from the centre. For example, fewer people should over time have centrist opinions on abortion, and more should believe it should never be legal or be legal in all circumstances; and fewer Americans should define themselves as ideological moderates and more should self-identify as strong liberals or strong conservatives. Figure 6.3 presents these theoretical distributions graphically. Most analysts would agree that opinion on any particular issue is not polarized in Figure 3a, is somewhat polarized in Figure 3b and is most polarized in Figure 3c. To recap, Fiorina's contention is that, on most issues, even the hot-button ones that allegedly define the culture war, the distribution of opinion in the American population is best represented by the normal bell-curve in Figure 6.3a.

The evidence on political positions appears to stack up in Fiorina's favour. His own work and that of DiMaggio *et al.* and Evans, based on exhaustive analysis of the available data, offer seemingly compelling evidence that Americans are not polarizing.[12] In the aggregate, the issue positions of Americans – on abortion, the role and reach of government, and so on – over the past four decades are best described as stable and centrist. Ideologically, a plurality of Americans still describe themselves as moderates, and only tiny percentages as extremely liberal or conservative. Adding moderates to 'don't knows' makes this group the majority.

Abramowitz's response,[13] based on the same data as Fiorina uses,[14] is that Americans hold increasingly coherent ideological positions across a range of issues – with fewer conservatives taking any liberal positions and fewer liberals taking conservative ones. DiMaggio *et al.* reached a similar conclusion regarding issue cohesion, although they called it issue constraint and consolidation. Fiorina argues in turn that issue coherence or consistency is not akin to polarization, because the overall distribution of positions on the issues has not changed – 6.3a or 6.3b in Figure 6.3 still best describes the distribution. But his focus on the aggregate distribution ignores the important individual-level changes occurring in the American population. That one is less likely to find a self-described ideological liberal expressing restrictionist views on reproductive rights or immigration and a self-identified conservative expressing liberal positions means that ideological sorting has occurred. Liberals and conservatives now differ more clearly and deeply on the issues because individuals have changed their issue positions. Moreover, ideological sorting is not restricted to the most politically knowledgeable and sophisticated citizens. Hetherington estimates that about three-quarters of Americans could be said to be sorted by ideology and party.[15] Fiorina's aggregate data mask this important individual-level change. Whether such sorting constitutes evidence of political polarization is, however, disputed. Abramowitz says it does and Fiorina it does not. In part, the dispute rests on the causes of any shifts. We return to this point in the conclusion. The dispute also rests on how one defines polarization and cannot be resolved empirically, but if a clearer ideological divide between liberals and conservatives based on an individual-level

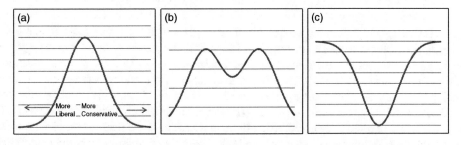

Figure 6.3 Normal distribution (6.3a), some polarization (6.3b) and polarized distribution (6.3c)

shift in issue positions does not constitute polarization then perhaps Fiorina may be accused of defining it out of existence.

Regardless of whether ideological sorting constitutes evidence of popular polarization, Fiorina has been criticized for underplaying the importance of issue salience. As Hetherington notes, 'polarization suggests an intensity that draws on attitudes that people hold deeply',[16] but Fiorina does not weigh issues according to their relative salience in public discourse or people's consciousness. Even if Americans are not more divided on cultural issues – with the issue distributions remaining constant, and perhaps even bell-shaped – 'salience can make issues seem more polarizing even if the distance between the groups remains relatively small. . . . If anything, the issue environment has become increasingly conducive to a culture war', argues Hetherington.[17] Hetherington offers the contrasting examples of civil rights in the 1960s and gay rights in the early twenty-first century. The preference distributions on both issues are very similar, but many more people identified civil rights as one of the most important problems facing America. It is perhaps this difference in issue salience, not the difference in preference distributions, which explains why civil rights was much more polarizing in the 1960s than is gay rights today.

While Hetherington does not conduct a rigorous analysis, his issue salience theory could potentially help explain part of the polarization puzzle. The puzzle is that Fiorina's issue distribution data show little evidence of polarization, yet a widespread perception remains that ordinary Americans are polarized and/or polarizing. If cultural issues have become more salient at the same time that the distribution of opinions has remained constant, then one could perhaps conclude that Americans are more polarized and America is experiencing a culture war. The remainder of this chapter tests Hetherington's salience theory.

First, an appropriate over-time measure of issue salience needs to be constructed. This is not straightforward, and there is no generally accepted instrument. However, Hetherington[18] and others[19] suggest that the most important problem (MIP) question may offer analytical leverage. The American National Election Studies (ANES) surveys have asked Americans to name the most important problem facing America roughly every two years since 1966. Because the question is 'open', respondents do not pick from a pre-existing list of problems but instead must consider unprompted the relative importance that they attach to various issues and pick the one they consider the most pressing. The question taps into Hetherington's understanding of issue saliency at the level of the individual citizen.

To construct our measure of issue saliency, the ANES MIP responses were scoured for any mention of cultural issues. Because issues evolve over time, the categories are not constant. Issues drop in and out of the response set. While this would normally be regarded as a potential problem by analysts, its flexibility is the key reason why the MIP question is an attractive measure. Table 6.1 sets out which categories are included in each year.

If Hetherington's issue salience theory is correct, the percentage of respondents mentioning cultural issues should increase over time. Figure 6.4 demonstrates that this is indeed the case. Apart from an uptick in 1970 and 1972, which was largely driven by anxiety over drugs, concern about cultural issues remained generally low in the 1960s and 1970s, despite a febrile political atmosphere generated by increasing opposition to the Vietnam War and growing concern over the rise of the anti-authoritarian and anti-traditionalist counter-culture. Even the Supreme Court's 1973 *Roe v. Wade* decision, which protected the rights of women seeking to terminate a pregnancy and is regarded as a staple of the culture war today, had no effect on the salience of cultural issues (it was not identified by any respondents as *the* most important problem). Concern began to increase again in the early 1980s, reaching its all-time high of 17.2 per cent when George H. W. Bush faced Michael Dukakis in the 1988

Table 6.1 American national election most important problem codes 1966–2004

ANES MIP code	Respondent mentions 1988–2004
45	Pro-abortion; pro-choice; the right of a woman to control her own body.
46	Anti-abortion; pro-life; 'abortion'.
320	Narcotics; availability of drugs; extent of drug/alcohol addiction in the US; interdiction of drugs coming to the US from foreign countries; alcohol- or drug-related crime; drug laws.
330	Women's rights; references to women's issues; economic equality for women; Equal Rights Amendment.
367	Against unregistered ownership of guns; legislative control of guns; 'control of guns'.
368	For gun ownership; right to have guns; against gun control.
380	General mention of moral/religious decay (of nation); sex, bad language, adult themes on TV.
381	Family problems – divorce; proper treatment of children; decay of family; child/ elder abuse (including sexual abuse); family values.
383	Problems of/with young people; drug/alcohol abuse among young people; sexual attitudes; lack of values/discipline; mixed-up thinking; lack of goals/ambition/ sense of responsibility.
384	Religion (too) mixed up in politics; prayer in school.
385	Homosexuality; protecting civil rights of gays and lesbians; accepting the lifestyle of homosexuality; granting homosexual couples the same rights and benefits as heterosexual couples; gay marriage.
765	Allowing/accepting gays in the military.

Year	Codes included by year
2004 =	45, 46, 320, 330, 367, 368, 380, 381, 383, 384, 385, 765
2000 =	45, 46, 320, 330, 367, 368, 380, 381, 383, 384, 385, 765
1998 =	45, 46, 320, 330, 367, 368, 380, 381, 383, 384, 385, 765
1996 =	45, 46, 320, 330, 367, 368, 380, 381, 383, 384, 385, 765
1994 =	45, 46, 320, 330, 367, 368, 380, 381, 383, 384, 385, 765
1992 =	45, 46, 320, 330, 367, 368, 380, 381, 383, 384, 385, 765
1990 =	45, 46, 320, 330, 367, 368, 380, 381, 383, 384
1988 =	45, 46, 320, 330, 367, 368, 380, 381, 383, 384

ANES MIP code	Respondent mentions 1974–86
45	Pro-abortion.
46	Anti-abortion.
49	Other specific reference to abortion.
320	Narcotics; general reference to drugs; drug addiction; pep pills, LSD, marijuana.
321	Against use of narcotics, LSD, marijuana.
322	For legalizing marijuana; for controlled use of narcotics, LSD, etc.
329	Other specific mention of narcotics/drugs/alcohol, etc.
330	Women's rights/liberation; general reference.
331	Pro-women's rights/liberation; for equal rights amendment.
332	Anti-women's rights/liberation; against equal rights amendment.
339	Other specific references to women's rights/liberation.
367	Against unregistered ownership of guns; legislative control of guns; 'control of guns'.
368	For gun ownership; right to have guns; against gun control.
380	General mention of moral/religious decay (of nation); sex, bad language, adult themes on TV.
381	Family problems – divorce; proper treatment of children; decay of family.
383	Young people; general reference to drinking, sexual freedom, discipline, mixed-up thinking, 'hippies', communication with young, etc.
384	Religion (too) mixed up in politics.

Table 6.1 Continued

Year	Codes included by year
1986 =	45, 46, 49, 320, 321, 322, 329, 330, 331, 332, 339, 367, 368, 380, 381, 383, 384
1984 =	45, 46, 49, 320, 321, 322, 329, 330, 331, 332, 339, 367, 368, 380, 381, 383, 384
1982 =	45, 46, 49, 320, 321, 322, 329, 330, 331, 332, 339, 367, 368, 380, 381, 383
1980 =	45, 46, 49, 320, 321, 322, 329, 330, 331, 332, 339, 367, 368, 380, 381, 383
1978 =	45, 46, 49, 320, 321, 322, 329, 330, 331, 332, 339, 367, 368, 380, 381, 383
1976 =	45, 46, 49, 320, 321, 322, 329, 330, 331, 332, 339, 367, 368, 380, 381, 383
1974 =	45, 46, 49, 320, 321, 322, 329, 330, 331, 332, 339, 367, 368, 380, 383

ANES MIP code	Respondent mentions 1966–72
363	Narcotics control; drug addiction; pep pills, LSD, marijuana, etc.
364	Problems of young people, e.g. drinking, discipline, mixed-up thinking.
365	Licensing, control of guns; other weapons.
380	Moral, religious decay of nation (general).
382	School prayers.
383	Problems of young people, e.g. drinking, sexual freedom, discipline, mixed-up thinking, hippies; communication with young; generation gap.

Year	Codes included by year
1972 =	363, 365, 380, 382, 383
1970 =	363, 365, 380, 382, 383
1968 =	363, 365, 380, 382, 383
1966 =	363, 364, 365, 380, 382

Notes: 2008 MIP question not yet coded by ANES; MIP question not asked in 2002; MIP numerical codes and associated wording are ANES's own; codes included by year selected by author.

presidential election. It dropped off over the next four years, perhaps as the first Gulf war and the recession diverted attention away from cultural concerns, but rose sharply from 1992 through the presidency of Bill Clinton, reaching 16.8 per cent in 2000.

The salience of cultural issues appears to have declined dramatically between 2000 and 2004 (the MIP question was not asked in 2002). This fall is particularly strange because some commentators identified the 2004 presidential election between George W. Bush and John Kerry as the time when cultural and moral issues came to the fore, a claim supported by data

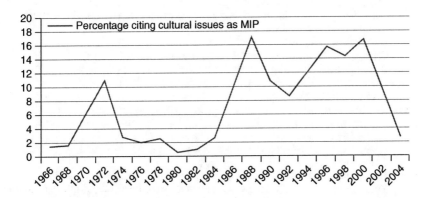

Figure 6.4 The salience of cultural issues, 1966–2004

Source: American National Election Studies. Figures compiled by the author. See text and Table 6.1 for details.

from the 2004 National Election Pool (NEP) exit poll, in which 22 per cent of respondents said 'moral values' was the most important issue determining their presidential vote. While the poll's methodology and the interpretation that moral values 'decided' the presidential election have been subject to scholarly criticism,[20] other surveys (by Pew and the *Los Angeles Times*, for example) confirm that moral values were a significant source of concern. Why did the ANES survey not pick up on this concern, or at least measure it at a much lower level than the NEP and other 2004 polls? The answer lies in a combination of factors to do with the respective survey designs and the important issues of the day. Most notably, the ANES changed the wording of the MIP question. In previous years, it had asked respondents to think about the present, but in 2004 it directed them to consider the past four years. Given that 9/11 had occurred during the specified four-year time period, America had engaged in wars in Afghanistan and Iraq, and respondents could select only their single *most* important concern, it is easy to understand why concern about cultural issues would be trumped by such events. We cannot know what the result would have been had the question not changed and events been different, but it is likely that they significantly diminished the number selecting cultural issues. We should thus be wary about the 2004 data point, and not conclude that cultural issues didn't matter. Unfortunately, the ANES has still not released the results of its 2008 MIP question.

In sum, and recognizing the 2004 data point is problematic, it seems appropriate to conclude that Hetherington is right. Thinking about issues in terms of their salience, rather than just their distribution, as does Fiorina, offers empirically interesting and theoretically important insights into the culture war debate. Even if Fiorina is correct, and Americans are not significantly more divided in terms of where they stand on the hot-button issues such as abortion, gay rights, family values and the role of religion in public and private life, it is very likely that they are more polarized because these issues have grown in importance over the past three decades. This finding poses a challenge to scholars who continue to reject the argument that ordinary Americans are engaged in battle over moral and cultural issues. It also allows observers to place recent events, such as the rise of the Tea Party and the vehement opposition of ordinary conservatives to the Obama administration, in the context of a polarizing polity. The apparently feverish climate of political discourse can in part be explained by the increased salience of cultural issues among ordinary Americans, not just political elites.

Causes of polarization

Has elite polarization caused ordinary Americans to become more polarized, or are elites responding, as perhaps they should in a democratic polity, to polarization at the mass level? Alternatively, it is possible that elite and mass polarization may be causally unrelated, and instead be the product of one or more other factors.

Despite the potentially messy causal relationships, Hetherington is clear that elite polarization is responsible for the increased salience of cultural issues at the mass level.[21] But how? One potential mechanism is that political operatives like Karl Rove, George W. Bush's close adviser, have adopted electoral strategies that seek to turn out the party's base rather than moderate voters.[22] To do so, parties, especially the Republicans, have focused their campaigns on divisive issues such as abortion, gay rights and school prayer that appeal to core supporters and motivate them to vote in large numbers. Alternatively, suggests Thomas Frank, Republicans may have used cultural issues to divide the Democratic coalition, splintering off conservative Democrats and realigning them with the GOP despite the fact that the Democratic Party best represents their economic interests.[23] As noted above, however, other scholars suggest that economics actually matters more today, not less as Frank suggests. An increasingly partisan and ideological media may also be part of the story, widening, or at least entrenching, ideological differences between partisans, as conservatives tune into Fox while liberals watch MSNBC, for example. The politically polarized nature of the blogosphere and talk radio may exacerbate this effect, suggests Hetherington.[24] A subsequent question, however, is why has the media polarized? Is it caused by the same things that are causing other aspects of elite polarization, or by the polarization going on in other parts of the elites' universe, such as Congress, or is it a response to technological developments and/or changing tastes at the mass level? The causal story is difficult to disentangle.

The causes of elite-level polarization are equally difficult to establish.[25] They are opaque, contested and many. Of the probable causes identified by Hetherington in his encyclopaedic review of the literature, perhaps the most notable is the Democratic Party's adoption of the civil rights agenda in the 1940s and 1950s and the subsequent loss of its southern hegemony.[26] The 'grand bargain' between northern liberal and southern conservative Democrats unravelled (where southerners had supported liberal economic programmes while northerners turned a blind eye to segregationist practices), producing more ideologically cohesive parties. The Democratic Party's congressional caucus became more universally liberal as its pro-segregation southern members lost their seats to conservative Republicans or switched parties. It is also likely that procedural changes enacted in the 1970s, particularly primary contests,[27] interacted with the growing radicalization of grassroots party activists to produce congressional and presidential candidates less representative of the median voter and more representative of each party's ideological poles.[28] While primaries were designed to weaken the grip of party elites and unsurprisingly have hitherto been interpreted as evidence of party decline, it appears they have in fact engendered party resurgence in both Congress and country. Of course, the subsequent question of why Republican Party activists have moved rightwards and Democratic ones leftwards is a thorny one. Any explanation should probably acknowledge the role of elite discourse and particularly the role elites play in framing issues,[29] but it is also likely that activists in turn played a role in elites' own polarization.[30] Such endogeneity makes it very difficult to pin down the relative contribution of the respective causes. That there are likely many other varied and interconnected causes – institutional, non-institutional and cultural[31] – further undermines efforts to settle on a robust explanatory model. More research in this area is required.

Consequences and solutions

The key consequence of polarization, say its critics, is a malfunctioning polity.[32] In the absence of very large majorities in both chambers of Congress, and particularly the Senate, the parties' failure to work together militates against the passage of important solutions to today's problems. Indeed, the parties are more likely to work against than with each other. For example, 'the single most important thing we want to achieve', declared Senate Minority Leader Mitch McConnell, is 'for President Obama to be a one-term president'.[33] Given that the Republicans' priority is defeating the incumbent president rather than addressing the financial crisis or growing the economy or rethinking America's role in the world, it is perhaps not surprising that only 12 per cent of the American people have a 'great deal' or 'quite a lot' of confidence in the US Congress (compared to 35 per cent in the presidency and 37 per cent in the Supreme Court),[34] and that only 10 per cent 'approve of the way Congress is handling its job'[35] – the lowest level since Gallup began asking this question in 1974. Yet the opprobrium of the American people has, hitherto, failed to refocus its members' attentions on substantive issues of policy and governance. At the time of writing, the institution is convulsed by partisan conflict, and there appears to be little prospect that the parties will emerge from their trenches in an *entente cordiale*.

Prospective solutions to elite polarization are varied. Those that require constitutional change – such as aligning the electoral terms of representatives, senators and presidents – will struggle to clear the hurdle of the constitution's own amendment procedure. Quirk's suggestion is to attack the problem at one of its alleged sources: the primary process.[36] This could be done at the state level and on a state-by-state basis, and would not require the congressional turkeys to vote for Christmas. California's new non-partisan blanket primary for state and congressional elections, approved by voters as Proposition 14 in 2010, arrays all prospective candidates on the same list irrespective of party affiliation. Its effects will be watched eagerly, but could include forcing politicians to seek out the median voter rather than those at the ideological poles.

Conclusion

The discussion above highlights a broad consensus among academics and observers of the political scene that American elites are deeply divided on cultural and social issues. No such consensus exists on the issue of polarization among ordinary Americans. Fiorina's and Abramowitz's work represents two sides of this debate. Much of the dispute between them is ultimately definitional. What Abramowitz sees as polarizing, Fiorina sees as sorting. There is no clear, scientific way to settle their disagreement and the debate in the wider literature. Nonetheless, this chapter is sympathetic to Fiorina's position that geographic, religious and party sorting does not constitute evidence of mass polarization.

It is less sympathetic to the idea that ideological sorting does not constitute evidence of mass polarization. We know that self-identified liberals increasingly hold fewer conservative positions on the issues and self-identified conservatives fewer liberal ones. The aggregate distribution of opinion may not have changed, with roughly stable numbers of liberal, moderate and conservative positions on any given cultural or social issue, but this masks an important change at the individual level. Liberals have moved towards the liberal end of the distribution and conservatives towards the conservative end. They are more divided ideologically because they have fewer overlapping value positions. Is that polarization or sorting? Probably both, but a firm answer depends in part on whether the shift is a consequence of real value change that pits more ideologically coherent liberals and conservatives against each other, or whether liberals and conservatives take more coherent positions across issues not because their opinions have fundamentally changed but because elite partisans are giving more clear signals about where they should say they stand. In other words, is the value change real or simply rhetorical? The answer is that we do not know. More research is required. Most likely, both processes are at work and interacting with each other. Importantly, however, public opinion is a combination of the two. When political scientists say that elites shape public opinion, they mean that elites influence what people think, feel and say without being able to distinguish clearly between them. Given that public opinion is what the public says its opinion is, we should probably, until we know better, interpret the data to mean that the public is more coherently divided ideologically because the public has told us it is more coherently divided ideologically. If this interpretation is correct, it undermines Fiorina's proposition that ordinary Americans are not polarized or engaged in a culture war.

Fiorina has also been criticized by Hetherington for fixating on the distribution of opinions and ignoring the relative importance of the issues under investigation. Even if there has been no change in terms of the distribution of opinion on hot-button cultural issues, Americans are likely to be more divided if those issues have grown in importance. Polarization, for Hetherington at least, is a product of opinion distribution and issue salience. To explore this idea, this chapter presented some new data on the salience of cultural issues in the US over the past four decades. The trend is clear. The number of Americans identifying cultural issues as the most important problem facing the country increased markedly during the 1980s and 1990s. Put differently, that these have become increasingly important to ordinary Americans suggests that the culture war is both an elite- and a mass-level phenomenon, whose reach should alarm all observers concerned about the health of American democracy.

Notes

1   Snowe, quoted in Michael Shear, 'Is Bipartisanship Back? Don't Count on It', *New York Times*, 1 March 2012.
2   Snowe, quoted in Shear, 'Is Bipartisanship Back?'
3   Keith Poole, 'Congressional Policy Shifts, 1879–2011', *Voteview Blog*, 15 February 2012, http://voteview.com/blog/.
4   Alan I. Abramowitz and Kyle L. Saunders, 'Is Polarization a Myth?' *Journal of Politics*, 70 (2008), 542.
5   Morris P. Fiorina, *Culture War? The Myth of a Polarized America* (New York: Pearson Longman, 2005), 8.
6   Ibid., 11–32.
7   Abramowitz and Saunders, 'Is Polarization a Myth?', 548.
8   Abramowitz and Saunders, 'Is Polarization a Myth?'
9   John Green, *Pew Research Center Forum on Religion and Public Life's* Faith Angle Conference, *December 2008.*
10 Morris P. Fiorina and Samuel J. Abrams, 'Political Polarization in the American Public', *Annual Review of Political Science*, 11 (2008), 578–580.
11 Ibid., 569.
12 Paul DiMaggio, John Evans and Bethany Bryson (1996), 'Have Americans' Social Attitudes Become More Polarized?', *American Journal of Sociology*, 10(3) (1996), 690–755; John H. Evans, 'Have Americans' Attitudes Become More Polarized? An Update', *Social Science Quarterly*, 84(1) (2003), 71–90.
13 Abramowitz and Saunders, 'Is Polarization a Myth?', 544–545.
14 Fiorina and Abrams, 'Political Polarization in the American Public', 573.
15 Marc J. Hetherington, 'Putting Polarization in Perspective', *British Journal of Political Science*, 39 (2009), 438.
16 Ibid., 429.
17 Ibid., 430, 435.
18 Ibid., 434–436.
19 Young Min, Salma I. Ghanem and Dixie Evatt, 'Using a Split-Ballot Survey to Explore the Robustness of the "MIP" Question in Agenda-Setting Research: A Methodological Study', *International Journal of Public Opinion Research*, 19 (2007), 221–236; Tom W. Smith, 'The Polls: America's Most Important Problems; Part I: National and International', *Public Opinion Quarterly*, 49 (1985), 264–274.
20 Howard Schuman, 'The Validity of the 2004 "Moral Values" Question', *The Forum*, 4(2) (2006), Article 5.
21 Hetherington, 'Putting Polarization in Perspective', 441.
22 Kevin Fullam and Alan R. Gitelson, 'A Lasting Republican Majority? George W. Bush's Electoral Strategy', in Andrew Wroe and Jon Herbert, eds, *Assessing the George W. Bush Presidency: A Tale of Two Terms* (Edinburgh: Edinburgh University Press, 2009).
23 Thomas Frank, *What's the Matter with Kansas? How Conservatives Won the Heart of America* (New York: Metropolitan Books, 2004).

24 Hetherington, 'Putting Polarization in Perspective', 443.
25 See, for example, Paul J. Quirk, 'A House Dividing: Understanding Polarization', *The Forum*, 9(2) (2011), Article 12.
26 Hetherington, 'Putting Polarization in Perspective', 421.
27 Morris P. Fiorina and Samuel J. Abrams, *Disconnect: The Breakdown of Representation in American Politics* (Norman: University of Oklahoma Press, 2009).
28 Alan I. Abramowitz, *The Disappearing Center: Engaged Citizens, Polarization, and American Democracy* (New Haven, CT: Yale University Press, 2011).
29 Marc J. Hetherington, 'Resurgent Mass Partisanship: The Role of Elite Polarization', *American Political Science Review*, 95 (2001), 619–631; Geoffrey C. Layman and Edward G. Carmines, 'Cultural Conflict in American Politics: Religious Traditionalism, Postmaterialism, and US Political Behavior', *Journal of Politics*, 59(3) (1997), 751–777; but see Kara Lindaman and Donald P. Haider-Markel, 'Issue Evolution, Political Parties, and the Culture Wars', *Political Research Quarterly*, 55(1) (2002), 91–110.
30 Edward G. Carmines and Geoffrey C. Layman, 'Issue Evolution in Post-War American Politics: Old Certainties and Fresh Tensions', in Byron E. Shafer (ed.), *Present Discontents: American Politics in the Very Late Twentieth Century* (Washington, DC: CQ Press, 1997).
31 This is Hetherington's typology in 'Putting Polarization in Perspective'.
32 Hetherington, 'Putting Polarization in Perspective', 427–429; Quirk, 'A House Dividing', 8–11.
33 Quoted in Jonathan Freedland, 'Barack Obama's Presidency, Three Years On – Is It Time to Give Up Hope?', *Guardian*, 19 January 2012.
34 Gallup Poll, 9–12 June 2011.
35 Gallup Poll, 2–5 February 2012.
36 Quirk, 'A House Dividing'.

7 The onward march of (asymmetric) political polarization in the contemporary Congress

John E. Owens

For decades now, congressional parties have been the most significant political organizations on Capitol Hill. Over this period, class and cultural issues have produced increasingly sharp ideological divisions between Democrats and Republicans, engendering congressional parties that are much more cohesive and ideologically polarized than those either of the mid-decades of the mid-twentieth century or anticipated by the US Constitution's framers. Parties now structure the contemporary congressional politics of most major legislation, treaties and nominations in ways not seen since the last decades of the nineteenth and the early twentieth century. Although rank-and-file members continue to demand particularistic benefits to meet constituency and re-election needs, and pursue individual policy agendas and interests, increasingly they see themselves first and foremost as party members. Armed with that pre-eminent perception, they vigorously promote and defend their party's brand while seeking to damage the opposing party's *brand*. Much more than previously, they insist on and depend upon central party leaders and coordinated party efforts to tease out from an increasingly complex and conflicted Congress *partisan* legislative products that distinguish their party from the opposition and will advantage their party in the next set of elections. Concomitantly, within this context, constituents reward party loyalty,[1] as voters and party activists have strengthened their partisanship and diverged increasingly from partisans in the opposing party – all at the same time that American voters care neither for the Congress as an institution nor its parties,[2] continue to want political leaders who are willing to make compromises,[3] and blame the parties for making US politics and government less civil.[4]

Accelerating (asymmetric) partisan polarization in the Congress

Over 220 or so years of congressional history, as Keith Poole and his colleagues have demonstrated, Congress members' preferences on House and Senate floor roll call votes have been simply structured: over that period, one dominant ideological dimension has tapped basic differences between members and separated the main parties.[5] In modern terms, this is the familiar distinction between liberals and conservatives that generally separates Democrats and Republicans over the role of government in US society and the economy. At different times, a second dimension tapping regional differences – variously, slavery, bimetallism, and civil rights for African-Americans – has emerged, but subsequently disappeared. In the mid-twentieth century, this second (civil rights) dimension emerged and divided northern and southern Democrats, but then declined, following the passage of the 1964 Civil Rights Act, the 1965 Voting Rights Act and the 1968 Open Housing Act, and by the turn of the century was almost extinct.

With the second dimension almost disappearing, both the congressional Democratic and the Republican parties became more ideologically homogeneous on a dominant liberal–conservative dimension, which came to account for over 90 per cent of Congress members' policy preferences.[6] Measured by Poole *et al.*'s DW-NOMINATE scores, where 1.0 is a strong conservative position and −1.0 is a strong liberal position, between the 91st House (1969–70) and the 106th and 111th Houses, the standard deviation of House Democrats' scores declined from 0.20 to 0.15, while those for the historically more cohesive House Republicans barely changed (from 0.17 to 0.16). Similar reductions were registered for Senate Democrats and Republicans.

As the congressional parties became more homogeneous ideologically, they became polarized, occupying separate ideological spaces on the liberal–conservative continuum, whereas 30 years ago the ideological spaces occupied by Democrats and Republicans in both chambers overlapped to some extent. Since the turn of the century, this has no longer been the case, as Figures 7.1 and 7.2 demonstrate. In the 91st House and Senate (1969–70), conservative and centrist House Democrats (largely from the South) shared the same ideological space with many centrist Republicans (primarily from the North-East) (top charts), but by the turn of the century (106th House and Senate), as the number of centrists declined significantly, just seven Democrats and 14 Republicans occupied the same ideological space in the House and a single Democrat in the Senate (centre charts). Ten years later (111th House and Senate), as the number of centrists declined further, House and Senate Democrats and Republicans achieved complete ideological separation (bottom charts). That is, in each chamber, every Republican is now more conservative than every Democrat, and every Democrat is more liberal than any Republican. In short, the congressional parties are now more polarized than at any other time since the end of Reconstruction in the 1880s.

For reasons that will be discussed later, there is little reason to think that this trend will change in the foreseeable future. Indeed, the most recent evidence for 2011 – the first year of the 112th Congress, in which partisan control was split between Republicans, who controlled the House, and Democrats, who controlled the Senate – shows that, partly as a consequence of the loss of many centrist Democrats in the 2010 midterm elections, polarization has accelerated even further and even more sharply than after the Republicans took over the House and Senate after the 1994 midterm elections, so that the ideological gap between the least conservative House and Senate Republican and the most conservative House and Senate Democrat is even wider than it was in the 111th Congress.

The recent acceleration of partisan polarization, however, has not been symmetrical. For, typically ignored in many journalistic (and some political science) accounts is that congressional Republicans have moved much more sharply to the right than have congressional Democrats to the left, never more so than since the inauguration of President Obama in 2009. Whereas mean House and Senate Democratic DW-NOMINATE scores have remained more or less stable since the late 1990s, those for House and Senate Republicans continued to accelerate towards even more conservative positions, pulling them further and further from their respective chamber means (Figure 7.3). Put another way, whereas the number of the most liberal House Democrats (DW-NOMINATE scores higher than −0.400) increased by 55 per cent between the 91st and 111th Congresses (1969–2010), the number of the most conservative Republicans (DW-NOMINATE scores lower than 0.400) increased 440 per cent.

Partisan polarization has been asymmetric not only in regard to the two parties, but also between the House and the Senate, as similar, albeit less dramatic, changes occurred in the Senate over the same period: while the number of the most liberal Democrats increased by 50 per cent, the most conservative Republicans increased 220 per cent. Thus, while House and Senate Democrats' mean (liberal) DW-NOMINATE scores remained more or less stable

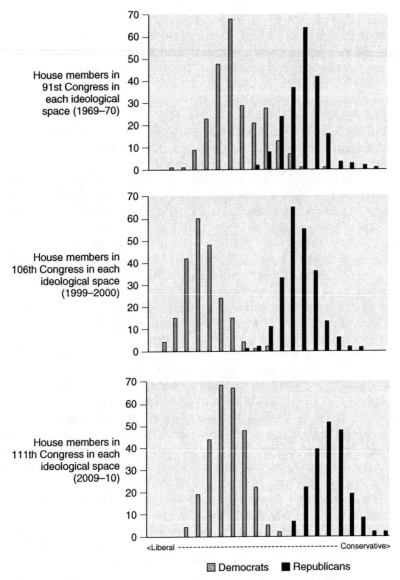

Figure 7.1 The growing ideological separateness of the House parties, 1969–2010

Note: First dimension DW-NOMINATE scores derived from voteview.com.

between the 106th and 111th Congresses (1999–2010) (respectively, −0.382 and −0.377, and −0.358 and −0.384), and House Republicans' mean scores accelerated from 0.487 to 0.623 (+28 per cent), Senate Republicans' mean (conservative) scores increased less sharply, from 0.376 to 0.448 (+20 per cent) – although, again, asymmetric polarization accelerated even further in the first session of the 112th Congress (2011).

Why has partisan polarization increased? And why has polarization been asymmetrical? As in previous periods of congressional history, we need to focus on what has been going on outside the Congress, as well as inside, including changes among voters, party activists, and Congress members and House and Senate leaders.[7]

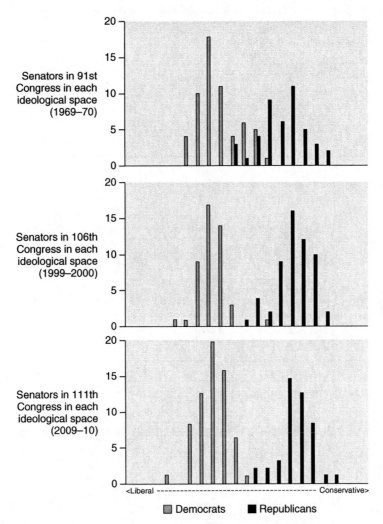

Figure 7.2 The growing ideological separateness of the Senate parties, 1969–2010

Note: First dimension DW-NOMINATE scores derived from voteview.com.

Increased (asymmetric) polarization in the congressional electorate

The most common explanation for increased partisan polarization within the Congress has to do with changes occurring within the electorate over recent decades. For a number of reasons – conservative white southern Democrats' negative responses to African-Americans' demands for civil rights,[8] growing social and economic inequality in the US within individual states,[9] more effective partisan redistricting[10] and increased ideological and geographic sorting – the two parties' voters have become dissimilar.[11]

Surveys conducted by the American National Election Study (ANES) and Gallup show that, despite a decline in partisanship from one in five to one in three voters and a small rise in the numbers of independents since the mid-1960s – many of the latter being ideologically similar to either Democratic or Republican partisans – at the beginning of the second decade of the twenty-first

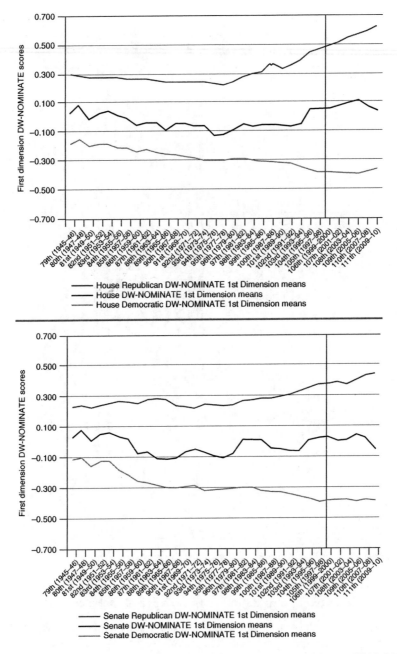

Figure 7.3 Asymmetric partisan and chamber polarization in the House and Senate, 1945–2010

century, 60 per cent of the US electorate continued to identify with one of the two main parties. Moreover, partisanship remains the most important force in US electoral politics. Voters' emotional-psychological, increasingly ideological, attachment to a party goes a long way to explaining why Americans exhibit the political attitudes that they do, how they evaluate candidates for office and why they vote as they do. The upshot is that those who identify with the Democratic Party are very likely to approve of *any* Democratic officeholder and very unlikely to disapprove of *any* Republican officeholder, and vice versa. Strong Democratic and Republican identifiers (whose numbers have increased since the late 1970s as overall partisanship has declined) are particularly likely to behave this way.

At the same time that partisanship has remained strong, US voters – partly as a consequence of rising educational levels and partly as a consequence of heightened ideological conflict among political elites, including congressional and presidential party leaders – have become much more capable of developing more coherent and consistent opinions and preferences across a range of different policy issues, much better able to apply ideological labels to the political parties, and much more likely to assign themselves ideological labels more closely and consistently related to their preferences on a wide range of domestic and foreign policy issues, such as government responsibility for jobs and living standards, health insurance, government services and spending, military spending, government assistance to African-Americans, abortion, and women's equality.[12] So, although they still do not articulate belief systems as elaborate or constrained as those of political activists and elites, over the last few decades an ideological sorting process has occurred, especially among those who are more politically engaged, and voters' ideological self-identification has become a much more reliable indication of their liberalism/conservatism and their partisanship.[13] Although the distribution of the political values and beliefs of all Americans has remained largely unchanged over the last 25 or so years,[14] the values and beliefs of Republican and Democrat identifiers now differ much more sharply than previously: whereas the gap between Republican and Democrat identifiers on 48 measures of political values was 10 per cent in 1987, in 2012 it was 18 per cent.[15] Indeed, partisan differences have now become much more significant than gender, age, race or class.

Importantly for present purposes, however, recent time-series research suggests that increased partisan polarization within the Congress – and more generally amongst other US political elites – has stimulated increased partisan-ideological sorting and polarization within the electorate by providing voters with much stronger cues on their parties' ideological positions and appeals. The two phenomena are effectively inseparable, with the causal arrow seemingly running from the elite to the mass level, not vice versa.[16] Using data from the Pew Research Center's 2012 report, Poole *et al.* have demonstrated high correlations between House and Senate polarization (measured by differences in members' first dimension scores) and the average percentage point difference between Democratic and Republican identifiers on Pew's series of political value questions (e.g., support for social safety net programmes, support for traditional family values, etc.) between 1987 and 2012 (House r=0.83; Senate r=0.80).[17]

The key change in patterns of electoral polarization occurred as voters responded in a polarized pattern to the policies and politics of the Reagan administration and the Republican congressional majorities led by Newt Gingrich.[18] As a result, American National Election Survey results show that, between 1972 and 2004, the percentage of conservatives who identified with the Republican Party rose from 57 to 63, while the percentage who called themselves 'liberal' fell from about 13 to 6 per cent. Over the same period, the percentage of 'liberal' Democrats increased from one-third to one-half, while those who identified themselves as 'conservative' declined from one-quarter to one-eighth. In short, voters' partisanship and ideological self-identification became highly correlated over this period at 0.63.[19] Voters also voted increasingly consistently for 'their' party: liberals voted for Democratic congressional candidates 86 per cent of the time (compared with 75 per cent in 1972) and conservatives voted for Republican candidates 79 per cent of the time. Since 2004, as the 2012 Pew survey shows, the link between voters' ideological self-identification and partisanship has strengthened even further: conservative Republicans increased their proportion of party identifiers to 68 per cent, as party centrists and 'liberals' dropped, respectively, to 26 and 5 per cent. Among Democrats, changes were less dramatic but nevertheless in the opposite direction: 'liberals' increased their proportion to 38 per cent, while party centrists declined to 38 per cent and conservatives to 20 per cent. As previously, the shift was greatest among the most active partisans.[20] At the same time, the correlation between ideological self-identification and voting increased.[21]

Notwithstanding this ideological-partisan sorting, however, since at least 1972 when the ANES began asking the question there have been about twice as many self-identified conservatives as there are liberals – as there are now;[22] and the vast majority identify with and vote for the Republican Party. Moreover, Republican voters' policy responses, which are not shared by Democratic or independent voters,[23] and have been driven by Republican politicians and, more recently, by the Tea Party,[24] have become much more uniformly conservative than Democrats have become uniformly liberal. That is, electoral polarization on the liberal–conservative/left–right continuum has been *asymmetric*: Democratic and Republican voters have not moved apart symmetrically, measured either by the numbers who are now at the extreme liberal and conservative poles or by the difference in party voters' mean positions. Instead, Republicans – particularly Republican activists and primary voters, who are less ideologically representative of the overall electorate than active Democrats[25] – have become much more heavily clustered at or near the extreme conservative pole than are Democrats, who continue to reflect a much broader ideological coalition and are less at the extreme liberal pole.[26] Gallup's 2010 and 2012 data show seven out of ten Republican voters identifying themselves as ideologically conservative, while only about 40 per cent of Democrats consider themselves liberal, the remaining Democrats calling themselves 'moderates' or 'conservative'.[27] The Pew Research Center's 2012 survey shows similar results: Republican conservatives outnumbered centrists by two to one, while liberals and centrists constituted the same proportions among Democrats. Moreover, Republicans and Democrats' political values have become most sharply polarized, as Republicans (and to a lesser extent independents) have expressed increasingly minimalist views on issues to do with the scope and role of government. Majorities of Republicans now say that they disagree that the government should guarantee every citizen enough to eat and a place to sleep (36 per cent agree, 63 per cent disagree) and take care of people who cannot take care of themselves (40 per cent agree, 54 per cent disagree) – compared with 2009, when Republican opinions on these questions were more evenly divided. In contrast, Democrats' opinions of these issues have remained stable over the last 25 years.[28]

Unsurprisingly, Republicans are also much more strongly motivated by their conservative ideology than are Democrats by their liberalism – in large part because of the increased emphasis on conservative ideology by Republican officeholders from Reagan, through Gingrich and forward to the Tea Party.[29] Republicans also remain much less willing to support political leaders who are willing to compromise (68 per cent in favour) than Democrats, amongst whom support has significantly increased (to 90 per cent) over the last 25 years.[30] As a consequence, Republican members of Congress, as well as other party officeholders, have a clearer, more uniform and more consistent sense of their party activists' expectations than do their Democratic counterparts.

How has greater ideological and partisan consistency among the electorate affected representation in the early twenty-first-century Congress?

The geographic effects of ideological and partisan sorting on congressional representation

Whether ideological sorting has led to geographic sorting within like-minded and segregated 'red' and 'blue' states and congressional districts[31] remains a contentious issue among political scientists. Bishop argues that over the last 30 or so years Americans have sorted themselves geographically, economically and politically into like-minded communities so that the percentages of voters living in counties lopsidedly voting for one party's presidential candidate almost doubled between 1976 and 2004.[32] Voters' preferences in presidential election returns, however, are often not consistent with how people vote in other elections. So, without further research, it is not possible to prove that geographic sorting has occurred.[33] Nonetheless, since the 1970s the ethnic composition of congressional districts and states, and the spread of income within them have become significantly more diverse,[34] strengthening socioeconomic and class segregation within and among them.[35] The spatial segregation of liberals and conservatives has also accelerated considerably since 2000, creating significantly greater ideological dissimilarity between counties and between states.[36]

Partisan redistricting was not a major cause of this segregation process,[37] but it undoubtedly assisted it. Between 1992 and 2002, the number of safe House seats rose from 281 to 356 – 82 per cent of the total.[38] On the eve of the 2002 elections, *Congressional Quarterly* rated just 48 House seats (11 per cent) as competitive.[39] Just four out of 382 incumbents seeking re-election lost. Two years later, just 37 seats were regarded as competitive (the smallest number in three decades). Just seven incumbents lost, as Democrats retained 98 per cent of the seats they won in 2002 and Republicans won 97 per cent of the seats they won.[40] Although the numbers of competitive House elections rose in 2006, 2008 and 2010, again the vast majority of seats held by one party in previous elections in the decade were retained by that party. Even in 2010, as Republicans made net gains of 64 seats to win a 242–193 House majority, Democrats retained 74 per cent of the seats they won in 2008, while Republicans won 98 per cent of theirs. (Thus, the same party as in 2008 won 84 per cent of seats.) Indeed, the trend over recent decades has been for congressional districts and states to become more consistently partisan for one party and for almost twice as many House members to be elected from safe districts as from districts where support for their party was weak.[41]

Although partisan retention rates for the Senate seats show wider fluctuations, nonetheless, between 1990 and 2010, Republicans' mean retention rate was 84.7 per cent and Democrats' mean retention rate was 82 per cent, and since the late 1970s the number of states sending mixed party delegations to the Senate has fallen from 27 to 17. Although over 50 per cent of senators continue to win election from competitive states, over 40 per cent are now elected from states safe for their party, compared with 25 per cent in the early 1970s.[42] As congressional districts and states have become more consistently partisan for one party, they have also elected representatives of the same party in presidential as well as congressional elections.

Polarizing partisan trends within the electorate, and ideological and geographic sorting among congressional districts and states tell only part of the story, however. A more important part of the story needs to focus on party activists, how their political incentives and roles have changed, and how these factors shape the respective parties' policy positions.

Party activists as agents of congressional polarization

From Downs forward,[43] it has been commonly assumed that parties are primarily interested in winning government office. Increasingly since the 1960s, however, within an open party nomination process, an increasing number of party activists have become more interested in advocating 'purist' issue positions than with winning congressional elections. As a consequence, they have pushed their party and its candidates towards extreme positions.[44] Indeed, this is exactly the position in which the supposed Republican presidential frontrunner and erstwhile centrist, now conservative, Mitt Romney soon found himself in 2012. In order to secure his party's nomination for president, he had to succeed first in convincing (conservative) party activists that he was at least as conservative as his competitors. John McCain (Republican, Arizona) – another Republican presidential candidate with centrist pretensions – found himself in the same position in 2008, as he also did in seeing off a more conservative primary challenger for his Arizona Senate seat in 2010.[45]

A considerable body of research has now shown that not only are both parties' activists more ideologically extreme than the electorate at large but opposing party activists' preferences have become much more polarized over recent decades.[46] More than this, the polarization process among party activists has been asymmetric, even more so than among the electorate: Republican activists have become much more uniformly extremely conservative than have Democratic activists become uniformly liberal.[47] Indeed, for Layman *et al.*, 'the main force behind partisan conflict extension in recent years has been the sharp growth in the presence of consistently conservative Republican activists'.[48] Conservative Republican activists, moreover, have become much more strongly committed to their party and their ideological preferences than have much less party-centred Democrats.[49]

Evidence of what Layman *et al.* call 'conflict extension' orchestrated by hard-line conservative Republican activists abounds, and is evident in press reports of Republican centrists in the House and Senate denigrated by their more conservative detractors as RINOs (Republicans in name only), often leading them to quit and be succeeded by more conservative substitutes. Centrist Senator Mark Hatfield (Republican, Oregon) was one of the first to come under intense pressure from Republican hard-liners following the Republican victories in the 1994 House and Senate elections, after he cast the deciding vote against his party's proposed balanced budget amendment. Seeing the writing on the wall in his state party, he retired, to be succeeded by the much more conservative Gordon Smith (Republican, Oregon). Other Republican centrists, including senators James Jeffords (Republican, Vermont), Lincoln Chafee (Republican, Rhode Island) and Olympia Snowe (Republican, Maine), have felt the same hard-line conservative pressure and followed suit or left the party, in Jeffords case precipitating a shift in partisan control of the Senate to the Democrats. Incensed by the election of President Obama, hard-line ultra-conservatives Republican activists – many of whom were members of the Tea Party movement – challenged and defeated less conservative Republican candidates in 2010, including three incumbent senators.[50] Two other incumbent Republicans, Kay Bailey Hutchinson (Republican, Texas) and three-term centrist Olympia Snowe (Republican, Maine), were subjected to intense pressure from Tea Party supporters in their home states, and opted not to seek re-election in 2012,[51] while another conservative, Richard Lugar (Republican, Indiana), was defeated by a more conservative challenger supported by the well-funded Tea Party. House Republicans – not all of them centrists – have also been subjected to similarly intense pressures and have either retired voluntarily or gone down to primary defeat.[52] Congressional Democrats have been subject to similar pressures from more liberal party activists, albeit not to the same extent.[53]

Extended analysis by Theriault has demonstrated that party activists' pressures in Congress members' districts and states has had as much effect on congressional polarization as the partisanship of their constituencies.[54] The more conservative Smith succeeded the centrist Hatfield in Oregon regardless of the state's slightly more Democratic hue, just as states with split-party Senate delegations, such as Iowa, New Mexico, Pennsylvania and Wisconsin, elect a conservative Republican and a liberal Democrat. Comparing the DW-NOMINATE scores of senators from the same party in unified state delegations (where support for the party is strong) with those of the same party from split delegations (where support for one party is weaker), Theriault finds that those from unified delegations were either more liberal or more conservative than their co-partisans from split delegations. Thus, on the basis of senators' scores for the 111th Senate, Democrats from unified delegations were 0.07 (or 24 per cent) more liberal than Democrats from split delegations, and Republicans from unified delegations were 0.09 (or 26 per cent) more conservative than co-partisans from split delegations. The explanation for these polarized patterns, which reflect a trend evident since the early 1970s, lies in senators responding to the more liberal and more conservative preferences of their party's activists, in addition to the partisan-ideological hue of their state's electorate.[55]

Partisan-ideological polarization has increased among the electorate, and particularly among party activists. These polarizing trends have also been asymmetric, with Republicans – and especially their activists – shifting to the right more than Democrats have moved to the left. Each of these trends has increased polarization within the Congress. But how have institutional changes within the Congress itself, including membership recruitment, changing relations between rank-and-file members and central party leaders, strengthened party loyalty and partisan behaviour among members, changes in central party leaderships' behaviour, House and Senate procedures, and voting rules?

Congressional leaders, institutional change and polarization

Over the last few decades, much attention in the congressional literature has focused on the re-emergence and subsequent strengthening of congressional party government – or 'conditional party government'[56] – many of the causes of which lie in the increased ideological homogeneity and polarization of the two parties and intensified inter-party wrangling, often for its own sake, which are all part of the respective parties' efforts to advance their party's brand and policy goals, and exert power, often at the expense of institutional reputation and civility.

Understandably, most of this literature has focused on the House, where more ideologically cohesive majorities and assertive majority leaders, such as Jim Wright (Democrat, Texas) and Newt Gingrich (Republican, Georgia), were able to exploit the chamber's majoritarian nature to change party and chamber rules and procedures to their party's advantage. Only very recently has the Senate received the same scholarly attention, even though senators have been subject to the same electoral pressures as House members to embrace their party brand, toe the party line and not cooperate with the other party – for the simple reason that they want their party to win the next set of elections, rather than the other party. As in the House, senators too have demanded stronger party mechanisms, which in turn have engendered stronger polarization within the chamber. Heightened electoral competition over the last few decades has also helped produce narrower partisan majorities in the Senate, as well as the House, and significantly increased the likelihood of frequent (sometimes sharp) shifts in partisan control of the Senate after each set of elections (or even between elections)[57] and frequent split-party control of the Congress and/or control of the presidency and the Congress. Each of these interrelated factors has served to enhance Senate polarization at the same time that the Senate's non-majoritarian character necessarily inhibits the emergence of the kind of party government that has re-emerged in the House.

Polarized and stronger party leaderships

While the Democrat and Republican parties in the House and Senate have become more homogeneous and separated, the ideological distances between the respective parties' central leaders (Speaker, Majority/Floor Leader, Majority Whip, and the Minority Leader and Whip), and between the committee chairs of the majority and the minority's ranking members have widened, especially in the House (and especially after Gingrich became Minority Whip in 1989).[58] Put differently, as the congressional parties have polarized increasingly, they have chosen leaders like Gingrich who have acted, and been encouraged to act by co-partisans, in a more combative and polarizing fashion than their predecessors in the 1970s and 1980s.[59] And, in order to deliver collectively desired *partisan* outcomes that diverge significantly from the chamber median, rank-and-file Democrats and Republicans in both chambers – but especially in the House – have changed chamber and party rules to endow central party leaders with stronger powers and greater resources, at the expense of congressional committees.

Decades of leadership strengthening in the House reached its apotheosis during the period of Republican rule between 1995 and 2006, during which time Republican speakers personally vetted or interviewed committee chairs, denied positions 14 times to the most senior committee Republicans,[60] including party centrists, such as Marge Roukema (Republican, New Jersey), Tom Petri (Republican, Wisconsin), Jim Leach (Republican, Iowa) and Chris Shays (Republican, Connecticut), and named more loyal party members in lieu.[61] Increasingly, Republican leaders have also made strategic use of the increased volumes of campaign money they are able to accrue both by favouring party-compliant rank-and-file members in the distribution of campaign contributions and by selecting committee and subcommittee chairs (or those likely to expect such positions when their party gained the majority) on the basis of their financial contributions to party funds.[62] More ideologically extreme leadership candidates' greater capacities to distribute campaign contributions to ideologically similar co-partisans, compared with their centrist opponents, have also enhanced polarization within the respective chambers. These same ideologically more extreme leaders then redistribute campaign money, which also helps ideologues win posts in the extended party leadership.[63]

After she became House Democratic Leader in 2002, Nancy Pelosi (Democrat, California) also strengthened her powers over committee assignments, rewarding party loyalists over more vulnerable members, and subjected all subcommittee leadership positions to party approval. When Democrats won control of the House in 2006, she became the first Speaker for almost 100 years to acquire control over all committee assignments.[64] Still, although House Democrats gave Pelosi these new powers, the less ideologically cohesive nature of her party's coalition and the need to help ensure the re-election of centrist Democrats, who had made winning a House majority possible in 2006 and 2008, meant that she could never pursue the kind of exclusive promotion policies that Gingrich and Hastert pursued. Indeed, Pelosi helped ensure that freshman 'Blue Dog' Democrats, such as Jason Altmire (Democrat, Pennsylvania) and Heath Shuler (Democrat, North Carolina), became subcommittee chairs in their first term, at the same time that other long-serving centrist members, such as John Spratt (Democrat, South Carolina), Collin Peterson (Democrat, Minnesota) and 'Blue Dog' Bart Gordon (Democrat, Tennessee), retained their full committee chairs. No contemporary Republican Speaker would be able to help centrist Republicans in these ways without risking his/her own position.

Senate party leaders, of course, have far fewer opportunities to *discipline* recalcitrant senators than do their counterparts in the House. Quite simply, in a non-majoritarian chamber where a single senator – as well as the minority party – can exercise significant veto power to thwart the majority leadership, they lack the disciplinary tools. Nonetheless, over recent decades majority leaders have been increasingly able to exploit the chamber's norms and traditions to control the floor agenda and induce the party-conforming behaviour demonstrated in the earlier analysis of senators' DW-NOMINATE scores. For it is increasingly the case that individual senators who seek to establish their individualistic or constituency *bona fides*, for example by having their legislative proposals debated on the floor, serving on a particular committee or using dilatory tactics on the floor to thwart objectionable legislation, need to enjoy fairly positive relationships with their party's leadership, and particularly if their party is in the majority.

The election of Trent Lott (Republican, Mississippi) as Senate Majority Leader in June 1996 signalled an important strengthening of Senate party leadership. An early disciple of Gingrich's confrontational approach in the House, Lott was an ambitious exponent of hard-line conservative positions who had won rapid promotion within his party.[65] He was a strong supporter of party government, siding with co-partisan hard-liners in an attempt to depose Hatfield from his chair of the Appropriations Committee in 1995 and, in 2001, pushing the Bush administration's hard-line conservative agenda, which triggered centrist Jeffords to desert his party and threw control of the Senate back to the Democrats. Lott's successor, Bill Frist (Republican, Tennessee), followed the trajectory set by Lott, as Bush's lieutenant in the Senate and as the first Senate leader to campaign openly against a Senate Minority Leader in that leader's home state. Over the complaints of party centrists, Frist acquired direct power to appoint Republican senators to over half of all vacancies on the Senate's most prestigious 'A' committees, thereby enhancing his capacity to enforce conservative conformity. With conservative party support in 2005 Frist also threatened to invoke 'the nuclear option', whereby he would introduce a novel floor procedure that would circumvent Democratic filibusters of President Bush's ultra-conservative judicial nominees and allow simple majority votes in order to exercise effectively the chamber's constitutional 'advice and consent' power (or rulemaking power). In response to this threat, Democrats threatened to shut down the Senate and prevent consideration of all routine and legislative Senate business. Ultimately, a compromise was reached without Frist's proposed action. Frist, however, then threatened centrist Arlen Specter (Republican, Pennsylvania) with the loss of his Judiciary Committee chair if he did not support Senate confirmation of Bush's judicial nominations. Specter felt obliged to give the necessary assurances.

Frist's successor, Mitch McConnell (Republican, Kentucky), has reportedly made similar threats in order to enforce party loyalty. Former senator then Vice President Joe Biden reported knowing 'at least seven [Republican] senators, who I will not name, but were made to make a commitment under threat of losing their chairmanships, if they did not support the leadership on every procedural vote'.[66] Although committee membership is less important to senators than it is to House members, McConnell has also taken advantage of Republican Conference rules requiring votes on committee chairs or ranking member positions, by reportedly threatening party colleagues with losing their committee assignments. During the 2009 health care debate, for example, Senator Chuck Grassley (Republican, Iowa) was reportedly threatened with the loss of his Judiciary Committee assignment, and Senator Olympia Snowe (Republican, Maine) with not being supported for a promotion to ranking minority member on the Commerce Committee when it became known that they were contemplating endorsing a health care reform bill supported by President Obama. McConnell also pressed Senator Lindsey Graham (Republican, South Carolina) to abandon bipartisan collaboration with Democratic senators on climate change and immigration in 2009–10. '[McConnell] doesn't twist arms', Snowe observed, 'so much as he reminds you how unhappy others will be if you go down this path – how hard it'll be – and the importance of sticking together.'[67]

Since leaders of the more ideologically diverse Democratic Conference must tolerate greater dissident behaviour, and so use their powers over committee assignments and chairs more as a defensive rather than an offensive mechanism,[68] the asymmetric effects on Senate polarization are obvious – and often blatant. Anticipating victory for his party a few weeks before the 2010 elections, Minority Leader McConnell declared that his 'single biggest' political goal in the new Congress was to ensure the re-election defeat of President Obama.[69] Several months later, McConnell perfunctorily put an end to lengthy bipartisan efforts by the so-called 'Gang of Six' senators – three from each party – to negotiate a grand deficit reduction package once the Republican leader told copartisans participating in the bipartisan talks that he, and only he, would negotiate with the Obama White House.[70] Quite simply, within the contemporary polarized context – and particularly when pressure on Republicans is so intense – where major legislation is at issue, the political stakes are just too high for leaders to allow co-partisans known for their individualistic behaviour, or who are cross-pressured by their states not being generally loyal for their party, to defect from the party line, especially if Senate arithmetic is tight.

Partisan agenda setting

Even more important to contemporary polarization than congressional leaders' disciplinary efforts, however, are their increasingly aggressive efforts to manipulate House and Senate procedures and decision processes to their party's advantage. In today's polarized congressional context, it is now assumed by both the parties in both chambers that the majority party will restrict the minority's opportunities for participation and influence and that the minority party will oppose and obstruct. The result is partisan polarization and conflict.

Following the logic of party government, majority leaders now exert much stronger control over the timing of legislation, privilege certain policy proposals over others, structure chamber members' decision choices through the amendment process and generally work to produce outcomes that favour the majority party at the expense of the minority party – all with a view towards promoting and protecting the party's brand and defending or enhancing the party's position in the next round of elections. Of course, the processes, organization and opportunities available for the majority party in the majoritarian House are different from those in the non-majoritarian Senate – although recent organizational changes fuelled by increased congressional partisanship and split-party government have strengthened party control in both chambers.

Probably the most drastic form of partisan agenda-setting in the House, which is a direct consequence of the recent increase in the ideological homogenity and polarisation of the chamber's parties, is that no speaker – and especially a Republican speaker – will bring any major legislation seen as important by the majority unless he/she is confident that it will pass.[71] In order to help achieve this outcome, the Speaker through the Rules Committee determines which measures reach the floor, and thus the policy alternatives on which members can vote, how long a measure will be considered, whether or not it will be subject to amendment, how many amendments, which amendments and in which order they will be considered, and when votes will be allowed. Increasingly, newly empowered majority leaders leading more united parties have used restrictive – and increasingly complex – rules that shape the chamber's agenda much more efficiently in line with majority party expectations and policy preferences.

In the period from the 99th to the first sessions of the 112th House (1985–2011), the percentage of rules that were restrictive (primarily limiting floor amendments) rose from 21.5

to 86 per cent,[72] reflecting the tighter grip imposed by successive House majorities on the floor. As recently as the 99th House, just over half of special rules were open or expansive. Now, the vast majority of rules are restrictive – almost exclusively so on 'major legislation'.[73] Despite each party regularly denouncing the party in power's 'gagging' practices and promising a more open floor process in the event that it forms the majority, the trend in recent years towards greater restrictiveness has continued under both parties, because restrictive rules enhance decision-making efficiency for the majority party, because they provide opportunities for the majority party to require the minority to cast electorally difficult votes while at the same time protecting their own side from such votes, and because they can ensure than the chamber reaches decisions favourable to the majority party. As Congressman John Dingell (Democrat, Michigan) once told members of the Rules Committee, 'If you let me write the procedure, and I let you write substance, I'll screw you every time.' Party leaders also do not view kindly dissent on a procedural vote, where the majority is seeking to structure the floor agenda.

With majority party leaders' greater use of restrictive rules, the minority party has been almost completely excluded from the formal amendment process, and been obliged to use motions to recommit and motions to instruct House–Senate conferees as their sole remaining vehicles of protest, albeit without any realistic expectation that they may thwart the majority's intent.[74] In turn, the majority party has retaliated by offering increasingly complex rules that structure floor consideration of their legislation in more intricate and restrictive ways – by, for example, forcing the House to proceed with, limit or end debate through self-executing clauses within rules, which allow members no choice but to accept or reject decisions made by majority leaders and embodied in the rule.[75] The effects on polarization and civility in the House are obvious.

Other procedural tactics used by House majority leaders have similar polarizing effects. Under periods of Republican rule, the majority party on a committee has regularly excluded hearing witnesses requested by the minority who might be expected to oppose the majority's legislative proposals. Since Gingrich's tenure as Speaker, they also regularly exclude the minority from and/or carefully manipulate the composition of conference committees with the Senate, assign a member of the majority leadership to oversee the work of each conference, and are heavily and directly involved in inter-cameral negotiations.[76]

Senate rules, of course, give individual senators and the minority party greater opportunities to obstruct the majority, the more so the smaller the majority party's plurality, and the greater the backlog of important legislation requiring floor votes. Fairly modest restrictions on floor debate – including a prohibition on filibusters on budget resolution and reconciliation bills (1974), a reduction to 60 in the number of senators required to invoke cloture (1975), and a limit of 30 hours on post-cloture debate (1986) – have not significantly undermined the chamber's tradition of unlimited debate. Nonetheless, as partisan unity and polarization have intensified, majority leaders have intensified their involvement in negotiating the content of major bills, in creating the necessary floor coalitions to pass or block legislation, and in negotiating with the House and the president to produce outcomes satisfactory to the majority party. In turn, minority parties have strengthened their efforts to obstruct the majority party's programme, thereby intensifying a procedural arms race wherein majority leaders devise new, innovative, procedural strategies to overcome minority obstruction by more easily achieving cloture. While by no means guaranteeing levels of majority party control or legislative success available to counterparts in the House, by increasingly exploiting chamber procedures, such as motions to table (to protect bills from floor amendments), filling the amendment tree (to deny minority senators the opportunity to offer floor amendments), budget reconciliation, budgetary points of order (particularly from the early 1990s on) and cloture (now used pre-emptively when there is a threat of a filibuster), on a case-by-case basis Senate majority leaders are now better able to exert a certain measure of agenda control that can prevent minority members from altering bills on the floor.[77]

The overall effect has been to enhance polarization. Especially after the Republicans took control of the Senate in 1995, a running procedural battle ensued between Lott and Democratic leader Tom Daschle (Democrat, South Dakota). But that battle was as nothing compared to events since the turn of the century, as more and more bills, including more minor ones, became subject to cloture petitions and votes. In the early years of the new century, Republican majority leaders also made common cause with the Bush administration to skirt round cloture requirements by extensive and unorthodox use of the budget reconciliation process – which does not allow for filibusters – to enact large tax increases and to propose oil drilling in the Alaskan National Wildlife Refuge.[78]

With Democrats taking control of the House and Senate in 2006, the frequency with which the Republican minority objected to the Democratic majority's unanimous consent (UC) requests reached unprecedented levels in the 110th and 111th Congresses (2007–10).[79] Objections to majority party UC requests averaged more than one per day when the Senate was in session, forcing Majority Leader Harry Reid (Democrat, Nevada) to find 60 votes for cloture on a wide range of bills, including the minimum wage, the 9/11 Commission's recommendations, immigration reform, energy, children's health insurance, domestic intelligence, climate change and others on which the parties were divided.[80] Frequent procedural spats occurred on the Senate floor as majority Democrats retaliated by objecting to Republican leaders' UC requests, by bringing up measures on the floor without clearance, which in turn generated more objections to UC requests, and by routinely moving immediately for cloture on bills and nominations.[81] With the return to unified party government brought about by President Obama's election in 2008, and Democrats committed to a large legislative agenda in the 111th Congress (2009–10), partisan polarization fuelled even higher levels of obstructionism by minority Republicans. Despite Democrats' 61–49 numerical majority (including two independents caucusing with Democrats), eight major pieces of legislation that received more than 50 votes in the Senate and had passed the Democrat-controlled House were stalled by Republican-led filibusters, six of them in the last three months of the Congress.[82]

Both Republican and Democratic Senate leaders have also resorted increasingly to using their privilege of being recognized first to deny floor amendment opportunities to the minority by filling up the amendment tree once cloture has been invoked. Once cloture has been invoked, all floor amendments must be germane, and the majority leader is then able to fill up all the available amendment slots with his own amendments.[83] Another procedural tactic increasingly used by majority leaders of both parties is to use the same privilege to offer a first degree amendment and then leave that amendment pending so that any other senator wishing to offer an amendment must first gain UC to set aside the pending 'place-holding' amendment temporarily, which then gives the majority leader the opportunity to object to that amendment.[84]

Like their House counterparts, Senate leaders have also become much more centrally involved in manipulating inter-cameral negotiations, with the effect of enhancing polarization. Thus, when House and Senate Republicans excluded the minority from meaningful roles in conference negotiations over Medicare reform and energy legislation in 2003 and 2004, Democrats retaliated by objecting to all UC requests to take other bills to conference.[85] Leaders from both parties have also used 'filling amendment tree' procedures to eliminate opportunities for senators to object to House amendments to a Senate bill or amendment that have been agreed in House–Senate negotiations.[86]

It is clear then that party leaders in both chambers have come to rely much more than previously upon procedural politics and votes inside the House and Senate to advantage their party's goals. In so doing, they have necessarily added to and intensified partisan conflict beyond substantive policy disagreements[87] and enhanced polarization. Party leaders in both parties in both chambers have strengthened their disciplinary and agenda setting powers. However, because of their more ideologically cohesive conferences, House and Senate Republican leaders have been more successful than their counterparts leading more ideologically diverse congressional parties in using and threatening coercion and sanctions to engender party loyalty. As the next section will show, the recruitment of a new generation of ideologically committed conservative Republican House members, who experienced firsthand Gingrich's combative style of partisan politics in the House, has also intensified asymmetric polarization.

The Gingrich Republicans

Between 1978 and 2006, 33 ideologically committed conservative Republicans who had served with Gingrich in the House were elected to the Senate. These 'Gingrich senators',[88] socialized by Gingrich through the Conservative Opportunity Society and then as Minority Whip and Speaker, changed the Senate by adopting Gingrich's confrontational approach, thereby helping make the chamber more polarized. As Rae and Campbell note:

> Many came to the House, after having been baptized by former minority whip Newt Gingrich (R.GA) into relentless and combative partisanship. Most of them saw the Senate as another forum to advance the cause of the Republican Party and their conservative philosophy on a national scale.[89]

More senior (conservative) Republican senators noticed the change at the time. 'So many House members have come to the Senate and brought the poison with them', noted Senator Alan Simpson (Republican, Wyoming). 'The rancor, the dissension, the disgusting harsh level came from those House members. . . . That's where it began.'[90]

Once elected, these 'Gingrich senators' were nearly twice as conservative as their co-partisans,[91] less likely than their Republican colleagues to support the confirmation of Democratic presidents' appointees, and more likely to support filibusters than their fellow Republicans. They include Senator Jim DeMint (Republican, South Carolina), who in 2009 claimed that health care reform could be President Obama's 'Waterloo'. That is, if the Republicans could stymie health care legislation, DeMint argued, they could stop Obama's entire legislative agenda.[92] Although some Republicans at first repudiated DeMint, not a single Republican in the House or the Senate voted for the final version of the legislation. DeMint again used the 'Waterloo' rallying call in 2011 to prevent a vote on raising the debt ceiling, 'even if it hurts the Republican Party politically'.[93] Just before he retired in 2010, another Gingrich senator, Jim Bunning (Republican, Kentucky), single-handedly prevented the Senate from extending unemployment benefits at a time of high unemployment. As with DeMint the previous year, some Republicans ridiculed Bunning for his strategy, but ultimately all but two Senate Republicans supported the strategy.[94]

While other factors were also at work, including pressure from conservative Republican activists, the direct effect of recruiting these 'Gingrich senators' has been to increase asymmetrically the ideological distance between the two Senate parties – 75 to 85 per cent of the increase, according to Theriault and Rohde by skewing Senate Republicans much further to the right.[95] Democrats who left the House to join the Senate had nowhere near the same effect.[96] Moreover, as the behaviour of a new generation of Republican senators, such as Rand Paul (Republican, Kentucky), suggests, even as Gingrich's direct effect on the Senate fades over time, the behaviour introduced indirectly by his disciples will likely continue.

The onward march of (asymmetric) partisan polarization

There is no shortage of examples of the effects of asymmetric partisan polarization on contemporary policymaking in Washington. The hyper-polarized fight over the debt increase in late 2011 is one of a number of recent episodes, with many Republicans under fierce pressure from Tea Party Republicans and their own leadership[97] vowing not to vote for *any* increase in the existing authority,[98] while others, including Senate Republican Leader McConnell, require any increase to be accompanied by 'serious' reductions in federal spending and no tax increases. House Republicans had also prepared the ground for this confrontation in a new package of rules approved on a straight party-line vote on the first day of the new 112th Congress in January 2011, which repealed the so-called Gephardt Rule[99] that obviated members casting a politically difficult vote by setting the debt limit automatically at the level projected by the most recent budget resolution.[100]

Although a last-minute compromise was ultimately agreed that allowed an increase in the debt limit, several aspects about the congressional politics of this episode support the argument made in this chapter. First is the evidence of asymmetric polarization. As an in-depth investigation by a *New York Times* reporter concluded:

> [Democrat] Obama managed to persuade his closest allies to sign off on what he wanted them to do, and [Republican House Speaker John] Boehner didn't, or couldn't. While Democratic leaders were willing to swallow either a deal with more revenue or a deal with less, Boehner's theoretical counteroffer, which probably reflected what he would have done if empowered to act alone, never even got a hearing from his leadership team.[101]

The proposed deal never received a hearing because Boehner could never muster majority support for it in the House Republican Conference, notably from the new members elected with the support of the Tea Party.[102] Contrastingly, Senate Republican leader Mitch McConnell (Republican, Kentucky) – hardly a centrist – took a less confrontational stance, fearing the political consequences for his party of inducing a debt default. In so doing, however, he provoked threats from conservative activists.[103] The Republicans' sharp shift to the right within the context of polarized politics is not only a far cry from the naïve anti-party expectations of the US Constitution's framers and, apparently, not what most Americans want,[104] but also causing concern among erstwhile party stalwarts.[105]

Second, there is the sheer level of uncertainty that such polarization engenders. Explaining its decision to downgrade the US's triple-A international credit rating for the first time ever, Standard & Poor's complained that '[t]he political brinksmanship of recent months highlights what we see as America's governance and policymaking becoming less stable, less effective, and less predictable than what we previously believed'.[106] More generally, Poole and Rosenthal draw the obvious conclusion from their analysis of increased polarization. While House and Senate mean liberal–conservative scores have remained more or less stable over recent decades (which one would expect in a competitive two-party system) – with the House mean becoming more conservative than that of the Senate (as a reflection of the greater incidence of Republican majorities during this period) – *policy outcomes* in each chamber have necessarily become much more volatile. That is, the decisions that the House and the Senate now make – and have made over the last 30 or so years – now depend much more on which party controls the chamber than they did previously. So, when the Republicans control a chamber, winning positions move to the right, and when Democrats are in the majority they move to the left.[107]

Third, partisan conflict over the debt crisis illustrates a wider conclusion reached by Sinclair:[108] in the contemporary context of more ideologically homogeneous congressional parties, narrow party pluralities and more powerful majority leaders willing and able to exploit procedural rules to achieve partisan outcomes, the probability of congressional–presidential agreement in writing major legislation significantly *decreases* under conditions of split-party government, and significantly *increases* under single-party government.

Notes

1 Jamie Carson, 'Electoral Accountability, Party Loyalty, and Roll-Call Voting in the U.S. Senate', in Nathan W. Monroe, Jason M. Roberts and David W. Rohde, eds, *Why Not Parties? Party Effects in the United States Senate* (Chicago, IL: University of Chicago Press, 2008), 23–38.

2 In February 2012, Gallup reported that just 10 per cent of respondents approved of 'the way Congress is handling its job'; 86 per cent disapproved – the highest level recorded since this question was asked in 1974; and, with partisan control of the House and the Senate divided between the parties, there was no significant difference in the disapproval rates of self-identified Democrats, Republicans or independents. At the same time, just 28 per cent of respondents approved of congressional Democrats and 26 per cent of congressional Republicans, and over three-quarters of registered voters said that most Congress members did not deserve re-election (Frank Newport, 'Congress' Job Approval at New Low of 10%: Republicans and Democrats Equally Negative', *Gallup.com*, 8 February 2012, accessed 10 February 2012 at http://www.gallup.com/poll/152528/Congress-Job-Approval-New-Low.aspx?utm_source=alert&utm_medium=email&utm_campaign=syndication&utm_content=morelink&utm_term=Politics).

3 Pew Research Center for the People and the Press, *Trends in American Values: 1987–2012. Partisan Polarization Surges in Bush, Obama Years*, 4 June (Washington, DC: Pew Research Center for the People and the Press, 2012), 55.

4 Michael R. Wolf, J. Cherie Strachan and Daniel M. Shea, 'Incivility and Standing Firm: A Second Layer of Partisan Division', *PS* (July 2012), 432.

5 Keith T. Poole and Howard Rosenthal, 'The Polarization of American Politics', *Journal of Politics* (December 1984), 1061–1079; Keith T. Poole and Howard Rosenthal, *Congress: A Political-Economic History of Roll Call Voting* (New York: Oxford University Press, 1996); Keith T. Poole and Howard Rosenthal, *Ideology and Congress*, 2nd rev. edn (New Brunswick, NJ: Transaction Publishers, 2007); Nolan McCarty, Keith T. Poole and Howard Rosenthal, *Polarized America: The Dance of Ideology and Unequal Riches* (Cambridge, MA: MIT Press, 2006).

6 This is not to say that issues such as affirmative action, welfare, Medicaid, subsidized housing and so forth do not remain related to race, but such issues are now primarily questions of redistribution that tap the main liberal–conservative dimension.

7 A fourth possible explanation to do with the effects of exogenous shocks on the Congress, such as war, crises or social movements, will not be discussed separately and directly in this chapter.

8 Alan I. Abramowitz, *The Disappearing Center: Engaged Citizens, Polarization, and American Democracy* (New Haven, CT and London: Yale University Press, 2010), 69–70; John Aldrich, *Why Parties? The Origin and Transformation of Political Parties in America* (Chicago, IL: University of Chicago Press, 1995); Edward G. Carmines and James A. Stimson, *Issue Evolution: Race and the Transformation of American Politics* (Princeton, NJ: Princeton University Press, 1990); Nelson W. Polsby, *How Congress Evolves: Social Bases of Institutional Change* (New York and

Oxford: Oxford University Press, 2003); Poole and Rosenthal, *Ideology and Congress*; David W. Rohde, *Parties and Leaders in the Postreform House* (Chicago, IL: University of Chicago Press, 1991).

9 Larry M. Bartels, *Unequal Democracy: The Political Economy of the New Gilded Age* (Princeton, NJ: Princeton University Press, 2008); Andrew Gelman, *Red State, Blue State, Rich State, Poor State: Why Americans Vote the Way They Do* (Princeton, NJ: Princeton University Press, 2008); McCarty *et al.*, *Polarized America*.

10 Jamie Carson, Michael H. Crespin, Charles J. Finocchiaro and David W. Rohde, 'Redistricting and Party Polarization in the US House of Representatives', *American Politics Research*, 35(3) (2007), 878–904; Sean T. Theriault, 'Political Polarization in the US Congress: Member Replacement and Member Adaptation', *Party Politics*, 12(4) (2006), 483–503.

11 Alan I. Abramowitz and Kyle L. Saunders (1998), 'Ideological Realignment in the American Electorate', *Journal of Politics*, 60 (1998), 634–652; Aldrich, *Why Parties?*; Gary C. Jacobson, 'Party Polarization in National Politics: The Electoral Connection', in Jon R. Bond and Richard Fleisher, eds, *Polarized Politics* (Washington, DC: CQ Press, 2000), 9–30.

12 Abramowitz, *Disappearing Center*, 34–61; Alan I. Abramowitz and Kyle L. Saunders, 'Why Can't We All Just Get Along? The Reality of a Polarized America', *The Forum*, 3(2) (2005); Alan I. Abramowitz and Kyle L. Saunders, 'Exploring the Bases of Partisanship in the American Electorate: Social Identity vs. Ideology', *Political Research Quarterly*, 59(1) (2006), 175–179; Philip E. Converse, 'Democratic Theory and Electoral Reality', *Critical Review*, 18 (2006), 297–329; Marc Hetherington, 'Resurgent Mass Partisanship: The Role of Elite Polarization', *American Political Science Review*, 93(3) (2001), 619–631; Geoffrey C. Layman and Thomas M. Carsey, 'Party Polarization and "Conflict Extension" in the American Electorate', *American Journal of Political Science*, 46(3) (2002), 786–802; cf. Morris P. Fiorina, Samuel J. Abrams and Jeremy C. Pope, *Culture War: The Myth of a Polarized America* (New York: Pearson Longman, 2005).

13 Alan I. Abramowitz, 'Disconnected, or Joined at the Hip?', in Pietro S. Nivola and David W. Brady, *Red and Blue Nation? Characteristics and Causes of America's Polarized Politics* (Washington, DC: Brookings Institution Press, 2008), 72–85, 72; Abramowitz, *Disappearing Center*, 40–43; Alan I. Abramowitz and Kyle L. Saunders (1998), 'Ideological Realignment in the American Electorate', *Journal of Politics*, 60(3) (2005), 634–652; Abramowitz and Saunders, 'Exploring the Bases of Partisanship', 175–187; Samuel J. Abrams and Morris P. Fiorina, 'The Big Sort That Wasn't: A Skeptical Re-examination', *PS: Political Science and Politics*, 45(2) (2012), 203–210, 208; Fiorina, Abrams and Pope, *Culture War*; Jeffrey M. Stonecash, Mark D. Brewer and Mark D. Mariani, *Diverging Parties: Social Change, Realignment, and Party Polarization* (Boulder, CO: Westview Press, 2003); B. Dan Wood and Soren Jordan, 'Electoral Polarization: Definition, Measurement and Evaluation', Paper delivered at the annual meeting of the American Political Science Association, Seattle, WA, 1–4 September 2011.

14 Pew Research Center, *Trends in American Values*, 99–100.

15 Ibid., 1, 19–23. Even when Pew extended the definition of party bases to include Democratic- and Republican-leaning independents, the extent of polarization over political values doubled between 1987 and 2012 (23–24).

16 Alan I. Abramowitz and Kyle L. Saunders, 'Party Sorting and Polarization in the American Mass Public and Political Elite', Paper presented to the annual meeting of the Midwest Political Science Association, Chicago, IL, 12–15 April 2012.

17 Christopher Hare, Nolan McCarty, Keith T. Poole and Howard Rosenthal, 'Mass and Elite Political Polarization', *voteview* blog, accessed 10 June 2012 at http://voteview.com/blog/.

18 Abramowitz, *Disappearing Center*, 169; Joseph Bafumi and Robert Y. Shapiro, 'A New Partisan Voter', *Journal of Politics*, 71(1) (2009), 8; Wood and Jordan, 'Electoral Polarization', 16–19.

19 Abramowitz, *Disappearing Center*, 45.

20 Alan I. Abramowitz, 'US Senate Elections in a Polarised Era', in Burdett A. Loomis, ed., *The US Senate: From Deliberation to Dysfunction* (Washington, DC: CQ Press/Sage, 2012), 66–84; Bafumi and Shapiro, 'New Partisan Voter'; Abramowitz and Saunders, 'Party Sorting and Polarization'.

21 Results from the Cooperative Congressional Election Study (CCES) show that 90 per cent of Democratic identifiers or leaners and 85 per cent of Republican identifiers or leaners voted for their own party's House candidate in the 2006 elections, while 94 per cent of Democratic identifiers or leaners and 87 per cent of Republican identifiers or leaners voted for their own party's Senate

candidate (Abramowitz, *Disappearing Center*, 56, 69). Jacobson reports similar findings for the 2010 elections (Gary C. Jacobson, 'The President, the Tea Party, and the Voting Behavior in 2010: Insights from the Cooperative Congressional Election Study', Paper presented to the annual meeting of the American Political Science Association, Seattle, WA, 1–4 September 2011).

22 Lydia Saad, 'Conservatives Remain the Largest Ideological Group in U.S.: Overall, the Nation Has Grown More Polarized over the Past Decade', *Gallup.com*, 12 January 2012, accessed 15 January 2012 at http://www.gallup.com/poll/152021/conservatives-remain-largest-ideological-group.aspx.

23 Joseph Daniel Ura and Christopher R. Ellis, 'Partisan Moods: Polarization and the Dynamics of Mass Party Preferences', *Journal of Politics*, 74(1) (2012), 283–288.

24 Alan I. Abramowitz, 'Partisan Polarization and the Rise of the Tea Party Movement', Paper presented to the annual meeting of the American Political Science Association, Seattle, WA, 1–6 September 2011; Jacobson, 'President, the Tea Party, and the Voting Behavior'; Robert Draper, *Do Not Ask What Good We Do: Inside the U.S. House of Representatives* (New York: Free Press, 2012), 3–10.

25 Kyle L. Saunders and Alan I. Abramowitz, 'Ideological Realignment and Active Partisans in the American Electorate', *American Politics Research*, 32(2) (2004), 285–309; Abramowitz, 'Partisan Polarization and the Rise of the Tea Party Movement'.

26 Wood and Jordan, 'Electoral Polarization'.

27 Lydia Saad, 'Conservatives Finish 2009 as No. 1 Ideological Group', *Gallup.com*, 7 January 2010, accessed 15 January 2012 at http://www.gallup.com/poll/124958/conservatives-finish-2009-no-1-ideological-group.aspx; Saad, 'Conservatives Remain the Largest Ideological Group'.

28 Partisan polarization increased from 23 to 41 per cent on government provision of a social welfare safety net, from 5 to 39 per cent on environmental protection, from 20 to 37 per cent on trades unions, from 17 to 33 per cent on government policies aimed at achieving equal opportunity, and from 6 to 33 per cent on the scope and performance of government. Pew Research Center, *Trends in American Values*, 4, 14, 51–53, 55–57, 62–63, 65–66.

29 Abramowitz, 'Partisan Polarization and the Rise of the Tea Party Movement'; Alan I. Abramowitz and Kyle L. Saunders, 'Ideological Realignment in the American Electorate', *Journal of Politics*, 60(3) (1998), 634–652; Bafumi and Shapiro, 'New Partisan Voter'; Saunders and Abramowitz, 'Ideological Realignment and Active Partisans', 293–294.

30 Pew Research Center, *Trends in American Values*, 55.

31 US commentators assign the colour red to the right party and blue to the left, contrary to the practice in almost all other democratic systems.

32 Bill Bishop and Robert Cushing, *The Big Sort: Why the Clustering of Like-Minded America Is Tearing Us Apart* (Boston, MA: Houghton Mifflin, 2008). See also Sean Theriault, *Party Polarization in Congress* (New York: Cambridge University Press, 2008), 93–95.

33 Abrams and Fiorina, 'Big Sort That Wasn't'.

34 Theriault, *Party Polarization in Congress*, 91–92.

35 Douglas S. Massey, Jonathan Rothwell and Thurston Domina, 'The Changing Bases of Segregation in the United States', *Annals of the American Academy of Political and Social Science*, 62 (2009), 87–89.

36 Gelman, *Red State, Blue State, Rich State, Poor State*, 130–136; Massey *et al.*, 'Changing Bases of Segregation', 85–87.

37 Abramowitz, *Disappearing Center*, 142–144; McCarty *et al.*, *Polarized America*, 59–67.

38 Gregory L. Giroux, 'House Races: An Election Bucking Tradition', *CQ Weekly*, 26 October 2002, pp. 2794–2795, accessed 3 March 2012 at http://library.cqpress.com.proxyau.wrlc.org/cqweekly/weeklyreport107-000000535952.

39 Ibid., 2795.

40 Gary C. Jacobson, 'Polarized Politics and the 2004 Congressional and Presidential Elections', *Political Science Quarterly*, 120(2) (2005), 199–218, 200, 202–203.

41 Jacobson, 'Polarized Politics'; Theriault, *Party Polarization in Congress*, 98–100.

42 Abramowitz, 'US Senate Elections in a Polarised Era', 37–38; Theriault, *Party Polarization in Congress*, 99–100, 102–103.

43 Anthony Downs, *An Economic Theory of Democracy* (New York: Harper & Row, 1957), 25.

44 Aldrich, *Why Parties?*, 187–194; Geoffrey C. Layman, Thomas M. Carsey, John C. Green, Richard Herrera and Rosalyn Cooperman, 'Activists and Conflict Extension in American Party Politics', *American Political Science Review*, 104(2) (2010), 326.

45 David Catanese, 'McCain Pays Heavy Reelection Price', *Politico.com*, 22 August 2010, accessed 22 March 2012 at http://www.politico.com/news/stories/0810/41339.html.

46 Aldrich, *Why Parties?*, 163–193; Geoffrey C. Layman and Thomas M. Carsey, 'Party Polarization and "Conflict Extension" in the American Electorate', *American Journal of Political Science*, 46(3) (2002), 786–802; Layman *et al.*, 'Activists and Conflict Extension', 330–331, 336; Gary Miller and Norman Schofield, 'Activists and Partisan Realignment in the United States', *American Political Science Review*, 97(2) (2003), 245–260; Theriault, *Party Polarization in Congress*, 113.

47 Layman *et al.*, 'Activists and Conflict Extension', 330–331, 336; Barbara Sinclair, *Party Wars: Polarization and the Politics of National Policymaking* (Norman: University of Oklahoma Press, 2006); Clyde Wilcox and Carin Larson, *Onward Christian Soldiers? The Religious Right in American Politics*, 3rd edn (Boulder, CO and Oxford: Westview, 2006).

48 Layman *et al.*, 'Activists and Conflict Extension', 332.

49 Ibid., 340–341.

50 In the 2010 Senate primaries, hard-line conservative Republicans defeated less conservative candidates in Alaska, Delaware, Florida, Kentucky, Nevada, Pennsylvania, South Carolina and Utah. In Alaska, Pennsylvania and Utah, the defeated candidates were incumbent senators, one of whom went on to win the general election as an independent. Bob Bennett, the three-term incumbent in Utah, however, was no centrist (his DW-NOMINATE score was at the median of all Republican senators), but his Senate behaviour was evidently not conservative enough for Utah Republicans, who opted instead for Mike Lee (Republican, Utah). Lee was one of the instigators of the Republicans' brinkman strategy on the debt limit in 2011.

51 Both Hutchinson and Snowe had upset hard-liners by not supporting Republican congressional leaders on a number of issues, including health care reform. Polls showed that Hutchinson and Snowe would easily win re-election from their states. In a sign of the times, both Hutchinson and Snowe were subject to rowdy protests by Tea Party supporters. Hutchinson's Republican successor is a hard-line Tea Party supporter. Ultra-conservative hard-liners also renewed their efforts in 2012 in Indiana and again in Utah.

52 Centrist 'casualties' include Marge Roukema (Republican, New Jersey) in 2002, Sherwood Boehlert (Republican, New York) and Joe Schwartz (Republican, Michigan) in 2006, and Wayne Gilchrest (Republican, Maryland) in 2008. However, conservative six-term Bob Inglis (Republican, South Carolina) was also trounced in his 2010 primary after upsetting Tea Party supporters on a number of issues, including suggesting that Republican voters not listen to conservative booster Glenn Beck and voting for a 2009 House Democratic motion to reprimand state colleague Joe Wilson (Republican, South Carolina) for shouting 'You lie' at President Obama during a speech to Congress. Other incumbent House Republicans faced Tea Party challenges in 2012, including Speaker John Boehner (Ohio), Energy and Commerce Committee chair Fred Upton (Michigan), Financial Services Committee chair Spencer Bachus (Alabama), Science and Commerce chair Ralph Hall (Texas) and newly elected members Larry Bucshon (Indiana), Richard Hanna (New York) and Alan Nunnelee (Mississippi), an erstwhile ardent Tea Party supporter. Tea Party challengers actually defeated several House Republican incumbents, including Don Manzullo (Illinois), Jean Schmidt (Ohio) and John Sullivan (Oklahoma).

53 In his state's 2006 Democratic primary, a more liberal anti-war Democrat defeated centrist Senator Joe Lieberman (Democrat, Connecticut).

54 Theriault, *Party Polarization in Congress*, 116ff.

55 Ibid., 119.

56 Rohde, *Parties and Leaders in the Postreform House*; Aldrich, *Why Parties?*; John Aldrich and David W. Rohde, 'The Consequences of Party Organization in the House: The Role of the Majority and Minority Parties in Conditional Party Government', in Jon R. Bond and Richard Fleisher, eds, *Polarized Politics* (Washington, DC: CQ Press, 2000), 31–72; John Aldrich and David W. Rohde, 'The Logic of Conditional Party Government: Revisiting the Electoral Connection', in Lawrence C. Dodd and Bruce I. Oppenheimer, eds, *Congress Reconsidered*, 7th edn (Washington, DC: CQ Press, 2001), 269–292.

57 Whereas partisan control of the House has changed only three times since 1980 (1994, 2006 and 2010), the Senate has changed seven times (1980, 1986, 1994, 2001 twice, 2002 and 2006), albeit once on the casting vote of the Vice President.

58 Theriault, *Party Polarization in Congress*, 135–138.

59 Aldrich, *Why Parties?*; John E. Owens, 'Late Twentieth Century Congressional Leaders as Shapers of and Hostages to Political Context: Gingrich, Hastert, and Lott', in Erwin C. Hargrove and John E. Owens, eds, *Leadership in Context* (Lanham, MD and Oxford: Rowman & Littlefield, 2003); R. Eric Petersen, Parker H. Reynolds and Amber Hope Wilhelm, *House of Representatives and Senate Staff Levels in Member, Committee, Leadership, and Other Offices, 1977–2010*, CRS Report for Congress R41366 (Washington, DC: Congressional Research Service, 2010); Rohde, *Parties and Leaders in the Postreform House*; Barbara Sinclair, *Legislators, Leaders, and Lawmakers: The U.S. House of Representatives in the Postreform Era* (Baltimore, MD: Johns Hopkins University Press, 1998); Sinclair, *Party Wars*.

60 Kathryn Pearson, 'Party Discipline in the Contemporary Congress: Rewarding Loyalty in Theory and in Practice', Unpublished Ph.D. dissertation, University of California, Berkeley, 2005, pp. 127–128.

61 House Democrats have also violated seniority to deny members committee chairs but very rarely on the grounds of ideology or party loyalty.

62 Damon M. Cann, *Sharing the Wealth: Member Contributions and the Exchange Theory of Party Influence in the US House of Representatives* (Albany, NY: SUNY Press, 2008), 32–33; Damon M. Cann, 'Modeling Committee Chair Selection in the U.S. House of Representatives', *Political Analysis*, 16(3) (2008), 274–289; Eric S. Heberlig and Bruce A. Larson, *Congressional Parties, Institutional Ambition, and the Financing of Majority Control* (Ann Arbor: University of Michigan Press, 2012), 159–196. Pearson reports that leaders told a House Republican that his subcommittee chair obligated him to contribute at least $50,000 to his party. Many members' contributions exceed these requests, especially contributions from rank-and-file members with ambitions of being a committee chair or future leader (Pearson, 'Party Discipline in the Contemporary Congress', 18). Peters and Rosenthal provide a similar example of requests to House Democrats, although some centrist Democrats failed to oblige with impunity (Ronald M. Peters and Cindy S. Rosenthal, *Speaker Nancy Pelosi and the New American Politics* (New York: Oxford University Press, 2010), 115, 278).

63 Eric Heberlig, Marc Hetherington and Bruce Larson, 'The Price of Leadership: Campaign Money and the Polarization of Congressional Parties', *Journal of Politics*, 68(4) (2006), 992–1005.

64 Peters and Rosenthal, *Speaker Nancy Pelosi and the New American Politics*, 69–70.

65 Owens, 'Late Twentieth Century Congressional Leaders', 69.

66 Biden, in Steve Benen, 'Political Animal', *Washington Monthly*, 30 June 2010.

67 In fact, in recent decades, seniority has never been violated in the appointment of Senate committee chairs.

68 Thus, when Senator Joe Lieberman (Democrat, Connecticut) lost his primary and won re-election as an independent, Democratic Majority Leader Harry Reid (Democrat, Nevada) allowed Lieberman to retain his chair of the Homeland Security and Governmental Affairs Committee. Reid's predecessor, Tom Daschle (Democrat, South Dakota), also used his assignment power to enhance the re-election chances of co-partisans, in one instance giving up his own seat on the powerful Finance Committee to Carol Moseley-Braun (Democrat, Illinois) in order to help her win re-election. When he was Minority Whip, Reid also gave up a Finance seat to encourage Charles Schumer (Democrat, New York) to remain in the Senate rather than run for Governor of New York (Allison Stevens, 'More Power to the Senate's Majority Leader?', *CQ Weekly,* 6 November 2004, pp. 2605–2606; Alan K. Ota, 'Senate GOP Gives Its Leader A Powerful New Tool', *CQ Weekly,* 20 November 2004, p. 2733).

69 Major Garrett, 'Top GOP Priority: Make Obama a One-Term President', *National Journal*, 29 October 2010.

70 Jay Newton-Small, 'Let's Make a Deal', *Time*, 4 June 2011.

71 This 'majority of the Majority' principle was first publicly enunciated by Speaker Dennis Hastert (Republican, Illinois). J. Dennis Hastert, 'Reflections on the Role of the Speaker in the Modern Day House of Representatives', Conference on the Changing Nature of the House Speakership: The Cannon Century Conference, Cannon Caucus Room, Library of Congress, 12 November 2003; John E. Owens , 'Style, Skills, and Context: An Interactionist Exploration of Dennis Hastert's Speakership', Paper presented to the annual meeting of the Southern Political Science Association, New Orleans, LA, 5–9 January 2005.

72 I am grateful to Don Wolfensberger of the Woodrow Wilson International Center for Scholars for providing the recent data. My codings of rules sometimes differ, however, from Wolfensberger's.

73 Barbara Sinclair, *Unorthodox Lawmaking: New Legislative Processes in the US Congress*, 4th edn (Washington, DC: CQ Press, 2012), 151.

74 Megan Lynch, *The Motion to Recommit in the House of Representatives: Effects, Recent Trends, and Options for Change*, CRS Report for Congress RL34757, 20 November (Washington, DC: Congressional Research Service, 2008), 18–19.

75 Wolfensberger's data show that in recent congresses over one-third of all special rules included self-executing clauses, compared with only 20 per cent in the early 1990s.

76 Jonathan Allen and John Cochran, 'The Might of the Right', *CQ Weekly Online*, 8 November 2003, pp. 2761–2762, accessed 11 December 2011 at http://library.cqpress.com/cqweekly/weeklyreport108_000000899550; Sarah A. Binder, 'In Memoriam: The Conference Committee', *American Prospect*, 21 December 2011, accessed 5 January 2012 at http://prospect.org/article/memoriam-conference-committee; Richard E. Cohen, Kirk Victor and David Baumann, 'The State of Congress', *National Journal*, 10 January 2004; Sinclair, *Unorthodox Lawmaking*, 91–95.

77 Bryan W. Marshall, Brandon C. Prins and David W. Rohde, 'Fighting Fire with Water: Partisan Procedural Strategies and the Senate Appropriations Committee', *Congress and the Presidency*, 26(2) (1999), 113–132; Chris Den Hartog and Nathan W. Monroe, 'Agenda Influence and Tabling Motions in the U.S. Senate', in Nathan W. Monroe, Jason M. Roberts and David W. Rohde, eds, *Why Not Parties?* (Chicago, IL: University of Chicago Press, 2008), 142–158; Richard Beth, Valerie Heitshusen, Bill Heniff and Elizabeth Rybicki, 'Leadership Tools for Managing the US Senate', Paper presented to the annual meeting of the American Political Science Association, Toronto, ON, 1–4 September 2009; Aaron S. King, Frank J. Orlando and David W. Rohde, 'Beyond Motions to Table: Exploring the Procedural Toolkit of the Majority Party in the United States Senate', Paper presented to the annual meeting of the American Political Science Association, Seattle, WA, 1–4 September 2011.

78 Sinclair, *Unorthodox Lawmaking*, 242–252.

79 The number of cloture motions offered increased by 342 per cent between the 97th and 111th Senates (1981–2010) and almost doubled between 2001 and 2010. Almost all of these motions were offered by majority senators and usually by their leadership.

80 With the help of two independents, Reid achieved a 69 per cent success rate in the 111th Senate. Indeed, over the last decade, majority leaders' success rates in invoking cloture (which are unrelated to the size of their party's numerical majority) have significantly increased, from a mean 39 per cent before 2001 to 54 per cent since (US Senate, *Senate Action on Cloture Motions*, accessed 8 January 2012 at http://www.senate.gov/pagelayout/reference/cloture_motions/clotureCounts.htm).

81 Steven S. Smith, 'The Senate Syndrome', *Issues in Governance Studies* (June 2010), 1–30, 9.

82 John E. Owens, 'A "Post-Partisan" President in a Partisan Context', in James A. Thurber, ed., *Obama in Office* (Boulder, CO: Paradigm Publishers, 2012).

83 Beth *et al.*, 'Leadership Tools for Managing the US Senate', 11.

84 Smith, 'Senate Syndrome', 13–14.

85 Allen and Cochran, 'The Might of the Right'; Richard E. Cohen, Kirk Victor and David Baumann, 'The State of Congress', *National Journal*, 10 January 2004, accessed 22 February 2012 at http://www.nationaljournal.com.libproxy.wustl.edu/njmagazine/nj_20040110_5.php.

86 Beth *et al.*, 'Leadership Tools for Managing the US Senate'.

87 Gary W. Cox and Mathew D. McCubbins, *Setting the Agenda: Responsible Party Government in the US House of Representatives* (Cambridge and New York: Cambridge University Press, 2005).

88 Sean Theriault, 'Party Polarization in the US Congress: Member Replacement and Member Adaptation', *Party Politics*, 12(4) (2006), 483–503; Sean M. Theriault and David W. Rohde, 'The Gingrich Senators and Party Polarization in the U.S. Senate', *Journal of Politics*, 73(4) (2011), 1011–1024.

89 Nicol C. Rae and Colton C. Campbell, 'Party Politics and Ideology in the Contemporary Senate', in Nicol C. Rae and Colton C. Campbell, eds, *The Contentious Senate: Partisanship, Ideology, and the Myth of Cool Judgement* (Lanham, MD and Oxford: Rowman & Littlefield, 2001), 8.

90 Quoted in Allison Stevens, 'Senators Pack a Sharper Edge', *CQ Weekly*, 13 December 2003, pp. 3069–3070.

91 Until the 100th Congress (1987–88), Republican senators who had served in the House were actually less conservative than party colleagues who had not served in the House. Beginning in

the 100th Congress, however, those recruited from the House were 56 per cent more conservative than their non-House colleagues (Theriault, *Party Polarization in Congress*).

92 Reid Wilson, 'DeMint: Americans Will "Take to the Street" on Healthcare', *The Hill*, 2 August 2011, p. A1.

93 Jordan Fabian, 'DeMint: If Vote to Raise Debt Ceiling is GOP's Waterloo, "Let It Be"', *The Hill*, 14 April 2011, p. A1.

94 J. Taylor Rushing, 'Bunning Filibuster Ends, Jobless Benefits Will Be Extended', *The Hill*, 2 March 2011, p. A1.

95 *Theriault* and *Rohde*, 'Gingrich Senators', 1014–1015. It is also the case that the behaviour of the Gingrich senators affected that of their non-House co-partisans, as well as that of Senate Democrats.

96 The effect on Senate polarization of House Democratic recruits from the same period was about one-sixth the magnitude of the Gingrich senators (*Theriault* and *Rohde*, 'Gingrich Senators', 1018–1020).

97 Matt Bai, 'Obama vs. Boehner: Who Killed the Debt Deal?', *New York Times Magazine*, 28 March 2012, accessed 31 March 2012 at http://www.nytimes.com/2012/04/01/magazine/obama-vs-boehner-who-killed-the-debt-deal.html?_r=1.

98 Mara Liasson, 'What Happens to the Tea Party after Election Day?', *NPR Morning Edition*, 28 October 2010, accessed 3 March 2012 at http://www.npr.org/templates/story/story.php?storyId=130870873.

99 Amongst other changes, the rules package also prohibited the consideration of legislation that would cause a net increase in mandatory spending, replacing the former House PAYGO rule, prohibited the consideration of a budget resolution containing budget reconciliation directives that would have the net effect of increasing mandatory spending, and allowed amendments striking unfunded intergovernmental mandates on the House floor, unless a special rule adopted by the House specifically prohibited such action. See Bill Heniff, *House Rules Changes Affecting the Congressional Budget Process Made at the Beginning of the 112th Congress*, CRS Report for Congress R41926 (Washington, DC: Congressional Research Service, 2011), 5.

100 House Republicans had also repealed the rule in 2001, but then in 2003 reinstated it, because they too found it useful to protect members from a difficult vote.

101 Bai, 'Obama vs. Boehner'.

102 On House Republican pressure on Boehner, see, for example, Draper, *Do Not Ask What Good We Do*.

103 Felicia Sonmez, 'McConnell Warns Default Could "Destroy" GOP Brand', *Washington Post*, 13 July 2011, accessed 10 January 2012 at http://www.washingtonpost.com/blogs/2chambers/post/mcconnell-warns-default-could-destroy-gop-brand/2011/07/13/gIQAPZTwCI_blog.html. See also Alexander Bolton, 'Senate GOP and Conservative Groups Clash on Healthcare Reform Repeal Votes', *The Hill*, 6 March 2012; Julian Pecquet and Alexander Bolton, 'McConnell Vows Full-Fledged Assault on Health Law amid Threat to His Leadership', *The Hill*, 1 March 2012.

104 Immediately after the agreement, congressional *disapproval* ratings rose to an unprecedented 84 per cent.

105 See, for example, Jim Rutenberg, 'Jeb Bush Questions GOP's Shift to the Right', *New York Times*, 11 June 2012.

106 Standard & Poor's, 'United States of America Long-Term Rating Lowered To "AA+" Due to Political Risks, Rising Debt Burden; Outlook Negative', 5 August 2011, accessed 1 December 2011 at http://www.standardandpoors.com/ratings/articles/en/us/?assetID=1245316529563.

107 Indeed, the mean winning position during the first session of the 112th House (2011) was the *most conservative* since the period of Republican rule in the late nineteenth and the early twentieth century, whereas the winning position in the Democrat-controlled 111th Senate, during which the number of Democrats varied between a 57- and a 60-seat supermajority, was the most liberal since the New Deal in the 1930s (Poole and Rosenthal, *Congress*; Poole and Rosenthal, *Ideology and Congress*; 'Congressional Policy Shifts, 1879–2001', *voteview* blog, 15 February 2012, accessed at http://voteview.com/blog?p=362.

108 Sinclair, *Party Wars*.

8 Never mind the details

Here's the Tea Party

Clodagh Harrington

As of 2008, we lost America to socialism.[1]

In 2010, Sidney Blumenthal observed that an unfortunate aspect of Barack Obama's style was that he tended to think in cases, not narrative. This works well for law professors, not so well for presidents. During the Reagan years, scholars were known to condescend that the former actor viewed his life – and the presidency – as a three-reel movie. How amusing, shallow, juvenile! Or was it? During the 2008 election campaign, pundits were quick to draw comparisons between Obama and Reagan regarding their awe-inspiring communication skills. However, whilst Obama may have been the intellectual giant of the two, he did not come close to his 1980s predecessor with regard to controlling the political narrative. Reagan made everyone feel that, despite any current adversity, matters would be resolved by sunset and good would triumph over evil. When discussing the gargantuan challenges facing the nation during his first two years in office, President Obama spoke to Americans as if they were grown-ups. He communicated cerebrally. As a result, voters were left feeling at best confused, at worst angry.

Enter the Tea Party. To call it a movement, in its early days at least, was an overstatement. Organizationally, the Tea Party in the period before November 2010 was akin to Al Qaeda prior to the Afghanistan and Iraq wars – that is, disparate and disconnected cells of discontented individuals or groups united mainly by what they stood against. If there was a driving Tea Party force prior to the 2010 elections, it was not a specific political agenda or mandate; it was something far more visceral: anger. One K Street consultant employed by the Tea Party explained to *Playboy* magazine that the key to getting the movement's message across was to pitch it to an individual's brainstem, rather than brain centre. In other words, the Tea Party message was to tap into the reptilian brain, rather than the logic centre.[2] Hence, when President Obama was appealing to voters for considered reflection on the complex set of problems facing the nation, the Tea Party message was lighting up the same neural pathways as road rage.

Referring to the 1960s Barry Goldwater movement, Richard Hofstadter's 1964 essay on the 'Paranoid Style in American Politics' could have been written with the Tea Party in mind. The examples and rhetoric were virtually identical. Only the names had changed. These instances, and a range of others including perceived conspiracies from Masons to Roosevelts, Catholics to communists, demonstrated how much political leverage could be obtained from the 'animosities and passions of a small minority'.[3] Hofstadter interpreted the paranoid style reoccurring over time as a result of a mental predisposition among a minority of the population to view the world in a particularly paranoid way. This paranoia could be activated 'chiefly by social conflicts that involve ultimate schemes of values and that bring fundamental fears and hatreds, rather than negotiable interests, into political action'.[4]

As in Hofstadter's thesis, within two years, despite its often unclear relationship with the Republicans, the Tea Party had a dramatic impact on the US political landscape, progressing from a state of mind to something requiring a K Street consultant. A key strengthening of the movement was to take control of the political narrative – something the Obama administration allowed to happen with surprising ease. Not that Tea Party anger was specifically focused on the president; it went far deeper and wider. Perennially, polls exist to demonstrate that a majority of Americans think that the country is going in the wrong direction. Those polled by NBC/WSJ, among others, said in 1996, 2005 and 2011 that the country was on the wrong track: 54 per cent, 63 per cent and 63 per cent respectively. So, whilst there was a noticeable rise in discontent during the post-9/11 years, the fury was brewing long before 4 November 2008.[5]

There was much cause for discontent. America's protracted and costly engagement in two wars, combined with broken immigration and health care systems, and a financial system suffering from cardiac arrest meant that, by any measure, being American was not what it used to be.[6] Initially, the rage was fiscal. And if there was someone to direct it at, it was the big government conservative George W. Bush, with his decidedly un-Republican expenditure and expansion. In some ways, the perceived ideological betrayal by Bush was harder to deal with than his successor's agenda. After all, big government Democrats were no surprise, but a Republican leader who failed to control spending and apply conservative principles when managing the economy was bound to stir discontentment. A key goal of the Bush presidency was to transform the American electorate by creating a durable Republican majority. His, or more accurately Karl Rove's, electoral strategy for 2004 ensured that those who had supported the incumbent financially would be rewarded with tax cuts; and those on the religious right who had voted for him expected hard-line conservative policies on the hot-button issues such as abortion and gay marriage. Receiving 50.7 per cent of the popular vote was hardly a landslide, but it was nonetheless an endorsement of his conservative agenda.[7]

Bush, as many saw it, let the side down. Fiscal conservatives were appalled at his plans to expand Medicare and increase federal spending. The budget surplus of $236.2 billion left by Bill Clinton became a $458.5 billion deficit by 2008. He also doubled the national debt to $10.7 trillion in the same period, allowing other countries to finance it.[8] So why didn't anyone take to the streets to protest about fiscal issues during the Bush years? Probably for a couple of reasons. Firstly, he was considered to be inherently on the same page as many of his critics. He may have caused disappointment and frustration among the religious right with regard to what it perceived as his insufficiently robust support for the Federal Marriage Amendment and government funding of stem cell research.[9] Despite this, he was 'one of them' and had mass appeal to evangelical Christians, particularly with his philosophy of 'compassionate conservatism'. However, a book written by former deputy director of Bush's Office of Faith-Based and Community Initiatives David Kuo claims that the administration, whilst hugging and welcoming evangelicals to the White House, also laughed and referred to them as 'nuts' in private.[10] Secondly, the ramifications of an economy in freefall were not fully felt until mid- to late 2008, by which time Bush's days were numbered. Even as late as January of that year, the president announced a $150 billion tax rebate – equivalent to $1,000 for every American household. The freefall began in March, and the Federal Reserve injected $236 billion into the American banking system. Bear Sterns received an emergency bailout from the Federal Reserve. In September, Lehman Brothers collapsed. In between, the list lengthened; Merrill Lynch, AIG, Freddie Mac and Fannie Mae – bailouts and rescue packages were cobbled together at lightning speed, as not only the US, but the global economy, teetered.[11]

By the final weeks prior to the presidential election, unemployment was nearing 10 per cent, with job losses averaging 500,000 per month. Home repossessions during the third quarter of 2008 numbered 765,558, and personal credit card debt stood at $900 billion.[12] If civilization is only ever three missed meals from anarchy, by late 2008 it was almost tea-time. The November election results sent a very clear message: the electorate was angry – very angry. The general consensus was that the Republican Party had lost its way, the country was beset with economic problems of epic proportions and the Great Recession had the potential to become a depression. In October 2008, President Bush signed the Troubled Assets Relief Program (TARP) into law. This bailout package was followed on 17 February 2009 by President Obama's American Recovery and Reinvestment Act (ARRA) stimulus bill. Ten days later, Tea Party protesters took to the streets. As Bush acknowledged in a 2010 interview with NBC's Matt Lauer, a majority of Americans polled believed that TARP was an Obama initiative, which helps to explain why protests started when they did.[13]

Electoral punishment of the Republicans had started in November 2006 and was compounded by the increased congressional shift of power balance two years later, not to mention the 52.9 per cent victory of the first African-American president of the United States. By November 2010, the Tea Party, in all its forms, was front-page news. Over a period of approximately 18 months, it had grown, evolved and fused into something high-profile and consequential. How did this happen? There were a couple of defining moments for the movement which launched its existence into the public consciousness. One was the impromptu speech on 19 February 2009 by CNBC's Rick Santelli, a live-on-air outburst about 'subsidizing the losers' mortgages' which instantly went viral and was dubbed 'rant of the year'.[14] In an interview with the *Chicago Sun Times*, Santelli took credit for igniting the movement, claiming 'I was the spark . . . that started it.'[15] Ironically, Santelli was addressing commodities traders on the floor of the Chicago Mercantile Exchange – a group hardly blameless in the financial crisis.[16]

Within 12 hours, a range of Tea Party websites were active and, by the following day, there was a Tea Party Facebook page.[17] Within days, dozens of protests were coordinated across the nation. The alternative ignition moment came three days earlier from the unlikely source of a 28-year-old mathematics teacher in Seattle. Not someone fitting the usual Tea Party demographic of white middle-aged, middle-income conservative or libertarian, Keli Carender had a facial piercing and wanted to become an actress. Her story spread instantly as the media got wind of her activities. She had made consistent but unsuccessful efforts to contact her senators to urge them to vote against Obama's stimulus package. So she decided to organize a 'porkulus' protest the day before the bill was due for signing. She contacted Michelle Malkin of *Fox News* in order to publicize the activity, and Malkin stated on her blog that 'there should be one of these in every town in America'.[18] The *New York Times* reported that Carender's original 'porkulus' did not attract enough supporters to eat all the pork, but she took a leaf from Obama's campaign book and noted the e-mail addresses of attendees. One week on, 300 supporters showed up, and six weeks later 1,200 came.[19] The maths teacher from Seattle became the poster girl for the movement. The Carender tale was endearing, inspiring even. But the protagonist was far from representative of the Tea Party as a whole.

The day of the first major protests was 27 February 2009 – this time focusing on President Bush's TARP legislation to bail out the banks and President Obama's ARRA stimulus package. An internet search for protest information on this date offers a wealth of information, from Youtube clips of speeches to photo galleries of events and endless blog commentary. The 4 July Tea Parties that year focused particularly on Obama's proposed health care reform. Again, events were spread across the country, and the blogosphere tone in reference to the day was one of bonhomie and camaraderie. An examination of the literature, websites, blogs and interviews with activists suggested they all reached the same conclusion: that, as with most populist movements, what the Tea Party really wanted was, in the words of *The Simpsons*' Ned Flanders, a 'return to the America of yesteryear, one which exists only in the minds of . . . Republicans'.[20] Much of the literature and rallying speeches painted a nostalgic picture of a lost world of political and moral clarity. There were constant references to 'taking our country back'.[21] Back to what? From whom? Critics suggested back from the African-American in the Oval Office to a time when his candidacy would have been unthinkable.

The 1980 census showed that the US population was then 226.5 million. By 2010, it was 308.7 million. In addition to this phenomenal increase, a Pew Research Center report projected that, by 2050, non-Hispanic white Americans would make up a minority of 47 per cent of the population. The report estimated that, with a 438 million population in 2050, 82 per cent of the increase would be due to immigration.[22] Although no racial demographics were available for the Tea Party movement in 2011, it is fair to say that it attracted predominantly white followers. There were some exceptions, and the non-white members argued that the movement was not inherently racist. Stories of racial slurs and images of racist posters were real, as highlighted by the NAACP.[23] Timothy F. Johnson, chairman of the Frederick Douglass Foundation, a black conservative group in favour of limited government spending and activity, told *CBS News* that critics claimed that, in order for someone to be a Tea Party supporter, he must 'hate himself'.[24] Tea Party supporters continuously claimed that any racist moments were isolated incidents and not representative of the movement as a whole. Despite the handful of non-white Tea Party followers, polls demonstrated that the average Tea Party supporter was middle-income, middle-aged and Caucasian. Parallels were drawn with the Reagan revolutionaries of the 1980s, but there was a notable difference in that the 18 per cent of Americans who considered themselves as Tea Party activists or supporters tended to be older (that is, over 45) and better educated. In addition, between 50 and 55 per cent of Tea Party supporters were women.[25] This is noteworthy, because traditionally the Republican Party, and the political right in general, has tended disproportionally to attract men.

A coherent agenda or a mish-mash of angry opposition?

Throughout its ascent, the key traits of the movement remained elusive. Labels were used for convenience but invariably offered an incomplete or even incorrect version of the reality. The reality was that there were some extremely diverse and often conflicting agendas that fell under the Tea Party umbrella. They were not all libertarian. Nor were they all conservative. Some had no time for Sarah Palin. Others thought she was worth every dime of her $100,000 speaking fee. In 2010, the *New Republic* reported that two-thirds of Tea Partiers supported Social Security and Medicare.[26] Even the association of Ron Paul and Sarah Palin with the movement demonstrated its diversity. Taking US foreign policy as an example, Paul repeatedly stated that 'we don't need to be the world's policeman' and publicly condemned US policy on Israel. Palin, in contrast, during her 2011 visit to Israel was reported to have 'out-Netanyahu'd Benjamin Netanyahu'.[27]

Many Tea Partiers stated that they wanted more government action on immigration. Cries for a Berlin-style wall between Mexico and the US suggested a requirement for a certain amount of government activity. On trade, aspects of the Tea Party's 'America-first' protectionist approach again appeared contradictory to some of the movement's more libertarian laissez-faire views. Regarding social issues, there were endless contradictions. Libertarians, as a rule, could not care less about gay marriage, abortion and stem cell research. Conservative Tea Partiers were continuously apoplectic on these issues. Such stances muddied the waters. If the original fuel of the movement was concern regarding the fiscal imprudence of big government, some found the emotional outbursts about abortion distracting or irrelevant.

However, emotional outbursts about abortion could not be dismissed by politicians. The presence of the religious right was felt by those chasing votes since long before Bush targeted them in 2004. Their political awakening is usually traced back to the Reagan campaign in 1980, and their concerns and priorities have been acknowledged, if not adhered to, since. The fact that the US was a centre-right country was not contested. The fact that a young, liberal, hyper-intelligent African-American with an Ivy League education was running for the Oval Office in 2008 instilled fear, if not horror, in the minds of many. The alternative, self-confessed 'maverick' John McCain, was not to everyone's taste. In early autumn 2008, there were rumours that he was considering former Pennsylvania Governor Tom Ridge or former Democrat Joe Lieberman as running mate. As both of these were known to be pro-choice on abortion, talk show host and opinion leader Rush Limbaugh rallied his listeners and 'declared war' against McCain. A 2008 Zogby poll showed that the $50-million-a-year pundit was considered the most trusted news personality in the US.[28] When he pontificated on a topic, his 20 million-plus listeners took note[29] – as did John McCain. *Newsweek* columnist Stryker McGuire described McCain's choice of the lightly travelled Christian evangelical Sarah Palin as his 2008 running mate as the choice of a man in a panic. The choice of this 'sudden, freakishly huge, full-fledged phenomenon', as described by Megan McCain, shocked voters and pundits and was testament to the steadily increasing impact of the religious right.[30] No one was talking Tea Party at that point, but within half a year anti-abortion and anti-stimulus activists found themselves on the same side of the street.

Parties

In the wake of Keli Carender's modest success in February 2009, a wave of Tea Party events followed. Tax Day was 15 April 2009 and therefore a fitting occasion for further displays of government-directed anger. The *New York Times* reported that approximately 750 events took place around the country, with attendance varying from dozens to thousands depending on the location.[31] The overall message was cohesive – to demonstrate against Obama's $787 billion stimulus package. The economic jargon surrounding quantitative easing and the dense detail of the Patient Protection and Affordable Care bill unnerved many, as they saw the economy spinning out of control and a government that appeared only to want to throw money at the problem.

As well as the ad hoc meetings and multifarious Tea Parties, larger, more formal events took place. By summer 2009, Tea Party websites were offering detailed instructions on how to get involved or mobilized. For that year's 4 July celebrations, enthusiasts were encouraged to be visible at their local parade. The website www.teapartypatriots.org advised 'patriots' to check if there were any existing Tea Party activities in their local area and, if not, to start some. Advice was very specific, offering guidance on everything from obtaining a permit to what sort of issues and slogans to put on banners and T-shirts. The bottom of the website page listed the movement's 'partners', which included Dick Armey's Freedom Works Foundation.[32] On 12 September 2009, *Fox News*, applauding coverage of the Taxpayer March on Washington, spoke of the tens of thousands of protesters who took to the streets with images of Obama as Hitler, signs that labelled him a communist, fascist and socialist, with particular emphasis on his health care plan. The march was the culmination of a nationwide tour of 34 cities over 7,000 miles, starting in Sacramento, California on 28 August with a gathering of 'taxfighters'.[33]

In February 2010, the Nashville Tea Party convention was held at the four-star Gaylord Opryland Hotel at a cost of $549, plus accommodation and transport. The event had 600 'delegates', with 1,100 attending the final evening with guest speaker Sarah Palin. Convention spokesman Mark Skoda told the *Washington Post* that the event intended to demonstrate how the movement had matured and evolved. However, not everything about the event suggested political maturity, as speaker Joseph Farah, editor of conservative website WorldNetDaily, questioned Obama's birthplace and called for continued pressure on the president to produce his birth certificate, which the president did in April 2011.[34] In addition, Farah's speech included accusations against the Obama administration for efforts to use 1960s-style Marxist theory to overthrow the 'American free enterprise system'.[35] Ex-Congressman Tom Tancredo's speech castigated RINOs (Republicans in name only) for conspiring with Democrats to boil Americans like frogs 'in the cauldron of the nanny state' and reminded his audience of the significance of President Obama's middle name. Hyperbole abounded. Americans were living under 'the Third Reich' after the 'Pearl Harbor' of Obama's election, having endured Roosevelt's First Reich and Lyndon Johnson's Second. Some within the Tea Party blogosphere suggested that sticking with more local, grassroots, street-level activities was truer to the movement spirit, rather than, for example, paying $89.99 at the convention for a silver tea-bag necklace. The event highlighted how diverging interests converged under the Tea Party umbrella, as for three days southern Christians shared space with secular libertarians. Writer Jonathan Raban attended the event and later recalled that disgruntled libertarians left some break-out sessions because of an overdose of prayers. There were also complaints that – in another nod to religion – no alcohol was served with dinner. Raban noted how the differences among delegates were highlighted by the forced proximity of the conference; in conversations on the smoking terrace he discerned that some viewed the conspiracy aspects of the gathering as tedious and as tending to undermine the group's larger objectives. However, whatever fissures were evident, the purpose of keynote speaker Sarah Palin's final evening address was to unify all present.[36] 'If you take 1,000 so-called Tea Partyers and ask them what this movement is, you'll get 1,000 different interpretations', said Mark Williams, a talk-radio host and chairman of the Tea Party Express. 'But they're all waving American flags and speaking out against the galloping socialist agenda.'[37]

On 28 August 2010, *Fox News* pundit Glenn Beck organized a 'Restore Honor in America' rally at the Lincoln Memorial in Washington, DC. CNN's John Avlon noted the more popular T-shirt slogans sported at the event, including 'We Came Unarmed (This Time)', 'Muslim Marxist', 'Barack Obama Supports Abortion, Sodomy, Socialism and the New World Order' and, doubtless the most confounding, 'Hands Off My Medicare'.[38] Not coincidentally, Beck chose the anniversary of Martin Luther King Jr's 'I have a dream' speech. Wearing a bullet-proof vest, Beck opened by announcing that 'Today, America begins to turn back to God.' Alveda King, pro-life activist and niece of Dr King, spoke at the event, stating that she wanted to honour her uncle and ask God 'to forgive us'. Attendees waved 'Don't tread on me' flags and distributed 'Dump Obama' flyers. Speaker Sarah Palin also compared their purpose to that of the civil rights movement. Beck's website claimed that hundreds of thousands attended. *CBS News* put the figure at somewhere around 87,000, whilst *Sky News* suggested 500,000.[39] Controversy ensued, as attendance estimates varied dramatically. Numbers notwithstanding, this 'non-political' event, as it was billed, was considered to be a success by various observers. Bill O'Reilly described the event as a big victory for Beck as he promoted a 'return to Judeo-Christian values'.[40] Others were less supportive. Writing for *Slate* magazine, Christopher Hitchens described the event as 'large, vague, moist and undirected, the Waterworld of white self-pity'.[41] Howard Dean did not mince words, calling Beck a 'racist hate-monger' and comparing him to 1930s populist Father Coughlin, known for his support of Hitler and Mussolini.[42] Despite the disparagement, for Beck and his supporters the day was a triumph.

Grassroots or astroturf?

In 2010, senior Obama adviser David Axelrod said of the Tea Party: 'In part, this is a grassroots citizens' movement brought to you by a bunch of oil billionaires'[43] – in other words, a very successful exercise in astroturfing. In 1985, Texan Democratic Senator Lloyd Bentsen coined the term 'astroturf' in a political sense when he was faced with an onslaught of generated mail presented as correspondence from the general public.[44] Various high-profile examples existed of this phenomenon, which was specifically prohibited by the code of ethics of the Public Relations Society of America. The Tea Party enjoyed presenting itself as a ramshackle, organically evolving movement. This may have been true, but it didn't take long for ideological and logistical control to come from sources such as the Freedom Works Foundation that were anything but ramshackle.

Writer and activist George Monbiot described the movement as 'one of the biggest exercises in false consciousness the world has ever seen'.[45] Monbiot outlined two types of astroturfing – one where no grassroots element ever existed and ones such as the Tea Party which start out as something genuine but are catalysed and mobilized from early on by vested interests. In the Tea Party's case, this interest came mostly in the form of 'the biggest company you've never heard of'.[46] A 2011 internet search for 'Koch Industries' resulted in 606,000 hits, offering information ranging from the Koch brothers' business website to www.opensecrets.org, listing their phenomenal lobbying and contribution record in Washington, DC. Prior to 2010, few had heard of the brothers with a combined worth then of $35 billion, or their business interests, but were more likely to be familiar with some of their not-for-profit activities. Hovering at the libertarian end of the Republican spectrum, Charles Koch funded the setting up of Citizens for a Sound Economy in 1984 (which later split into Americans for Prosperity and the Freedom Works Foundation), founded the Cato Institute in 1977 and established the Americans for Prosperity Foundation in 2005. David Koch held a particularly deep animosity towards President Obama and funded a range of climate-denial groups. According to a 2011 Greenpeace report, Koch Industries had to date funnelled $55 million to delay policies and regulations aimed at stopping global warming. Koch industries – the second-largest private corporation in the US – was mostly an oil company, with a poor environmental record.[47] Koch Industries' response to the Greenpeace report was to say that it 'distorts the environmental record of our companies', and David Koch condemned the actions of the 'radical press'.[48] However, founder of the Center for Public Integrity Charles Lewis said:

> The Kochs are on a whole different level. There's no one else who has spent this much money. The sheer dimension of it is what sets them apart. They have a pattern of lawbreaking, manipulation and obfuscation. I've been in Washington since Watergate and I've never seen anything like it. They are the Standard Oil of our times.[49]

Liberal blogger Lee Fang described the Kochs as 'the billionaires behind the hate'.[50] So why the hate? Writing for the *New Yorker*, Jane Mayer offered some context for the Koch agenda, in an article that brought a stinging rebuttal from the Kochs.[51] Fred Koch had a lifelong paranoia about the Soviet Union and communism, which his sons inherited and translated into deep distrust of the US government, particularly of Roosevelt's New Deal. The brothers adhered to the Austrian school of free market economic ideals, particularly the writings of Friedrich von Hayek. In June 2010, *Fox News* host Glenn Beck promoted Hayek's 1944 work *The Road to Serfdom*, which resulted in it becoming a number one best-seller on Amazon. Tea Party activists warmed to Hayek's promotion of unfettered capitalism. The Koch brothers also embraced the work of Robert LeFevre, who favoured the abolition of the state, thought the New Deal was a horrible mistake and argued that 'government is a disease masquerading as its own cure'.[52] In 1956, when Lefevre opened the Freedom School in Colorado Springs, Charles Koch provided financial support. In 1979, David Koch ran on the Libertarian vice-presidential ticket with candidate Ed Clark, who was offering a further-right alternative to Ronald Reagan. Clark told *The Nation* that his supporters were preparing for a 'very big Tea Party' because people were 'sick to death of taxes'.[53] Koch's wealth allowed their campaign to be largely self-funded, and they received 1.06 per cent of the popular vote – the highest of any libertarian presidential candidate to date but still far short of anything meaningful.

From this juncture onwards, the Koch brothers took a step back from direct involvement in politics. They continued to spend hundreds of millions of dollars via their charitable foundations, along with contributions to lobbying groups, Republican campaigns and political action groups. Interviewer Brian Doherty described Charles Koch's goal as to 'tear government out at its root'.[54] As the brothers increasingly regarded elected politicians as merely 'actors playing out a script', the logical way to progress and alter the direction of America, according to a Koch friend, was to 'influence the areas where policy ideas percolate from: academia and think-tanks' – hence support for the Cato Institute, Citizens for a Sound Economy, the Institute for Justice, the Institute for Humane Studies and the Bill of Rights Institute, among others.[55]

The Kochs were hardly the first to think of such a strategy, but the extent of their efforts and capacity were, in the words of Media Matters' Ari Rabin-Havt, 'staggering'.[56] Conservative economist and historian Bruce Bartlett argued that the problem for the libertarian movement was that it was all chiefs and not enough Indians, as the presidential election results demonstrated. As the Tea Party emerged, 'everyone suddenly sees for the first time that there are Indians out there – people who can provide real ideological power'.[57] The K Street consultant quoted in *Playboy* magazine offered a fascinating insight into the netherworld of astroturfing, stating: 'the cynical among us think [the Tea Party] is a group of peasants with pitchforks controlled by an underground cabal of Glenn Beck, wealthy donors and the guys who killed JFK'.[58] However, despite the disparaging tone, he admitted that 'this cause is worthier and more real than anything I've done in the past'. Describing the 'colorful characters' behind the organization, he said: 'none of them were prom king, none of them went to college east of the Appalachians (even the Jews) and a lot of them smoke a pack a day just because they're not supposed to'.[59] He recalled a visit to a St Louis Tea Party event in 2010 full of 'angst-ridden Caucasians sitting in lawn chairs with signs such as "My daughter is nine years old and already $41,000 in debt"'. Highlighting the incoherence of the Tea Party, he explained:

> you have to understand the state of the Republican Party to understand how there can still be oxygen in the room for the Tea Party. Bush mangled the GOP brand into a grotesque form that conservatives haven't recognized in five years.[60]

This is insightful and accurate but does not tell the whole story. Just as the Tea Party was not all about whether Obama had a US birth certificate, neither was it all about George W. Bush going off piste with the Republican agenda. According to Rasmussen polls, the specific events that triggered the Tea Party into existence were the Bush and Obama bank bailouts.[61] However, concerns ran deeper than this. The simplistic option to blame the government for the nation's financial woes was tempting and yet also carried weight. Polls demonstrated that there was a real feeling among Americans that their country was losing its international standing and credibility. Since the late 1970s, the government has given major incentives to the wealthy whilst reducing measures of support for the average citizen. The wealthy have benefited and profited, this giving them further opportunity to advance their agenda and financially support the Tea Party. The naivety of the 'blame government' approach was beneficial for corporate supporters of the Tea Party, and conveniently no one mentioned the extent of Wall Street's responsibility for the economic crisis. All of the Tea Party dialogue centred on cutting government programmes as the panacea for all ills. It did not address crucial issues such as increased poverty, wealth disparity and the impact of mass unemployment.[62] The Tea Party seized the political narrative, everyone listened and the government did not respond in a sufficiently coherent manner.

The 2010 elections and beyond

In the 2010 midterm elections, the Tea Party candidates ran as economic conservatives and those who won seats remained true to their word. By March 2011, the government came within 20 minutes of a shutdown, with Speaker of the House Boehner under pressure from hard-liners within the GOP to 'face off' the president over agreement on the budget. Despite agreement among experienced Republicans that a government shutdown would simply benefit the Democrats, Boehner's own position was under threat from hard-liners within his own party if he was not seen to be sufficiently robust in his confrontation with the president over the extent of spending cuts.[63]

Whilst exact measurement of who was a Tea Party candidate in 2010 was a somewhat imprecise task, a reasonable yardstick was to consider those who had self-identified as Tea Partiers or those who had been backed by groups within the movement. Based on this criterion, the Tea Party achieved a string of high-profile victories across the nation, with Michele Bachmann among the most visible. The outspoken evangelical Republican congresswoman for Minnesota since 2006 became head of the Tea Party Caucus in Congress. She embodied the often challenging balance between remaining true to Tea Party principles and embracing the Republican Party that she represented in Congress, describing the Caucus as a 'receptacle' that was there to listen, rather than to be a mouthpiece.[64] The Caucus was met with cautious optimism from national coordinator for the Tea Party Patriots Dawn Wildman, whose response was to take a 'wait-and-see approach to find out how they will actually be representing the ideas and efforts of the tea party patriots all over the nation'.[65]

Tea Party philosophy suggested that incumbents and self-appointed leaders were anathema to their agenda, but without some figure-heads the movement could hardly progress beyond a protest stance. After the 2010 elections, Bachmann announced her bid for House Republican Conference Chair, crediting herself with keeping the Tea Party within the Republican parameters and therefore enabling the party's House victory in 2010. Republican response to her bid was mixed. Her fundraising skills were unparalleled, but some within the party perceived her stance as being overly dogmatic. By November 2010, Bachmann had withdrawn her candidacy and publicly voiced her support for Jeb Hensarling. The bid demonstrated how tensions could emerge when a party member's own message conflicted with the larger Republican agenda.

Bachmann's 2012 presidential bid, launched in July of the previous year, pledged to give Americans 'independence from government'. Immediately, a *Des Moines Register* poll showed Bachmann's support almost level with her more mainstream Republican rival Mitt Romney, and her popularity remained high throughout August and September 2011.[66] The website www.ontheissues.org outlined Bachmann's stance on the key issues – all predictably hard-line and socially conservative – but the fine print remained elusive. She would repeal Obamacare. But how? In the television debates, her charisma and capacity for slick sound-bites were evident, helped by her telegenic appearance, but there was little scope for offering anything deeper during these 60-second exchanges.

The Pew Research Center's 2011 quadrennial study of the American electorate noted that 'the most visible shift in the political landscape' since 2005 'is the emergence of a single bloc of across-the-board conservatives. The long-standing divide between economic, pro-business conservatives and social conservatives has blurred.'[67] Bachmann personified this fusion as 'the candidate Sarah Palin was supposed to be'.[68] The Minnesotan was not the only contender to hold the right of centre stage. Republican presidential candidate Herman Cain presented himself as an outsider in the race, but this unique selling point was undermined by revelations that he had worked for years as a motivational speaker for the Koch Broth-ers-funded Americans for Prosperity group. As well as donating heavily to the Tea Party, the Koch Brothers contributed to the American Legislative Exchange Council, the lobbying group linked to former UK Defence Secretary Liam Fox's Atlantic Bridge organization.[69] Cain's campaign manager and a number of aides previously worked for Americans for Pros-perity (AFP), and Cain himself credited his 9-9-9 formula for saving the US economy to a businessman who served on the AFP advisory board.[70] AFP's agenda included decreasing public and private sector union strength, undoing Obama's health care legislation and under-mining environmental regulation, all of which were considered advantages from the Tea Party perspective.

Media comparisons between the Tea Party's least preferred candidate Mitt Romney's 2012 bid and Nelson Rockefeller's 1964 campaign were not particularly accurate. Nelson Rockefeller was genuinely a moderate Republican, running against a hard-line conservative, Barry Goldwater, and the choice between the two men was clear and wide. Romney – pre-viously considered a reasonably liberal Republican – was no longer so moderate by 2011. Whilst it suited his conservative opponents to paint him as a moderate, or even liberal, in reality little in his 2012 bid could have upset the Tea Party. He was, as conservative radio host Rush Limbaugh put it, 'all three legs of the conservative stool'. In order to appeal to the twenty-first-century solidly conservative GOP base, Romney needed to shed his moderate image.[71] However, there was a clear tension between the Republican Party's electoral priori-ties and the Tea Party's self-image as a beacon of ideological purity.[72] A study by Karpowitz *et al.* examined the extent to which Tea Party activity translated into votes in the 2010 elec-tions – a difficult task considering that one of the key traits of the Tea Party movement was that it did not have a centralized organizational structure or anything resembling a national mandate. A table detailing determinants of Republican 2010 General Election voter share demonstrates that Tea Party endorsements generally had a minimal statistically determinable impact on the Republican vote share. Writing in 2011, Karpowitz *et al.* concluded that the day of reckoning between the Republicans and the Tea Party was yet to come.[73]

The literature suggests that the Tea Party's bark was worse than its bite and that, whilst Tea Partiers may have cheered such escapades as the Austin man who flew a plane into his local IRS building in February 2010 to demonstrate his displeasure regarding taxation, they were less likely to carry out such stunts themselves. Immediately afterwards, a *New York Times* blog appeared entitled 'The First Tea-Party Terrorist?'[74] The conclusion was, more or less, that he was not. Joseph Stack had myriad grudges against the government, but the newspaper acknowledged that he could not to any meaningful extent represent the Tea Party, as its only core unifying theme was populist rage. Commentator Gary Younge observed that the Tea Party was not a new phenomenon; it was simply the hard right with a new title. Previously, individuals such as Father Coughlin, Huey Long and Joseph McCarthy loudly banged their drums. In recent times, groups including the Birthers, Oath Keepers, Glenn Beck watchers, Rush Limbaugh listeners and other assorted hard right groups lacked a unifying identity. In 2009 the Tea Party was considered an insurgent, inchoate entity. By late 2010, it was a force to be reckoned with.[75] The twenty-first-century Father Coughlins had access to 24/7 media in a way their predecessors could only have dreamed of, along with financial support from those who saw the benefits of decreased, if not paralysed, government. At times, repellent language can mask a genuine point, and so the paranoia that agitates many of the fringe elements is further agitated. Much of the misery that has beset America in recent years has been too complex easily to explain. The near collapse of the economic system, caused by so few and afflicting so many, and the confusion and distortion surrounding the raucous, bitter health care debate have been exploited by talk show hosts and partisan politics to fan a rabid ignorance that looks for simplistic blame via soundbites.[76] The final word is far from written on the Tea Party and its impact. After a stratospheric rise, it warrants note as a significant – if temporary – force to be reckoned with. The movement's sense of rage and urgency was compelling, if not new.

> The paranoid spokesman sees the fate of this conspiracy in apocalyptic terms. . . . He is always manning the barricades of civilisation. He constantly lives at the turning point: it is now or never in organising resistance to conspiracy. Time is forever just running out.[77]

For all the Tea Party's momentary fire and brimstone, Hofstadter's 1964 essay acts as a telling reminder of the likelihood that this movement will settle into place as another momentary interlude in the nation's greater political narrative.

Notes

1 Charly Gullett, *The Official Tea Party Handbook* (Prescott, AZ: Warfield Press, 2009), 23.
2 Anonymous, 'Rogues of K Street', *Playboy* (July 2010), 4.
3 Richard Hofstadter, 'The Paranoid Style in American Politics', *Harper's Magazine* (November 1964), 1.
4 Richard Hofstadter, *The Paranoid Style in American Politics* (London: Jonathan Cape, 1966), 39.
5 NBC/WSJ poll (and others), 'Direction of the Country', http://www.pollingreport.com/right.htm.
6 Gary Younge, 'For White Americans, Things Aren't What They Used to Be', *Guardian*, 21 November 2010.
7 Jacob Weisberg, 'How Was It for You?', *Guardian*, 13 December 2005.
8 Kate Zernike, *Boiling Mad: Inside Tea Party America* (New York: Times Books, 2010), 16.
9 Associated Press, 'Bush's Gay Union Stance Irks Conservatives', 26 October 2004.
10 Julian Borger, 'Aides Say White House Mocked Evangelicals', *Guardian*, 14 October 2006.
11 Neil Mathieson, 'Three Weeks That Changed the World', *Guardian*, 28 December 2008.
12 Catherine Clifford, 'Foreclosure Filings Spike 71%', *CNN Money*, 23 October 2008.
13 George W. Bush interview with Matt Lauer, *Dateline* NBC, 8 November 2010.
14 Rick Santelli, 'Rant of the Year', *CNBC*, 19 February 2009.

15 Rick Santelli interview, *Chicago Sun Times*, 19 February 2009.
16 *Huffington Post*, http://www.huffingtonpost.com/2010/09/20/rick-santelli-i-sparked-t_n_731249. html.
17 www.teapartypatriots.org; www.reteaparty.com; wwwteapartyexpress.org; www.facebook. com/teapartypatriots.
18 http://michellemalkin.com/2009/02/15/taxpayer-revolt-porkulus-protest-in-seattle/.
19 Kate Zernike, 'Unlikely Activist Who Got to the Tea Party Early', *New York Times*, 27 February 2010.
20 'Home away from Homer', *The Simpsons* (Fox, 2005).
21 Dean Reynolds, 'Palin: It's Time to Take Our Country Back', *CBS News*, 17 September 2010.
22 Jeffrey Passel and D'Vera Cohn, 'Immigration to Play Lead Role in Future US Growth', Pew Research Center, 11 February 2008.
23 Huma Khan, 'NAACP vs. Tea Party: Racism Debate Heats Up as Sarah Palin Joins the Fray', *ABC News*, 13 July 2010.
24 Associated Press, 'Black Tea Party Supporters Take the Heat', *CBS News*, 7 April 2010.
25 Kate Zernike and Megan Thee-Brenan, 'Polls Find Tea Party Backers Wealthier and Better Educated', *New York Times*, 14 April 2010.
26 Barry Gewen, 'How the Tea Party Is Wrecking Republican Foreign Policy', *New Republic*, 4 December 2010.
27 Ibid.
28 Zogby poll, November 2008, www.imao.us/wp-content/.../2008/11/media_project_poll_info.pdf.
29 Paul Farhi, 'No Rush to Measure Limbaugh's Ratings', *LA Times*, 9 March 2009.
30 'The Palin Girls Don't Share', *Daily Beast*, 16 September 2010, accessed at http://www. thedailybeast.com/articles/2010/09/17/the-palin-girls-dont-share.html; Stryker McGuire, 'Bush May Be Going: But the Religious Right Is Fighting Fit', *Guardian*, 7 September 2008.
31 Liz Robbins, 'Tax Day Is Met with Tea Parties', *New York Times*, 15 April 2009.
32 www.teapartypatriots.org; www.freedomworks.org.
33 http://open.salon.com/blog/richard_rider/2009/08/27/richard_rider_honored_as_tax_fighter_of_ the_year/comment.
34 Jonathan Raban, 'At the Tea Party', *New York Review of Books*, 25 March 2010.
35 http://www.youtube.com/watch?v=JyoCRC-oT0A.
36 Raban, 'At the Tea Party'.
37 Phillip Rucker, 'Tea Party Convention Begins in Nashville', *Washington Post*, 5 February 2010.
38 John Avlon, *Wingnuts: How the Lunatic Fringe Is Hijacking America* (New York: Beast Books, 2010), 39.
39 Brian Montopoli, 'Glenn Beck "Restoring Honor" Rally Crowd Estimates Explained', *CBS News*, 31 August 2010.
40 Dan Gilgoff, 'At Rally, Beck Positions Himself as New Leader for Christian Conservatives', *CNN Belief Blog*, 28 August 2010; Bill O'Reilly, *Talking Points*, Fox News, 30 August 2010, accessed at http://video.foxnews.com/v/4325074/big-victory-for-glenn-beck.
41 Christopher Hitchens, 'White Fright', *Slate* magazine, 30 August 2010.
42 Howard Dean on 'Morning Joe', *MSNBC*, 30 August 2010.
43 Jane Mayer, 'Covert Operations', *New Yorker*, 30 August 2010.
44 Ryan Sager, 'Keep Off the Astroturf', *New York Times*, 18 August 2009.
45 George Monbiot, 'Toxic Brew', www.monbiot.com, 25 October 2010.
46 Ibid.
47 Greenpeace, 'Koch Industries: Secretly Funding the Climate Denial Machine', 2011.
48 Andrew Goldman, 'The Billionaires' Party', *New York Magazine*, 25 July 2010.
49 Mayer, 'Covert Operations'.
50 Ibid.
51 www.kochfacts.com/kf/holdingnewyorker.
52 Brian Doherty, *Radicals for Capitalism* (New York: PublicAffairs, 2007), 312.
53 Mayer, 'Covert Operations'.
54 Doherty, *Radicals for Capitalism*, 602.
55 Mayer, 'Covert Operations'.
56 www.commoncause.org/ (United States).
57 Mayer, 'Covert Operations'.

58 Anonymous, 'Rogues of K Street', 1.
59 Ibid., 2.
60 Ibid.
61 Dan Weil, 'Rasmussen: Tea Party Shows Weakness of Republican Establishment', *Newsmax*, 19 September 2010.
62 E. J. Dionne, 'The Tea Party Is Winning', *Washington Post*, 21 February 2011.
63 John Bresnahan and Jake Sherman, 'John Boehner: Democrats "Win" in Government Shutdown', *Politico*, 5 April 2011.
64 Janie Lorber, 'Republicans Form Caucus for Tea Party in the House', *New York Times*, 21 July 2010.
65 Associated Press, 'Michele Bachmann: Tea Party Caucus Not Movement Mouthpiece', 21 July 2010.
66 http://www.realclearpolitics.com/epolls/2012/president/us/general_election_bachmann_vs_obama-1941.html.
67 Ryan Lizza, 'Leap of Faith: The Transformation of Michele Bachmann', *New Yorker*, 15 August 2011.
68 Ezra Klein, 'Michele Bachmann Is the Candidate Sarah Palin Was Supposed to Be', *Washington Post* blog, 19 May 2011.
69 Alex Spillius, 'US Elections 2012: Fresh Doubts over Herman Cain's Credentials', *Daily Telegraph*, 17 October 2011.
70 'Herman Cain's Deep Ties to Koch Brothers Key to Campaign', *Washington Post*, 16 October 2011.
71 Steve Kornacki, 'Why Mitt Romney Is Not a Moderate', *Salon.com*, 17 October 2011.
72 Christopher F. Karpowitz, J. Quin Monson, Kelly D. Patterson and Jeremy C. Pope, 'Tea Time in America: The Impact of the Tea Party Movement on the 2010 Midterm Elections', *PS: Political Science and Politics*, 44 (2011), 303–309.
73 Ibid.
74 Robert Wright, 'The First Tea Party Terrorist?', *New York Times* blog, 23 February 2010.
75 Gary Younge, 'The Tea Party Is Not New', *Guardian*, 7 November 2010.
76 Avlon, *Wingnuts*, xi.
77 Hofstadter, *Paranoid Style in American Politics*, 29–30.

9 The Sarah Palin phenomenon

The Washington–Hollywood–Wall Street syndrome in American politics, and more . . .

Clive S. Thomas

From virtual obscurity as a small town mayor and Governor of Alaska, a minor state politically, Sarah Palin was thrust into the national and international spotlight on 29 August 2008 when John McCain nominated her as his vice presidential running mate on the Republican ticket. And, even though the McCain–Palin ticket was defeated, this did not push Palin into obscurity – quite the contrary.

In effect, she became a national and international celebrity – a superstar. Palin appeared on the covers of *Time, Newsweek* and the *Economist*, and was the subject of thousands of media stories from New York to Rio, from Seattle to Copenhagen, and some lengthy articles in publications such as *Vanity Fair*.[1] She had her own television programme, *Sarah Palin's Alaska*, watched by tens of millions of her fans, authored two books, and was the subject of several others.[2] One particularly enlightening popular book, *Game Change*, was also made into a television film in early 2012.[3] Palin spawned a cottage industry, with her image featured on fridge magnets, greetings cards, calendars and Sarah Palin dolls, and a surge in the demand for lookalike spectacles.

In 2012 she still had greater name recognition in the United States and abroad than most members of the US Congress, including its leaders, and more than US Vice President Joe Biden. She became a broker in American politics, sought after by many Republicans seeking re-election or running for the first time. In fact, she is a phenomenon equalled by few, if any, politicians in the US or abroad in recent years. Palin is a phenomenon in three ways: she is an exceptional person, with an aptitude for public speaking and relating to certain people; her story is unusual, significant and in some ways unique in American politics; and the holistic phenomenon of which Sarah Palin is the core is something that cannot be totally explained – it belongs, in some degree, to the surreal. A synthesis of these three senses of phenomenon is an enlightening way to describe Palin's career both in Alaska and in national politics. Phenomena can, of course, be positive or negative, or a combination. Palin epitomizes these complexities of political and social phenomena. She became and remains a phenomenon despite often being woefully uninformed on many issues, ill prepared in speeches and dealing with the press, and the butt of many jokes for her lack of general knowledge and misuse of the English language. She often does not seem interested in politics, and is a very divisive person, with die-hard supporters and major detractors. Given the sharp contrast between her positive and negative attributes, how can we explain Palin's continued prominence in the United States and around the world? And what does the Palin phenomenon tell us about American politics, past and present?

This chapter seeks to answer these questions. In regard to one aspect of Palin being a phenomenon, there is far from a definitive answer to the first question: commentators disagree over Palin's personal motives for being in politics. Nevertheless, we offer an explanation of her continuing prominence. This helps in answering the second question, the major of the two that we explore. The argument presented here is that the Palin phenomenon is a classic case of the Washington–Hollywood–Wall Street political syndrome, representing the connection that many American politicians are able to forge between politics, entertainment (in some cases celebrity status and stardom) and making small fortunes. More specifically, the Palin phenomenon provides insights into American populism and conservatism (particularly social conservatism), continuing racism in the United States, and the polarization of contemporary national politics.

Yet, while the Palin phenomenon has been ever present in American politics since 2008, this is a short time for major academic studies to appear. Those published deal with Palin in the context of women and continuing sexism in politics, and women as candidates from a political marketing perspective.[4] None addresses the broader questions posed in this chapter. This necessitates that the sources for this chapter include radio and television stories, newspaper and magazine articles, popular books written by and about Palin, survey data on attitudes to Palin, conversations with Alaskan politicians, journalists and political observers, and the observations of the author, who followed Palin first-hand in Alaska and in national politics before, during and after her nomination as a vice presidential candidate.[5]

Palin's personal background, political career and personality: background, family life and personal experiences

Palin's background and family life offer insights into her actions in politics and her continued prominence, as does her personality, even if there is considerable disagreement on who is the 'real Sarah Palin'.[6] Sarah Louise Palin was born on 11 February 1964 in Sandpoint, Idaho. Soon after, her family moved to Alaska, eventually settling in Wasilla, then a town of under 1,000 inhabitants just north of Alaska's largest city, Anchorage. In high school she was on the basketball team that won the state-wide championship in 1982, earning her the nickname of 'Sarah Barracuda' for her competiveness. In school she was also head of the Fellowship of Christian Athletes, was very religious and attended the Assemblies of God Church in Wasilla, and her commitment to religion continues. This essentially Pentecostal faith (though Palin does not describe herself as Pentecostal) adheres to a strict moral code: it opposes smoking, drinking, dancing, and sex outside of marriage.

In 1984 Palin won the Miss Wasilla beauty contest and came third in the Miss Alaska contest. After attending several universities she eventually graduated from the University of Idaho in journalism in 1987. She returned to Alaska to work as a sports reporter for Anchorage television stations and a local newspaper. In August 1988 she eloped with her high-school sweetheart, Todd Palin. The couple have five children. The two most well known are Bristol, born in 1990, and Trig, born in 2008 when Palin was Governor of Alaska. Both before and after becoming governor, Palin was very much a family person and a home-lover. Only in 2006, at the age of 42, did she get a passport. And Sarah Palin is very much a mother – a mom – and involved with her family.

Palin's personal and family life has been colourful and full of trials and tribulations. This private life became very public after her vice presidential nomination. From eloping with Todd, to Bristol being an unwed mother, with the birth of Palin's first grandchild in 2008, to fights with Bristol's boyfriend, Levi Johnston, to Trig Palin being born with Down's syndrome, to the arrest of her sister-in-law (Todd Palin's half-sister) for burglary in 2009, to Bristol's celebrity status on the television programme *Dancing with the Stars*, this is the stuff of which soap operas are made and great fodder for the tabloids.[7]

From small town mayor to the world stage

Palin has been a life-long Republican, registering as such in 1982. However, the first ten years of her political career were spent in non-partisan local government in Wasilla, first as a city council member and then as mayor for two terms. Her first foray into state politics occurred in 2002, when she ran unsuccessfully in the primary election for the Republican nomination for Lieutenant Governor. Then, in 2003, Governor Murkowski appointed her to the Alaska Oil and Gas Conservation Commission, but she resigned from this position in January 2004.

In 2006 Palin ran for governor and won both the primary and the general election easily, beating two-term governor Tony Knowles in the general election. In the campaign Palin divulged few specifics about the policies she would pursue if elected, but often stressed that she would let the people decide on many issues, including abortion and other highly charged issues. She got elected as an outsider Republican and was seen as a sort of maverick in not conforming to many of the ideas and policies of the state Republican establishment. In July 2009, eight months after being part of the losing McCain–Palin ticket, she unexpectedly resigned as governor after only two and a half years in office.

Palin's tenure as governor falls clearly into two parts – that before her nomination by McCain and the time after. Before August 2008, she was the most popular governor in Alaska history, at one time reaching an over 90 per cent approval rating, which made her one of the most popular governors in the nation.[8] She annoyed many hard-core Republicans by working across party lines with the House Democratic minority in the Alaska legislature and, consequently, was very popular with them. She pushed popular – in essence populist – legislation such as ethics reform and a tax increase on the oil industry. Yet, despite her apparently strong religious views, Palin did not push family-value issues such as anti-abortion and anti-gay marriage. In fact, on most issues, including major development versus environmental issues, she was silent, though she did have a traditional Alaskan conservative bias toward economic development. Even in these years, however, there was another, less visible and less amicable side to her governorship, which would surface after McCain nominated her.

From taking America by storm with her electrifying, if in parts disingenuous speech, at the Republican nominating convention in early September and paralysing the Democrats for a month, to gaffes with the press showing her lack of knowledge and interest in politics, and the reports of the problems she caused the McCain campaign (well documented in *Game Change*), Palin found her public image in Alaska taking a nose-dive by December of 2008 as she was embroiled in increasing controversy.[9] Part of the reason was likely that, after her exposure to national politics and international prominence and the future promise that that held, Palin's interest in Alaska seemed to wane considerably. Eventually she also alienated most of the legislature, who overrode her veto of the acceptance of some federal monies because it was based on her misunderstanding of conditions for the state receiving the funds.

Personal, sometimes intense and occasionally vitriolic conflict and controversy were, in fact, a hallmark of Palin's entire time in public office. This began when she was Mayor of Wasilla with a run-in with the city librarian and the sacking of the chief of police. While on the Oil and Gas Conservation Commission, she brought an ethics complaint against a member, who was forced to resign. Then she joined an action against the state attorney general, claiming he had a conflict of interest. As governor she became embroiled in several scandals, including the so-called 'troopergate affair', where she fired the state public safety commissioner, allegedly because he would not fire her former brother-in-law, who had been involved in a nasty divorce with her sister. The state legislature hired an investigator to pursue the matter. She was cleared of this charge. Other ethics complaints filed against her by private citizens for alleged misuse of state travel funds were also dismissed.

Various accusations included her apparently mercenary turn-around on issues like the 'bridge to nowhere' (a project in Ketchikan in south-east Alaska where she first supported receiving federal funds but then claimed she had said 'no' to them as 'wasteful government spending' after she got the nomination as vice president), and her apparent abandoning of Alaska during and after her vice presidential run. These and other revelations about her during the campaign soured many Alaskans on Palin. A major irony was that she had made a political career, in part, by exposing what she considered unethical behaviour in politics, and had pushed ethics legislation in her first year as governor. So great was the contrast between the pre- and post-August 2009 Sarah Palin that in the spring of 2012 her approval rating fell to just 33 per cent in Alaska.[10] Nevertheless, in March 2012 nationally she was more popular among Republicans than any of the party's presidential candidates, including Mitt Romney, who eventually was nominated.[11]

Palin the enigma: her personality, psyche and goals

Few politicians in the United States or around the world have had their personalities, psyche and intentions analysed as has Sarah Palin. The truth, however, is that no one has the definitive answer on this. As a result, assessing her psychology has become a mini-industry in itself. Assessments run the gamut. At one end are many of her detractors, who see her as lazy, a quitter, and vindictive: a self-serving person with a large ego and narcissist tendencies who craves attention, but is not particularly interested in anything, including politics, other than her family and her own advancement at any price. At the other end are her supporters, who see her as a charming, charismatic and caring person with the interests of America at heart. Neither of these assessments stands up to close scrutiny. A more balanced assessment comes from synthesizing the perspectives of those who have worked with her and know her well (as far as anyone can) and through her own actions, statements and writings.

From this synthesis, six of Palin's characteristics come through time and time again. These are that she is enigmatic, is very concerned about her image, has difficulty taking criticism, is often opportunistic, can be very tenacious and is often erratic. Observations by three Alaska journalists and two nationally known journalists and the theme of the book and film *Game Change* appear to encapsulate her personality, psyche and goals.

Julie O'Malley wrote an editorial in the *Anchorage Daily News*, in November 2009, at the peak of Palin's popularity and when speculation about her running for president in 2012 was in full swing, titled 'She's Everywhere But Don't Ask Where Palin Is Coming From'.[12] In other words, Palin was prominent in the media and travelling all across America, but her motives, goals and intentions were far from clear. Two journalists from the *Alaska Dispatch* commented: 'We knew she possessed a special political charisma, but her success in Alaska seemed more the result of chance and circumstances than a calculated vision for her home state, her smarts or her background.'[13] David Brooks of the *New York Times* observed: 'She [Palin] does not have a political strategy, she has a media strategy.'[14] And, in a review of the TV film *Game Change*, Roger Ebert described Palin as 'the greatest actress in American political history'.[15]

The portrayal of Palin in *Game Change* provides ample evidence to support these perspectives but goes further. It shows her as, on the one hand, a very charismatic politician who can hold a crowd and get them to cheer enthusiastically for her and as able to relate to people on a very personal level. On the other, it shows her as woefully uninformed about current political issues, egotistical, hard to deal with, insensitive to the needs of others, erratic, prone to temper tantrums, and tenacious to her own detriment.[16]

Apart from these general traits, specific ones are apparent that throw light on Palin's role in politics and the contrasting way that she is viewed by her supporters and detractors. One is the ability to relate to people in a very personal way. As a relatively young mother of five, and in the eyes of many an attractive woman, she had an appeal to both men and women, if for different reasons. Many young mothers saw her as one of them; and many men saw her as a sex symbol. Her eschewing of some traditional Republican policies and casting herself as a maverick helped her relate to many Alaskans and Americans fed up with partisan political wrangling. An aspect of her maverick status is that she often seemed to play by her own rules. One example is her clear flouting of the rules she had agreed upon in the vice presidential candidate debate with Joe Biden.[17] She simply refused to answer some questions, and gave statements of her own choosing. Another example is her use of the social media sites Facebook and Twitter during the 2008 presidential campaign, but particularly after resigning as Alaska governor.[18] Her resignation from two public offices could also be seen as playing by her own rules.[19]

Palin playing by her own rules can also be viewed as a negative aspect of her personality. Her maverick tendency can be seen as an aspect of selfishness and not wanting to play by the Republican Party rules, and also as an attention-getting device. Palin's use of social media can be viewed as her way of escaping the scrutiny and often ridicule of the media. And resigning in the middle of her terms in public office could be seen as irresponsible, illustrating an inability to carry through on commitments and a lack of interest in politics. Many Alaska politicians who know Palin well strongly confirm this lack of interest.[20]

The resignations from office, championing of causes like public ethics, and apparent lack of engagement and interest in politics may well be explained by another personality trait that Palin displays – the desire for popularity and a flair for the theatrical. Political commentator Ron Reagan (son of President Reagan) has often commented that Palin is always running for something but mainly 'for attention!'[21] She seeks the limelight and was intoxicated by the adulation she received in the 2008 campaign. At the same time, she gets very defensive and often angry at criticism or when people disagree with her; and the evidence shows that, if she can, she works to get back at them. Her first book, *Going Rogue*, contains many parts justifying her actions and inactions and includes several swipes at those she had differences with, including her former legislative director, John Bitney.[22]

By all accounts, Palin was very hurt by being caricatured by actress, comedian and producer Tina Fey on the television comedy programme *Saturday Night Live*, and by her portrayal in *Game Change*. This pursuit of adulation, but inability to take criticism and laugh at herself, plus her often unfeeling attitude towards others, fuelled the speculation that she is a narcissist.[23] This intense need to be seen as popular may also help explain her apparent disengagement from politics and tendency to quit half-way though political appointments. Exposing a potential conflict of interest, as she did on the Oil and Gas Commission, and winning an election earned her accolades and were good for her ego. But doing a job in politics is often tedious, thankless and far from the public view, and may involve conflicts and being disliked by many.

Palin's apparent desire for attention and approval and the limelight may also help to explain her very opportunistic record in politics. In fact, she has been opportunistic to the point of disingenuousness in some instances. These include the 'bridge to nowhere' issue and being the standard bearer for right-wing conservative causes, such as those espoused by the anti-government Tea Party movement, including opposition to President Obama's health care reforms. From being a moderate Republican Governor of Alaska, bent on consensus building, Palin became a spokesperson for the conservative right wing during and after the 2008 election, making her one of the most divisive politicians in recent American history. This is what it took to keep her in the public eye and advance her cause. Though, as Julia O'Malley commented, it is unclear exactly what that cause was or remains.[24] All indications are that Palin does not know herself and has no grand plan other than self-aggrandizement. But no one knows for certain, and this uncertainty about her thoughts, goals and motives, the enigma that is Sarah Palin, is probably a major part of the Palin phenomenon.

Continuing prominence, 2008–12

Even following the 2008 McCain–Palin defeat, next to President Obama, Sarah Palin was likely the most talked- and written-about person in the United States. Palin was, indeed, everywhere! It was hard to escape her (and her family) in the media, in conversations and in public and private debates about her positives and negatives and her future intentions. Palin was a guest commentator on mainly right-wing news programmes, like *Fox News*. She became perhaps the most famous user of Facebook and Twitter, using them to get her political and other messages across in a forum protected from liberal critics. And she toured the country supporting candidates for the 2010 election and endorsed others, mainly right-wing Tea Party candidates or those in sympathy with the Tea Party. She, in fact, became the Tea Party's unofficial standard-bearer. In addition, she made very controversial, in some cases inflammatory, statements, such as those about health care reform in 2009 and 2010, the shooting of Arizona Representative Gabrielle Giffords in January 2011, and the Secret Service scandal involving prostitutes in April 2010. All this annoyed liberals and pleased many conservatives. The media ate it up, and kept Sarah Palin in the national limelight.

An early indication of the phenomenal interest in Palin, whether out of the hope or fear that she might get elected, came in the vice presidential debate with Senator Joe Biden on 2 October 2008. Over 73 million Americans (out of a population of 300 million) watched that debate, far more than any other vice presidential debate in television history. In numbers it ranked second to the presidential election debate of 28 October 1980 between President Carter and Ronald Reagan, which drew 81 million viewers (out of about 230 million Americans).[25] While Biden's views were probably of interest to many, likely it was Palin that most viewers tuned in to see.

It was, in fact, speculation over whether Palin would seek the 2012 Republican nomination for president that was a major reason why she got so much media exposure from Obama's victory in November 2008 until she decided not to run in early October 2011. Right up to the end of this period, Palin was characteristically enigmatic (or indecisive), and this sent the press into a frenzy of speculation.[26] She was, in fact, the leading contender. As such, she was the subject of a cover story in *Newsweek* magazine in July 2011 in which she declared 'I Can Win.'[27] Her failure to make a decision, however, began to alienate some Republicans, and she finally announced that she would not run.[28] Despite this annoyance, and disappointing her supporters for not seeking the presidency and having taken a dive in popularity in her home state, in March 2012 and close to four years after being nominated by McCain she was still very popular with Republican voters and more so than any Republican presidential candidate.

Sarah Palin's personal and political life, her psychology and her continuing popularity, in fact her star status, tell us much not only about her psyche but also about American politics.

In many ways she epitomizes what is described in this chapter as the Washington–Hollywood–Wall Street political syndrome; she also provides a perspective on the nature of American politics in the opening years of the twenty-first century.

The American economic and political environment, 2008–12

From mid-2008 to the national elections in November 2012, the United States experienced a confluence of economic and political conditions that had not occurred since the Great Depression and which produced circumstances ripe for the re-emergence of populism.

With a few minor downturns, American economic prosperity advanced steadily for 60 years after the Second World War. This was particularly so during the Clinton and George Bush, Jr administrations from 1993 onward. To be sure, the American economy, particularly its industries, had been under pressure since the early 1980s and saw the gradual transfer of many forms of manufacturing to countries with much lower labour costs in the Far East and Central America. But these changes were incremental and did not generate major public concern. All this changed with the world economic crisis that hit in the late summer of 2008. Unemployment soared to over 10 per cent; people saw the value of their houses, investments and retirement funds cut by 25 to 50 per cent; and major previously bedrock American companies, like General Motors and many in the financial services industry, either went bankrupt or sought assistance from the federal government to survive.

Fumbling to find its feet, the Obama administration that took office in January 2009 passed a stimulus package to dole out to the states and communities to try to boost the economy and bring down unemployment. It was only partly successful. By the summer of 2012 unemployment was still over 8 per cent, though the stock market had rebounded and house prices had partially recovered. Many blamed the federal government, and particularly President Obama, for these continuing problems, even though in reality the president has little control over the economy.

These economic woes spilled over, of course, into politics and exacerbated increasing political polarization in Congress and in the nation. Many Americans could not accept an African American in the White House, although this was rarely vocalized explicitly. A statement made by Senate Minority Leader Mitch McConnell – that 'the single most important thing we want to achieve is for President Obama to be a one-term president' – both helped explain and added to the polarization between the president and the Republicans.[29] In particular, the Republicans directly confronted the president on many issues, but particularly regarding his proposal for a new national health care system. The Republicans and their allies dubbed this 'socialism' and a government takeover of health care. Although a proposal was eventually passed, and in June 2012 upheld by the US Supreme Court against conservative challenges, this proved to be one of the most divisive issues since the 1960s and the Vietnam War.

The severe economic recession and concerns in many quarters regarding the policies of the Obama administration and, in some states, concern about immigration and competition with American workers rallied many conservative elements in America and spawned a new conservative force, the Tea Party, though this was more a movement than a coherent party. The movement was essentially reactive, expressing anti-immigrant sentiments, opposition to big government, and some racism, sometimes disguised in rhetoric, sometimes overt. The Tea Party elected several members of Congress in the 2010 midterm elections who vowed to change 'politics as usual' in Washington, DC by refusing to compromise and ending pork-barrel legislation.

This strong conservative reaction was bolstered by conservative TV and radio talk show hosts, like Rush Limbaugh, Glenn Beck and those on *Fox News*, all vocalizing the anti-government, anti-Washington, DC and anti-Obama rhetoric. Some of their comments and 'calls to arms' bordered on, and sometimes crossed, the line to demagoguery. In some ways, the right-wing Republican reaction also bordered on political paranoia. Its political and media advocates often claimed that they were working to rescue the Constitution and save America's democracy. Underlying all this was an intolerance of dissenting views and a political self-righteousness on the part of these commentators.

This confluence of circumstances between 2008 and 2012 provided textbook conditions for the re-emergence of populism, but these populist sentiments needed crystallizing and a leader. In an unofficial way Sarah Palin became that leader whether she intended to do so or not.

Explaining the Palin phenomenon and what it tells us about American politics

Sarah Palin's short but eventful four years on the national stage have much to say about American politics, past and present. Yet it is also evident that, while politics was the vehicle that she used (intentionally or through opportunism), the Palin phenomenon cannot be explained by politics alone.

Many of the obvious insights that the Palin phenomenon provides into US politics relate to American political exceptionalism. A major one is the way that America recruits some of its national politicians, including its presidents. These can come from the entertainment, corporate, military or sports world as much as politics. And those who do come from politics, like Palin, may be very obscure figures before they are catapulted on to the national political stage. Who, for instance, had heard of Barack Obama before his memorable speech at the 2004 Democratic Convention? But four years later he was elected president. Linked to this is the cult of personality in American politics, often trumping party affiliation and identification. This, in turn, allows for the maverick or independent political operative, which John McCain once claimed to be, Senator Joseph Lieberman of Connecticut (Al Gore's vice presidential running mate in 2000) has played to his advantage, and Sarah Palin has used as a means to her success. The instant political stardom that many of these politicians acquire put them in the Washington–Hollywood political syndrome and eventually into the Washington–Hollywood–Wall Street syndrome, as they rake in the cash from their national and often international prominence. Neither Palin nor Obama would have risen to such political prominence in virtually any other western democracy.

Other insights relate to the nature and state of American democracy, past, present and probably future. There are five of these, and Sarah Palin, while not instituting any of them, became their unofficial but powerful symbol, their avatar, intentionally or not.[30] How intensely or superficially she supported these causes is both hard to determine and irrelevant to the fact that she did and was able to keep in the political limelight by doing so. These five are: populism; the political prominence of social conservatism and family values; the ability of a small minority to have influence out of proportion to its numbers; political polarization; and a general political intolerance of opposing viewpoints.

Populism

The Palin phenomenon is the latest manifestation of a recurring aspect of American radical conservatism in political life that has strong populist overtones. The version that emerged following the economic crisis of 2008, and the election of Barack Obama, had many of the traditional elements of populism, but with some variations. Traditional elements of populism that manifested themselves were: the victim complex (victims of Wall Street, big business, the elite, Washington, DC, among other forces); racism and anti-immigrant sentiments; extolling the virtues of ordinary citizens; the longing for some bygone age when all was well; the need for radical solutions to deal with the perceived problems; and a leader who symbolized the movement and championed its causes with a charismatic zeal. Sarah Palin became that leader and relished the role.

Two new elements of this post-2008 populism, or at least new versions of a combination of the anti-elitist, anti-government and victim elements, are anti-intellectualism and a strong antipathy to the so-called liberal media. Often the focus of anti-intellectualism is the fact that Barack Obama went to Harvard, as did many of his close associates. The inference is that these are 'not ordinary people' who are the stuff of America. But, as journalist Leonard Pitts, among others, observed, this anti-intellectualism in Palin's statements lauded 'mental mediocrity' and 'mythologized' the native intelligence of ordinary folks as superior to the intelligence of well-educated members of society.[31] Palin's excoriating of the liberal media, which encapsulates how many of her supporters feel, is intertwined with the other elements of what the Palin phenomenon has to say about American politics, which we explore below.

One element of early expressions of American populism that is not part of the new variety was support for a positive role for government in putting right perceived wrongs and injustices. This had been part of the populism of the late nineteenth century and of the 1930s. It was less characteristic of the George Wallace variety of populism in the 1960s, where opposition to federal interventions to further racial integration held centre-ground. In the Palin and Tea Party-led version of populism, government is similarly seen as the problem, having become too big, too self-serving, too corrupt, and generally 'broken', as many Tea Party politicians and supporters argue. So modern American populism is anti-government as well as anti many other things.

Social conservatism and family values

This broad ideology focuses on the preservation of traditional values, based on a deep religious commitment and a particular view of morality, especially the preservation of what it considers family values. Thus social conservatives emphasize the sanctity of marriage between a man and a woman (and thus oppose gay marriage and government benefits for gay couples). They oppose abortion, euthanasia, assisted suicide, and embryonic stem cell research, and generally promote the sanctity of life. The religious element leads social conservatives to favour government aid to religious schools, a policy that many would argue is contrary to the separation of church and state in the US Constitution.

Under the broad political umbrella of American conservatism, social conservatives are on the far right of the Republican Party. Estimates and statistics vary, but they probably constitute less than 30 per cent of the Republican Party and less than 15 per cent of the American electorate.[32] Unlike many other conservatives, particularly libertarians, social conservatives support an increased role for the national government in the social affairs of its citizens, generally supporting whatever these conservatives see as morally correct choices and discouraging or outright forbidding those it considers morally wrong.[33] In addition, they have a particular view of the US Constitution that supports their agenda. They view this as how the Founding Fathers intended the nation and society to develop, and condemn all alternative views and interpretations of the Constitution. Thus social conservatism manifests elements of authoritarianism and intolerance.

With her strong religious commitment, Sarah Palin became the unofficial but willing and enthusiastic champion of this cause. She has pushed it in speeches around the nation and in entries on Facebook and Twitter, despite her own suspect credentials as a social conservative. This does not seem to matter to those who support family values, especially as Palin has been a big critic of the nemesis of the social conservative cause – Barack Obama. This is even more so since Obama came out in favour of same sex marriage in May 2012.

The ability of a small minority to exert disproportionate influence

Many of America's Founding Fathers, particularly James Madison, had a fear of the 'tyranny of the majority': that a majority of citizens could ride roughshod over the interests and needs of a minority. This was one reason why they built checks and balances into the Constitution of 1787. What many of them likely did not envision was the sort of 'tyranny of the minority' that can be imposed by a small, determined group – something made possible by these very checks and balances. This power of the minority has become a hallmark of American politics and has manifested itself on many occasions, most notably the South's ability to impose racial segregation for almost a hundred years following the Civil War. There are other less far-reaching but nevertheless significant examples of this minority power.

One of these relates to the influence of the right wing of the Republican Party, particularly the social conservatives. Since the early 1970s this faction has been able to control the party platform and insert many of its policy goals into it. However, these goals have not generally been followed by many party leaders, and particularly not by presidential candidates, as appealing to the centre, particularly for nationwide office, is key to getting elected. All this was true until the election of Barack Obama as president. Since then, an unofficial coalition of three vocal and politically active minorities – social conservatives, joined by those promoting populist sentiments, and Tea Party supporters – has been the driving force in American national politics and in many states. This unofficial political coalition has been able not only to exert major influence over the policy agenda, but also to hold the balance of power in many instances.

Leading up to and during the 2010 midterm elections these groups, partly through the actions and speeches of Sarah Palin, got major publicity and ran candidates for election. The success of Tea Party and anti-Obama forces in the congressional elections and their political inflexibility put the new Republican leadership in the House of Representatives in a difficult position in working to keep newly elected Tea Party members from undermining the unity of the Republican majority. Moreover, the national success of the combination of these minority movements forced potential Republican nominees for president to move to the right to reflect these minority positions, even though this might hurt the eventual nominee.

None of these potentially destructive political hazards for the Republican Party seemed to bother Palin as she voiced the concerns of all three minorities. Not running for office gave her the luxury of making statements that would have little immediate political consequence for her. Palin personified this view of what was wrong with America and its politics according to these amorphous minority viewpoints. Through turning her basketball reputation of 'Sarah Barracuda' into a political barracuda of fiery, often demagogic speeches, she acted as a sort of unifying force for these political minority perspectives.

Political polarization

It was in her attacks on President Obama, congressional Democrats, the so-called liberal media and anyone who disagreed with her that Sarah Barracuda was at her most animated and was able to draw a clear line between her supporters and detractors. Her actions exacerbated the atmosphere of political polarization that dogged American politics after Obama's 2008 presidential victory. This was certainly not the first time that intense polarization had occurred in America, as the pre-Civil War period, the Vietnam War and the years of President Bill Clinton's second term attest, but following the November 2008 election this polarization was particularly vitriolic and uncompromising and tended to dominate the actions of right-wing Republicans. Polarization was further fuelled by right-wing radio and television commentators, though some Democrats and liberals – particularly liberal television political talk show hosts, like MSNBC's Keith Olbermann – added to the polarization.

One significant aspect of this polarization, involving Obama and his detractors on the conservative right, was the claim that Obama was not born in the United States but in Kenya or somewhere else. This controversy dragged on. It was related to a broader issue of conflict between Palin and Obama supporters and detractors as to which of the two was more and less qualified to be president. As set out in Article II, Section 1 of the US Constitution, there are only two requirement to qualify a person to be president: to have been born in the United States; and to have reached 35 years of age. Both sides dug in their political heels on the issue. Palin's supporters saw her experience as governor and her personal and family values as good qualifications. Her detractors, including journalist Leonard Pitts and, most recently, McCain's major 2008 presidential campaign strategist Steve Schmidt, saw Palin as patently unfit to be president for many of the reasons regarding her shortcomings in politics related above.[34] The intensity of the debate and the nastiness it generated on both sides contributed to the widening gap between various liberal and conservative segments of American society. Most of all, however, this political polarization was likely a reaction among segments of American society to the first African American resident in the White House. In this regard, it is worth asking the question: would this polarization have been so intense and so dominant in American national politics had Hillary Clinton been the Democratic nominee and eventually elected to the presidency?

To be sure, Sarah Palin did not instigate this polarization, but she certainly took advantage of it and helped intensify it. In fact, her personality, style and willingness to do what it took to stay in the national limelight made her one of the foremost symbols of this widening political divide. On the one hand, there were her supporters and defenders in the media who came to her defence on almost every controversy. These supporters defended many clearly inaccurate or disingenuous statements and actions, such as Palin's assertion during the health care reform debate that there would be 'death panels' set up to decide who would get life-saving medical treatment and who would not.[35]

Her personal attacks on politicians were met with return fire from her detractors, such as journalists like Leonard Pitts, and from members of the public. One letter to the editor commented that hearing Palin's voice was as grating as 'chewing on tin foil'.[36] There was a downward spiral of a widening gap between Palin's supporters and her detractors. Neither side would give any quarter, regardless of the accuracy, suspect nature or plain inaccuracy of Palin's statements.[37] Civility was cast aside in American politics in the nation and in Congress.

This polarization, in which Palin was a central figure, has three major insights to offer into American politics. First, as the nature of the American political system means power is shared between Congress and the president, compromise and middle-of-the road politics are essential to get things done. The political polarization that occurred after 2008 made policy-making at the national level difficult at best, and sometimes impossible. Second, the politics of personality, and attacks on personalities, came to dominate over the substance of policy. And third, at least on the Republican side, there was a rewriting of recent American political history, especially invoking the name and supposed role of former President Ronald Reagan. He was invoked as a champion of the policies of the Tea Party, and as an anti-government and strong family values advocate. Reagan may have been some of these. On the other hand, he was certainly a politician who understood the need for compromise, bipartisanship and civility in politics. Palin intimated that she was a new Ronald Reagan, but his son Ron Reagan bristled at this suggestion.[38]

Intolerance of opposing viewpoints

The Obama presidency and the confluence of other circumstances have unleashed a particularly intense and vituperative brand of intolerance, often at odds with American traditions of free speech and toleration of opposing views. Though it has no monopoly on intolerance, this phenomenon is very evident on the right of the Republican Party. Here, it is mixed with a sort of moral crusade to put America right by imposing a particular view of the Constitution, denying the major element of pluralist politics that values compromise, and imposing social values held by a small minority. On these and other issues, there is closed-mindedness and a degree of authoritarianism that Sarah Palin has championed – consciously or unconsciously. This would be less of a problem if these views were politically marginalized, but their supporters have gained positions of influence and hold the balance of power in many key policy situations. Overall, this could have serious consequences for American democracy.

Other factors that account for the Palin phenomenon

Because her role in politics does not explain the Palin phenomenon completely, we need to identify other factors to account for it. One that is likely of comparatively minimal significance is that she was from Alaska. Certainly, the appeal of her television show *Sarah Palin's Alaska* helped maintain the limelight and added a dimension to her image. But, after Palin rose to national prominence, her political style, value system and personal combativeness, among other traits, said more about her personality and ambitions than about Alaskan politics and political culture. Alaska is, in fact, much less 'different, odd and mystical' than popular myth in the United States and abroad holds. Alaskans are Americans and share most American cultural values. And, while the state is conservative in many ways, it is pragmatic and not dogmatically conservative. Indeed, it is far more moderate than the forces that Sarah Palin represents nationally.[39]

So we need to identify other factors that add to the political core of the Palin phenomenon. Five are particularly instructive: serendipity or being in the right place at the right time; her enigmatic personality; her looks, ability to relate to certain people, and occasional charismatic performances; her family situation; and, perhaps most importantly, the role of the media.

Being in the right place at the right time has been a major factor in the Palin phenomenon. Her lodging of ethics complaints before she became governor got her publicity and a positive reputation in a period when Alaska was going through some political scandals. Her run for governor was done in a year when the incumbent Republican governor, Frank Murkowski, ran for re-election as one of the most unpopular governors in Alaska history. Palin would likely not have been able to beat even a moderately popular Republican governor in the primary as she did Murkowski. Moreover, that year no really strong Republican candidates ran, and her Democratic opponent had recently been defeated in a US Senate race and had a record to defend as a two-term governor. Then McCain chose her in an attempt to get the female vote, among other reasons. An African American won the White House and a major recession ensued: both enabled her, intentionally or not, to tap populist sentiments after the defeat of the McCain–Palin ticket.

Also, the three movements of social conservatism, populism and the Tea Party were looking for a leader, a symbol to represent and push their cause. Again, serendipity knocked at Palin's political door. She was far from an ideal leader, but she tried hard and did what was needed. As a consequence, most of the members of the three movements embraced her enthusiastically.

Being enigmatic, vague or non-committal in her intentions, having a rather mercurial personality, and exhibiting a roller-coaster set of erratic behaviours from charm to anger: these characteristics fed a fascination with Palin among the public and media. The major example of this was her keeping the nation guessing as to her intentions in the 2012 presidential race. More broadly, a sort of national pastime developed of trying to guess Palin's overall intentions. Was it her intention to make it big in politics, become a superstar or make a pile of money? Or was it a combination of all three? Whatever it was or is, the media lapped it up and literally millions of words and hours and hours of television and radio time were devoted to speculating about her intentions.

Then there are Palin's looks and her ability to be charismatic and relate to people. It is a fact that women in American politics are still viewed differently from men, and not only by men but by women too. This is not to say they are not taken seriously. It is to say that they are still seen as women and often viewed in the role that women have in society as wives and mothers and in some cases judged by elements of the electorate, and particularly men, in terms of their femininity or sex appeal. While there are no statistics to prove it, there is no doubt that much of Palin's appeal to men was her youth and good looks compared with most female politicians. In this regard, the question can be posed: would Sarah Palin have been so popular if she had been a late-middle-aged, dowdy female politician?

Then there is her populist appeal as a 'regular mom' and an ordinary person that endears her to many women and men. She has an uncanny ability to relate to people and can be extremely charming when she wants to be. She is, in her ability to relate to people, on a par with Ronald Reagan – whatever his son might say. She can also, on occasion, give nothing short of an electrifying speech and get a crowd almost mesmerized and cheering wildly for her. This was the case at the 2008 Republican convention. And Palin has a family which is perfect for a prime-time soap opera and for front-page exposure in tabloids like the *National Enquirer*. There are Palin's five children, her unmarried daughter Bristol with a child, the feud with Levi Johnston, the father of Bristol's child, her fisherman husband, her divorced sister (the person precipitating 'troopergate') and her thieving sister-in-law.

There are two perspectives on Palin's family situation: that of her supporters and that of her detractors. Her supporters see commitment to family as adding to Palin's charms and 'ordinariness'. Her detractors see her as selfishly exploiting her family for her own personal aggrandizement, particularly by dragging her children around the country on her campaigns and speaking tours. Palin's detractors particularly deplore her exploiting the Down's syndrome condition of her son Trig.

Whether or not Palin is a good mother is of no direct concern to us here. What is important is that the issue was, like many other aspects of her actions and personality, subject to much debate and controversy that kept people talking about her and kept her in the limelight. In fact, the confluence of additional factors identified here, combined with her political career and role, added up to keep her as front-page news, and probably will for some time to come. Again, we can pose a question: if Sarah Palin had not been in the right place at the right time, so enigmatic, attractive and good with people, with a soap opera-worthy family, would she have been in such demand as a speaker and star attraction at major political events and command major fees, fees that placed her among the top ten circuit speakers in the world?[40] And would she have been so attractive to the media who became fixated and obsessed with her?

In fact, if there is one major reason for the Palin phenomenon it is the American media's attention to her. Without this she would have been a passing fad. In a sense the media, both in the United States and internationally, made Palin and continue to do so. Despite a degree of initial fear, evidenced for instance in moderator Gwen Ifill's reluctance to keep Palin to the rules she had agreed to in the 2008 vice presidential debate, eventually the media did expose Palin's inadequacies in a major way. There were several interviews where she made herself look foolish. Palin's actions, attitude, statements and faux pas opened her up to the widely seen parodying by Tina Fey, who bears a striking physical resemblance to Palin. However much the parodies hurt Palin's feelings, she rode them for all they were worth. Lampooning Palin did not seem to reduce her great appeal among her strong supporters.

This major media attention to Palin was true of both the conservative media like *Fox News* and the more liberal media like MSNBC. And, despite her demonstrated lack of knowledge and understanding of many issues, she was invited on to news programmes, mainly conservative ones, to comment on events. There was a lively discussion among both some politicians and reporters and members of the public as to why there was so much media attention to Palin given her shortcomings. Among politicians, Mike Huckabee, former Arkansas governor, 2008 presidential contender and early favourite for the 2012 nomination, wondered why Palin got all the attention.[41] Reporter Michael Carey of the *Los Angeles Times* chided all the media attention given to the release of e-mails in June 2011 of Palin's time as governor.[42] Many of the major television networks set up operations in Juneau in anticipation of the release of the tapes and tried to hire local experts as commentators.[43] Nothing much was found in all 24,000 pages of these e-mails.

The media attention to Palin was probably due to three main factors. First is the combination of reasons, both political and personal and family related, explained above. She was a major personality and the press reported on her. Second, she was a person whom her detractors 'loved to hate', and the more they disliked her and saw her as a nonentity who had made the big time and was unqualified to be president, the more they hated her. So they were and remain fascinated by her, in some cases possessed and fixated on her, and cannot help following her every move, hoping she will self-destruct. Meanwhile, the media continues to cover her and the liberal media enjoys lampooning her. Third, media managers know a money-maker when they see one, and Sarah Palin is a money-maker for them. Public radio and television have to cover her because so do other media. The upshot is that it is a vicious cycle of giving prominent coverage to her because everyone else does.

And more – a phenomenon larger than the sum of the parts

Picking up on the 'and more' in the title of this chapter, even when we combine the political elements, the Hollywood aspects and the Wall Street angle, all this still does not entirely explain the Palin phenomenon. The total phenomenon is larger than the sum of the parts. There is 'more' to the explanation – there has to be!

Palin made so many mistakes, was ridiculed by the media, was shown to be disingenuous on many occasions, even lied, was clearly misinformed and appeared to be 'dumb' in many ways. So why was she not more or less universally dismissed and pushed aside, as was, for example, Dan Quayle (George Bush, Sr's Vice President, 1989–93), who made many bloopers, such as that he wished he'd studied Latin more in school after a visit to Latin America? Was this any worse than Palin not understanding that the Queen is not the head of government in the United Kingdom, or her not knowing the details of Paul Revere's ride during the Revolutionary War? Not only was she not dismissed for her lack of knowledge or misuse of the English language, but she was actually rewarded for it. None other than the highly respected *New Oxford American Dictionary* made her word 'refudiate' their word of the year in 2010.[44] How can all this be explained?

Furthermore, why did her apparent disingenuousness on several issues, from political ethics to federal government aid, not get her into deeper political hot water than it did? Other politicians who have gone down this road were much more severely damaged. It is difficult to explain. There is obviously a certain personal, political, cultural, even religious chemistry that combined to make Palin a phenomenon in the mercurial, hard-to-explain sense of the word 'phenomenon'. There is an element of surrealism about it.

Conclusion: the Washington–Hollywood–Wall Street American political syndrome – and more

Judging by media coverage, name recognition and the demand for her time and support of her by certain politicians, since 2008 Sarah Palin has been as prominent a figure in American politics as Barack Obama, if for different reasons. In their own ways they are both phenomena and very much products of the American political system and American culture. In fact, in the case of the Palin phenomenon, it says as much about American culture as it does about American politics, plus a lot about Palin.

In regard to American politics and the nature of American democracy, Palin's career has both positive and negative insights to offer. It illustrates the egalitarian nature of that democracy, where an ordinary citizen from a minor state can rise to national political prominence and challenge the political elite. It also shows how a political leader can enthuse a segment of the population who might not normally be interested in politics. Much of this reaching out to ordinary people was done through Facebook and Twitter, new political media in American politics. So, in this regard, again even if unintentionally or for selfish reasons, Palin has contributed to a new dimension in American political campaigning.

Less positive perhaps is the ability of someone ill informed and probably with motives other than promoting the national welfare to rise to political prominence through serendipity and Hollywood-like appeal. The Palin phenomenon also brings into relief the stark contrast between the theory – the supposed ideal of American democracy – and manifestations of its political reality. It shows how a minority viewpoint can come to hold the balance of power in politics, that political intolerance lurks just below the surface and is easily exposed, and the willingness of segments of the population to follow someone because of personality and charisma and regardless of political ability, credibility and ethical standards. This shows how paper-thin and how soft is the underbelly of the world's oldest democracy. The reason why journalist Leonard Pitts wanted Palin to declare and run for president is that he thought it might bring America to its senses and work to defeat what he saw as such an unqualified candidate.[45] By implication, it would restore his faith in American democracy and show that it was alive and well and deep-rooted. That test did not come in 2012. It may come in 2016 if Palin decides to run.

Yet Palin's brief and eventful rise to national and international stardom and the small fortune that she and her family have made from this through politics would not have been possible without the Washington–Hollywood–Wall Street syndrome aspect of American culture. A particular American factor is that Palin was simultaneously able to take advantage of all three of these elements. In particular, she was able to have a major influence on politics (or at least the media saw her as having influence) even though after July 2009 she held no political office and seemed more interested in promoting her image and making money.

There is no equivalent to this American phenomenon of the interrelationship of politics, entertainment and raking in the cash in the political culture or broader culture of other democracies. There are more or less clear lines between political careers and entertainment and making small fortunes in other democracies. Palin is certainly an extreme example of the Washington–Hollywood–Wall Street syndrome, but many American politicians fall into this syndrome after holding office. Much of this is due to the nature of the media in the United States and the apparently insatiable appetite of Americans for being entertained by famous, infamous, controversial and charismatic individuals in and out of politics.

Notes

1. See, for example, Todd S. Purdum, 'It Came from Wasilla', *Vanity Fair* (August 2009); Michael Joseph Cross, 'Sarah Palin: The Sound and the Fury', *Vanity Fair* (October 2010); Joshua Green, 'The Tragedy of Sarah Palin', *Atlantic Monthly* (June 2011).
2. Palin's two books are: *Going Rogue: An American Life* (New York: HarperCollins, 2009); and *America by Heart: Reflections on Family, Faith and Flag* (New York: HarperCollins, 2010). The most revealing books about Palin are: Scott Conroy and Shushannah Walshe, *Sarah from Alaska: The Sudden Rise and Brutal Education of a New Conservative Superstar* (New York: PublicAffairs, 2009), a very balanced treatment; and Frank Bailey, with Ken Morris and Jeanne Devon, *Blind Allegiance to Sarah Palin: A Memoir of Our Tumultuous Years* (New York: Howard Books, 2011) – Bailey, a former aide to Palin when she was governor, focuses on her weaknesses. Stephen Mansfield and David A. Holland, *The Faith and Values of Sarah Palin* (Lake Mary, FL: FrontLine, 2010) is pro-Palin. There are two other somewhat sensationalist but, in parts, revealing books: Joe McGinniss, *The Rogue: Searching for the Real Sarah Palin* (New York: Crown Publishers, 2011); and Geoffrey Dunn, *The Lies of Sarah Palin: The Untold Story behind Her Relentless Quest for Power* (New York: St Martin's Press, 2010).
3. John Heilemann and Mark Halperin, *Game Change: Obama and the Clintons, McCain and Palin and the Race of a Lifetime*, reprint edn (New York: Harper Perennial, 2010), published in Britain as *Race of a Lifetime* (London: Penguin, 2010).
4. See, for example, Nathan A. Heflick and Jamie L. Goldenberg, 'Objectifying Sarah Palin: Evidence That Objectification Causes Women to Be Perceived as Less Competent and Less Fully Human', *Journal of Experimental Social Psychology*, 45(3) (2009), 598–601; Diana B. Carlin and Kelly L. Winfrey, 'Have You Come a Long Way, Baby? Hillary Clinton, Sarah Palin, and Sexism in 2008 Campaign Coverage', *Communication Studies*, 60(4) (2009), 326–343; and Brian J. Brox and Madison L. Cassels, 'The Contemporary Effects of Vice-Presidential Nominees: Sarah Palin and the 2008 Presidential Campaign', *Journal of Political Marketing*, 8(4) (2009), 349–363.
5. Amanda Silverman, 'The First Palinologist?', *New Republic*, 1 December 2009, published online at http://www.tnr.com.
6. Unless separate references are listed, this personal and professional background on Palin is a composite of the various sources above.
7. Zaz Hollander, 'Todd Palin's Half-Sister Arrested for Burglary', *Anchorage Daily News*, 3 April 2009.
8. 'Public Opinion of Sarah Palin, September 17, 2007', Hays Research Group, Anchorage, AK, September 2007.
9. Tony Hernden, 'Sarah Palin Popularity Rating Takes a Dive', *Telegraph*, 29 December 2008, reporting a CNN poll conducted in early December 2008.

10 'Alaska Icy on Sarah Palin: Poll', *Huff Post Politics*, the online political report of the *Huffington Post*, 5 May 2012.

11 See the *Alaska Dispatch* [an online daily newspaper], 'Palin Watch' section for 21 March 2012, 'Sarah Palin More Popular than Any GOP Presidential Candidate, Poll Finds'.

12 Julie O'Malley, 'She's Everywhere But Don't Ask Where Palin Is Coming From', *Anchorage Daily News*, 28 November 2009, p. A-5.

13 Amanda Coyne and Tony Hopfinger, *Crude Awakening: Money, Mavericks, and Mayhem in Alaska* (New York: Nation Books, 2011), ix.

14 Quoted in Alan Boraas, 'Palin Aims to Offend Liberals and Entertain Conservatives', *Anchorage Daily News*, 22 January 2011, p. B-4.

15 Roger Ebert's Journal, *Chicago Sun-Times*, 5 March 2012.

16 Heilemann and Halperin, *Game Change*.

17 Patrick Healy, 'Cordial but Pointed, Palin and Biden Face Off', *New York Times*, 2 October 2008.

18 Julie O'Malley, 'The Lady Doth Refudiate on Twitter, Methinks', *Anchorage Daily News*, 21 July 2010, p. A-3; 'Palin Emerges as Facebook Phenom', *Yahoo News*, 19 September 2009, http://www.politico.com/news/stories/0909/27344.html.

19 Dan Balz, 'Yet Again, Palin Plays by Own Rules', *Washington Post*, 4 July 2009.

20 The author has talked to several Alaska public figures from both political parties, including Senator John Coghill, Representative Berta Gardner and former Representative Harry Crawford, who all attest to Palin being disengaged or uninterested in most policy issues.

21 Jennifer Epstein, 'Ron Reagan: Palin is a "Soap Opera"', *Politico*, 4 February 2011, http://www.politico.com/news/stories/0211/48871.html.

22 Sean Cockerham, 'Portrayal in Palin Book Irritates Former Aide', *Anchorage Daily News*, 23 November 2011.

23 Maureen Dowd, 'Now, Sarah's Folly', *New York Times*, 5 July 2009.

24 O'Malley, 'She's Everywhere'.

25 Lisa de Moraes, 'Biden and Palin Draw Record 73 Million to the Veep Show', TV Column, *Washington Post*, 4 October 2008.

26 Brian Naylor, 'Palin Offers No Clues on Presidential Ambitions', NPR [National Public Radio] report on *Weekend Edition Sunday*, 11 September 2011.

27 Peter J. Boyer, 'Palin Plots Her Next Move', *Newsweek*, 18 July 2011, pp. 32–39. The quote by Palin is from the cover, on which her picture appeared.

28 Martin Kaste, 'As the "Un-candidate", Palin Tests GOP Patience', NPR, *Morning Edition*, 21 September 2011; Rachel Weiner, 'Sarah Palin Not Running for President', *Washington Post*, 5 October 2011.

29 Michael M. Memoli, 'Mitch McConnell Comments on 2012 Draw White House Ire', *Los Angeles Times*, 27 October 2010.

30 Leonard Pitts, Jr, 'Dear Sarah: Say It Is So, Run for President', *Miami Herald*, 16 February 2010.

31 Ibid.

32 See various Gallup polls at http://www.gallup.com/poll/154889/Nearly-Half-Identify-Economically-Conservative.aspx?utm_source=tagrss&utm_medium=rss&utm_campaign=syndication. See also 'Support for Tea Party Falls in Strongholds, Polls Show', *New York Times*, 29 November 2011, http://www.nytimes.com/2011/11/30/us/politics/tea-party-support-falls-even-in-strongholds-survey-finds.html. ABC News, 'Tea Party Movement Looks Stalled; Half Like It Less as They Hear More', 15 April 2012, http://abcnews.go.com/blogs/politics/2012/04/tea-party-movement-looks-stalled-half-like-it-less-as-they-hear-more/.

33 See Milan Zafirovski, *Modern Free Society and Its Nemesis: Democracy, Economy, and Conservatism* (New York: Lexington Books, 2008), especially chap. 1.

34 Pitts, 'Dear Sarah: Say It Is So'; Max Whittaker, 'A Career Resurrected after McCain and Palin', *New York Times*, 8 June 2012.

35 Rachel Weiner, 'Palin: Obama's "Death Panel" Could Kill My Down Syndrome Baby', *Huff Post*, the online newspaper, 7 September 2009.

36 Monique Lussier, 'Tea Party Needs New Poster Child', letter to the editor, *Anchorage Daily News*, 29 November 2010.

37 Ross Douthat, 'Palin Made Mistakes, But Elites Treated Her Unfairly', Comment, *Anchorage Daily News*, 8 July 2009, p. A-11.

38 Epstein, 'Ron Reagan: Palin is a "Soap Opera"'.

39 Clive S. Thomas, 'Alaska', in Donald P. Haider-Markel, ed., *Political Encyclopedia of U.S. States and Regions*, 2 vols (Washington, DC: CQ Press, 2008), vol. 1, 353–364.

40 '10 Highest Paid Public Speakers In the World', Universities.com, http://www.onlineuniversities.com/blog/2010/04/10-highest-paid-public-speakers-in-the-world/.
41 Frank James, 'Mike Huckabee Wonders Why Sarah Palin Gets So Much Attention', NPR [National Public Radio], 6 December 2010.
42 'Does Sarah Palin Warrant the Media Attention She Gets?', *Los Angeles Times*, Opinion, 15 June 2011.
43 Becky Bohrer, 'State Poised to Release Palin Emails', *Anchorage Daily News*, 10 June 2011, p. A-3.
44 Andrew Malcolm, 'Sarah Palin's "Refudiate" Named Dictionary's Word of the Year', *Los Angeles Times*, 15 November 2010.
45 Pitts, 'Dear Sarah: Say It Is So'.

10 Contemporary elections

Philip John Davies

The midterm elections of 2010 were considered a success for the Republican Party. Control of the US House of Representatives changed in favour of the Republicans, who with 64 seats more than they had taken two years previously in 2008 achieved a 242- to-193-seat majority. The GOP also made gains in the US Senate, but the Democrats, bolstered by two senators elected as Independents who chose to form part of the Democratic caucus, remained in the majority in that chamber, by 53 to 47. The presidency was not on the ballot in 2010 and so, by default, the executive branch remained in the hands of Democrat President Barack Obama, first elected in 2008.

At the end of their successful 2010 campaign and election the Republicans were jubilant that their congressional seat gains and their resulting total number of House seats were the largest the party had enjoyed since the first half of the previous century. They must simultaneously have felt dismayed that an election result so comprehensively in their favour left them in charge of just one chamber in the federal government.

That disappointment is, of course, in part an inbuilt feature of the US political system. In the words of Richard Hofstadter, the Founding Fathers, led especially by the political philosophy of James Madison, believed that 'a properly designed state . . . would check . . . one branch of government with another in a harmonious system of mutual frustration'.[1] Among the tools embedded in the US Constitution to reinforce these checks, the impact of staggering the terms of office in the different branches and chambers of federal government was demonstrated well in 2010.

The mood of the voting electorate in 2010 was strongly for the Republicans, as opinion polls and election results both strongly indicated. But since the presidency and two-thirds of the US Senate were not on the ballot, the impact of that public feeling was diluted in terms of the party's share of national political offices. The 2010 result meant that at the opening of Congress in January 2011 the United States found itself with a federal government where authority was divided between the two major political parties. This has often been a feature of US government in recent years.

The American public is not unused to divided government of this kind, and it is not solely a feature of Washington politics. The 50 states generally model their political structures to reflect the national system, and with the exception of Nebraska, which uses a unicameral, non-partisan form of state government, all the rest feature party political competition for all the seats in two chambers of their legislature and for the state's executive officers, the governors. The 2010 elections nationwide left 34 of the nation's states with governments in which the governor and both chambers of the state's legislature were controlled by the same party, with the Republicans controlling about twice as many states as the Democrats. While unified party control of state government was the result in two-thirds of states, a substantial minority ended up with control of state government divided between parties. Fifteen states came out of the 2010 elections with some form of divided government, including Rhode Island, where an Independent governor faced a Democrat-controlled legislature.

It would appear that the US electorate is at least not uncomfortable with a degree of divided government. The late scholar and Director of the University of Connecticut Roper Center Everett Carll Ladd interpreted this as a positive affection for divided government on the part of some split-ticket voters, who would divide their votes between candidates of different parties, according to the offices being filled and issues of the day, in an act that he called 'cognitive Madisonianism', at least in part designed to increase the frustration between branches and chambers by adding to the natural differences of constituency the extra element of party clash and thereby pushing elected representatives towards negotiation and inter-party compromise as a necessary condition for efficient governance.[2]

If Madisonianism is an inbuilt element of a Constitution essentially drafted from a model written by James Madison, neither 'cognitive Madisonianism' nor divided government is an automatic consequence. A Gallup poll in June 2010 found 30 per cent of respondents favouring divided government, as opposed to 27 per cent who felt unified party government would be best, with 39 per cent feeling that this factor made no difference to the conduct of government. Using time series data, analyst Jeffrey Jones points out that, while aggregate public opinion figures on this issue have altered fairly modestly in a decade, they do demonstrate a reactive quality. When Democrats are in power, the Republican reaction against single party government increases, while more Democrats think it is a good idea. When Republicans are in power that breakdown shows the reverse reaction in the partisan groups.[3] It seems clear that no strong commitment exists among the American electorate to defend unified party authority for its own sake, but neither does there seem to be an overbearing demand for divided party government. Nevertheless in a system where the two major political parties may win or lose elections by quite small numbers of legislative seats, public votes or Electoral College votes, a relatively small proportion of split-ticket voters can have an impact.

Recent elections have indicated that the political parties have been relatively balanced in their electoral success. Election results have often left parties to deal with the realities of sharing divided control of branches and chambers of federal government, but unified party domination of American national government sometimes seems not far away. Four of the six federal elections from 2000 to 2010 resulted in unified party control, and both political parties have envisioned the possibility of that situation continuing to their advantage.

The closely contested election of 2000 resulted briefly in Republican control of the presidency, House and Senate. Controversy surrounded the presidential election, but a Supreme Court decision on 12 December, more than a month after the poll, halted further consideration of the very close presidential vote in Florida and propelled Republican George W. Bush to the White House. His 271 Electoral College votes legitimately trumped Democrat Vice President Al Gore's 266 in spite of the latter's popular vote advantage of about half a million. The victory may have been confirmed only six weeks before the scheduled inauguration, but the Bush team had been preparing for the presidential transition since the day after the election, and the electorate, having seen the political and legal process stagger to a conclusion, accepted the result with reasonable grace, and so it was that President George W. Bush followed in his father's footsteps to the presidency, restoring the White House to the Republicans after the interruption furnished by the Bill Clinton administration.

Bush's 2000 Court-imposed victory did not show much in the way of a coat-tails effect to benefit other federal office seekers in the Republican Party. In the House of Representatives the Republicans were a couple of seats down on their previous result, but they remained the majority party, and a four-seat Republican loss in the Senate left them with 50 seats and the Democrats with 50, but the Republicans in control of that chamber by the casting vote of the Republican vice president. In both chambers of Congress, and in the presidential election, the margins were tiny, but the significance of this close set of election results remains that George W. Bush's presidential victory helped steer his party to a position of unified party leadership in both legislative chambers and the executive for the first time in almost half a century.

With such a close result any administration would still be left with significant strategic and logistical problems of political management, but President Bush, Vice President Cheney and their team appeared ready to govern as boldly as they might be able. The advantage of leading through unified party control of the federal government was real, even if not giving the Republicans carte blanche. Unfortunately for his party, President Bush did not manage to hold this advantageous position for long. The inability of the Bush administration to resolve a dispute on agricultural policy with their own Senator Jim Jeffords of Vermont resulted in his decision to leave the GOP on 24 May 2001 to become an Independent, and consequently led to the re-emergence of a Democratic Party majority in the Senate, and the reinstallation of divided government at the federal level.

The 2001 terrorist attacks on New York and Washington, DC transformed the context of the Bush presidency. While not wholly assured, President Bush's public responses to the perceived threat achieved a combination of reassurance and reaction that met with the approval of most Americans, and public support for the way the president was doing his job grew to the highest levels ever recorded. Even at a time when voters had many other issues on their minds, this level of approbation was likely to be a factor in the 2002 and 2004 elections, when the Republicans gradually increased their majority in the House and took a clear majority of Senate seats.

By 2002 Bush had led his party to a position where it held authority simultaneously in both chambers of congress and the executive. Bush's 2004 re-election over Democrat Senator John Kerry was closer than an incumbent might have expected, but it was a clear victory, and Bush was now accompanied in Washington, DC by 232 Republicans in the House of Representatives and 55 in the Senate. They had not achieved a higher number of seats in both chambers simultaneously since the elections of 1928. This was also the best series of federal election results the Republicans had seen since the 1920s, a decade that saw the final years of a period of Republican domination that stretched back with brief interruptions to the US Civil War. Karl Rove, key adviser to President Bush, was one senior Republican strategist who saw in this series of Bush elections the opportunity to establish another long period of unified Republican control of the federal government.[4]

If George Bush's GOP was at an electoral highpoint at the opening of the 109th Congress in January 2005, problems emerged that would shatter the Republican dream of an extended period of unified party authority in the federal government. The party of the incumbent president usually does not do well in the second midterm elections, and conditions were gradually shifting to produce a 'perfect storm' for the Republican Party to face.

In August 2005 Hurricane Katrina made landfall on the Gulf Coast, flooding New Orleans and leaving a trail of damage and destruction across the region. The response of the Bush administration was faltering and inadequate, severely undermining public confidence in the Republican's management of the public agencies under their control. In addition, in January 2006 Jack Abramoff, a lobbyist closely associated with the Republican Party, pleaded guilty in federal court to charges including the corruption of public officials and as the ripples of the Abramoff case spread it became clear that Republican heads might fall. In an unrelated case

Republican Representative Randy 'Duke' Cunningham (California) had in November 2005 pleaded guilty to fraud, bribery and tax evasion charges. Another Republican Representative, Mark Foley (Florida) stepped down after revelations concerning messages sent to male congressional pages. These resignations and indictments undermined the reputation the party in the areas of financial probity and moral leadership.

On the foreign policy front there was growing and continuing public concern about the invasion and occupation of Iraq. Concern was expressed about the quality of the nation's intelligence gathering and analysis and the apparent absence of an exit strategy. Public approval for the job being done by the president was being negatively affected, falling to 38 per cent on the eve of the 2006 midterm elections, a figure lower than recorded for the incumbent president in all post-war midterms except Harry S. Truman's in 1946.[5]

In the 2006 midterms the Republican Party lost 30 seats in the US House of Representatives and six in the US Senate. Even given the shock of these losses to a party that had recently been looking forward to a period of sustained political authority, an argument can be made that the Republicans did not do as badly as they might have in the circumstances. Midterms in the sixth year of an administration are notoriously tricky, and the Bush administration's electoral performance was well within the norm. The party building that had occurred in Bush's first term had helped cushion the electoral blow in 2006, but the Republicans had still lost control of both House and Senate to the Democrats. With Bush not up for election in 2006 this returned the federal government to a position of divided party government. Furthermore, with the administration's public approval ratings continuing to decline, and the Republicans facing the problem of having to choose a candidate to replace the term-limited Bush before the 2008 general election, it was now the Democrats' turn to see the potential to take firm control of the federal government.[6]

This was widely reported as the first presidential election campaign since 1928 featuring no attempt by an incumbent president or vice president to gain their party's nomination, and Michael Nelson goes so far as to say that:

> Not since George Washington was unanimously chosen as the first president in 1788 had there been an election in which it was clear from the outset that neither the incumbent president nor the incumbent vice president would be on the ballot.[7]

The unusual openness of the election prompted many hopefuls to enter the field. This emphasized a trend that has been apparent in recent elections, as active campaigning for the nominations started earlier than ever, and some hopefuls for the nomination invested heavily only to disappear from the race at a very early stage.

Among the Republicans, Jim Gilmore, former Governor of Virginia, declared, but became an early casualty, withdrawing from the race six months before the primary season opened. Former Governor of Wisconsin Tommy Thompson left the race about the same time, after a poor showing in an Iowa straw poll. Sam Brownback, then US Senator from Kansas, lasted three months longer. After nearly three years of campaigning Tom Tancredo, then US Representative from Colorado, pulled out of the race just days before the Iowa caucus. Duncan Hunter, then US Representative from California, did not last through January 2008. The battle between the Republicans left competing for the party nomination was more brief than had been expected, with none of the following – Ron Paul, US Representative from Texas and the 1988 Libertarian Party nominee for the presidency, Fred Thompson, former US Senator from Tennessee and TV actor, Rudy Giuliani, former New York City mayor, Mitt Romney, former Governor of Massachusetts, and Mike Huckabee, former Governor of Arkansas –

managing to match the steady progress to the nomination of Senator John McCain of Arizona. By March it was clear that McCain would be the Republican nominee.

There was a similar range of Democratic hopefuls. Senator John Edwards (North Carolina), Senator Evan Bayh (Indiana), Senator Joe Biden (Delaware), General Wesley Clark, Governor Howard Dean (Vermont), Senator Chris Dodd (Connecticut), Senator Russ Feingold (Wisconsin), Representative Dennis Kucinich (Ohio), Senator Mike Gravel (Alaska), Governor Bill Richardson (New Mexico), Governor Tom Vilsack (Iowa) and Governor Mark Warner (Virginia) had some early presence in the nomination contest. Many of these too did not have the campaign strength to reach the first hurdle of the primaries, and almost all fell out of the race very soon thereafter, leaving Senator Barack Obama and Senator Hillary Clinton to battle through the whole of the presidential primary season before it became clear that Obama would be the nominee.

The party with the most contentious primary battle is traditionally felt to be at a disadvantage in the general election, but while the Democratic contest had taken three months longer than the Republican race to confirm the nominee the Republicans appeared to come out of the nomination period most wounded. McCain had emerged from a field that represented the cross-cutting ideological and cultural divisions in the Republican Party. The evangelical Huckabee, the libertarian Paul and the Mormon Romney had commanded support from enthusiastic minorities, but not enough broad support within the party to take the nomination, yet at the same time their supporters were not energized by the thought of a McCain administration. These voters were very unlikely to defect to support a Democrat, but without enthusiasm for a candidate some were just not likely to turn out. On the other hand the Democrats, even after a gruelling and very costly campaign, did not disturb the fault lines of their own electoral coalition, and their campaign had a compelling cultural resonance, since the Democrats were making a choice between a woman and an African-American. Either would be an exciting first for a major US political party. Once the Clinton campaign conceded, the two camps managed the difficult post-primary healing process with some skill, symbolized by Senator Clinton casting her delegation's votes for Obama at the Democratic National Convention in August.

The polls indicated a close race, but other actions were symptomatic of a different feeling. Obama chose a traditional vice presidential candidate, the well-established Senator Joe Biden, to balance the Democratic ticket and appeal to the mainstream. McCain chose the unknown, untraditional and untried Governor of Alaska, Sarah Palin, in an apparent attempt to unbalance feminists while appealing to the Republican right. Incumbent President Bush's public approval ratings continued to fall, further dampening Republican hopes. The September bankruptcy of Lehman Brothers shook the financial world and signalled a banking crisis of historic proportions that eliminated whatever chances the Republican campaign may have had. As the issue of the economy became more salient, overshadowing issues like terrorism and defence (where McCain's experience resonated with the electorate), so Obama's attraction waxed and McCain's waned.

The Democrats were working from the solid office-holding base in Congress that they had established in 2006. They had another advantage in the 2008 elections, since about two-thirds of the Senate seats being contested in that year's elections were currently held by the Republicans. The GOP presented a large target in 2008, and the Democrats were having a good year. November 2008 brought Obama victory with around 53 per cent of the vote, and a lead over McCain of about 7 per cent. The last Democrat to obtain a higher proportion of the presidential vote was Lyndon Johnson in 1964. The last non-incumbent Democrat to obtain a higher proportion of the presidential vote was Franklin Roosevelt in 1932. While no landslide, the 2008 presidential election was a considerable success for the Democrats. Added to this the Democrats did unexpectedly well in the Senate elections. They won 59 seats, although the Minnesota election was so close as not to be confirmed until July 2009. Before then, in April, incumbent Senator Arlen Specter (Pennsylvania) had crossed the floor to join the Democrats, providing the Democrats with a 60-seat majority. More gains in the House brought the Democrats to a 257-to-178 lead over the Republicans. Once again the USA had a unified party government. The Democrats had taken control from the Republicans, and one party had come out of the elections in authority simultaneously in the White House and both chambers of Congress for the fourth time in five elections. This rare occurrence in recent decades fired the imagination of both major political parties.

There had not been such a series of elections resulting in unified party control at federal level since the 1960s. At that time the Democrats were enjoying an extended period of success in congressional elections, and in the elections of 1960 and 1964 the voters had put first John Kennedy and then Lyndon Johnson into the White House. These mid-twentieth-century elections marked the end of an era when unified party control was more often the result of federal elections, and the beginning of a generation of divided government.

From the earliest US federal elections up to and including the elections of 1966 the result had been unified party control of the presidency, the US Senate and the US House of Representatives 73 per cent of the time.[8] In the generations from 1896 to 1966 the average had been slightly higher, at 81 per cent. This consistent preference in the American electorate for unified party government came to an abrupt halt in 1968, not to show any signs of returning for another generation. From 1968 up to and including 1998 unified party government results occurred in only 19 per cent of election years. From a norm throughout US history of 73 per cent unified party government, and an early twentieth-century standard of 81 per cent the situation had completely reversed. In the last third of the twentieth century divided government resulted in 81 per cent of election years, making this generation of elections unique in American electoral history.

It might be expected that the leading strategists of both major parties must at times have yearned for a return to the time when elections tended to produce unified party control. In a system already structurally separated and balanced by the terms of the US Constitution, extra-constitutional structures such as political parties provide the oil for the grinding wheels of government – nowhere more obviously than in the legislative process, where both chambers of Congress and the president are involved in the making of the laws, and the political community has to work against the background of varying constituency interests and regional differences embedded into the federal government structure in order to create law that appears fair, reasonable and fit for purpose to the electorate.

But Democrat and Republican leaderships might well hark back to different unified eras. The Democratic Party was dominant in federal government for a generation from the 1930s to the late 1960s. There were occasional Republican successes, certainly enough to see that the Democrats did not get everything their own way, but the GOP breakthroughs were brief in these decades. This Democratic ascendancy, coming after the economic debacle of the Great Crash of the late 1920s, itself followed an even longer period of Republican domination at the national level. From 1860, when Abraham Lincoln came to the presidency and led the nation at a time of Civil War, to the late 1920s it had been the Republican Party that was dominant and the Democrats who were winning occasional but unsustained breakthroughs.

That had been the nature of electoral politics in the USA for more than a century up to the late 1960s: extended periods of unified party control by first the Republicans and then the Democrats, with the out-of-favour party retaining enough broad-based support to maintain its competitive challenge and occasionally to break through and have a brief period of its own unified party control. The less common appearance of divided party control usually signalled a shift into one of the temporary breakthrough periods or, in the late 1920s and early 1930s, a period when authority was shifting for some time from one party to the other.

Realignment theory attempted to explain these cycles, identifying that the shifts between party dominance were associated with 'critical elections' or brief series of critical elections, when the electorate were responding to factors such as significant shifts in the key issues that underpinned the identification of political differences, sometimes prompted by national crises such as war, or major economic threat and restructuring. Change appeared associated with periods of sharp growth in the electorate, and especially the entry of groups with different agendas to those that had become traditional in those times, and accompanying shifts in the electoral coalitions supporting the political parties. And, while there was sometimes a break between old party agendas and the ambitions of new electorates, there were changes in the parties themselves as they adapted to the shifting context of federal politics. The Republican Party of the 1860s, emerging from various grassroots predecessors and radical in the moral underpinnings of its stand on the US Civil War and its aftermath, was very different to the Republican Party of the 1920s, a middle-class, business-supporting entity that in the end could not envision the kind of leadership needed to tackle the economic crisis of the time, but which had till then satisfied the electorate through a substantial period of immense economic change and expansion.

For eight years after the 1968 election a Republican president faced a Democratic Congress, but in the wake of Republican President Nixon's Watergate scandal it was Democrat Jimmy Carter who won the presidential election in 1972, and Democrats hoped they were back to the historical norm of unified political authority and to the post-New Deal norm of Democratic Party dominance. This expectation failed when Carter lost to Ronald Reagan in 1980, and the Republicans also gained a majority in the US Senate. When Reagan was re-elected in 1984, again with a Republican majority in the Senate, he and his party in their turn hoped that this indicated a return to the historical norm of unified party control in federal government, only in favour of the Republicans, who felt that a restructured political majority in their support was due, and had somehow been derailed, possibly by the ripples from Watergate, as well as the reduced trust in government evident in the wake of the Vietnam War. President Reagan showed how conscious was commitment of the party leadership and strategists to nurturing the birth of this remodelled political majority when he declared, at his re-election in 1984, that 'realignment is real'.[9] But, if he was not wrong in his assessment, he was certainly premature.

Contrary to the hopes of President Reagan and his Republican colleagues the federal elections of the last third of the twentieth century continued in contrary mode. When Reagan left office Republican George H. W. Bush entered the White House, but, rather than seeing his party take the essential step for unified party control of adding the House of Representatives to its holdings, his party lost ground, he faced a Democrat-controlled Congress, and his relatively weak executive performance again gave the Democrats the opportunity to look forward to consolidating their position. This they did in the election of 1992, which put President Bill Clinton in the White House, and elected Democrat majorities in both House and Senate, but once again this was not to be a return to the stability of previous political eras. Only two years later the Democrats had again lost control of the Senate and, more shockingly for them, had lost control of the US House of Representatives, something that had only happened twice (in 1946 and 1952) since the end of the 1920s.

The Republicans held on to Congress, and while they failed to unseat President Clinton in 1996 they looked forward to 2000 as an election year from which they could emerge in control of both the presidency and Congress, and from which base they might establish a long-term position of national political authority. The Republican Party's qualified success in 2000, followed by considerable gains in 2002, prompted President Bush's senior adviser Karl Rove to voice his sense of the re-established potential for the Republican Party:

> things are beginning to move in one direction. . . . Something else more fundamental is happening there, but we will only know it retrospectively, in two years or four years or six years [when] we look back and say the dam began to break in 2002.

In particular he claimed a 'pretty dramatic' growth in Republican identification among young voters, a shift in the gender gap that has generally given the Democrats a significant advantage among women voters, and indications of Republican Party attraction to Hispanic voters, especially on family values issues. Each of these factors, opined Rove, could contribute to 'a significant trend' towards the building of a generation-long Republican majority.[10]

As we have seen, the early elections of the twenty-first century brought some of what Rove hoped for. There was a series of Republican victories unlike any since the 1920s. Economic crisis at home and military stalemate in Iraq helped the Democrats interrupt that series of election results and in 2008, led by the first non-white US president, achieve a Democratic victory encompassing the presidency, House and Senate. The 2010 elections burst any emerging Democratic bubble, as the congressional results swung sharply towards the Republicans, and the Democrats lost seats everywhere and lost control of the House, bringing divided government back to the capital.

America's voters did not give the Obama administration a long honeymoon. In October 2008 Republican candidate John McCain, who had thus far benefited from a public perception that he had leadership experience that Obama may have lacked, had lost this advantage. In a Gallup poll only two-thirds as many felt that McCain 'has a clear plan for solving the country's problems' as had the same expectation of Obama.[11] At the same time it was becoming clear that the issue concerns of the remaining swing voters matched more closely those of Obama supporters than McCain supporters. While the economy ranked top for all groups, Obama supporters and swing voters agreed that jobs, health care, education and energy were the next most important issues, while, of these, McCain voters included only energy, alongside taxes, terrorism and Iraq, in their top five.[12] While this disjunction worked to the Democrat candidate's advantage in the 2008 election it also helped to identify and structure the strong opposition that coalesced against the administration once in office.

It can be argued that the Obama White House initially showed considerable skill in its legislative work. By choosing issues carefully, compromising when necessary and adopting a clear leadership role when appropriate the president gained a notable success rate in promoting legislation through Congress. On issues where the president took a position in his first year of office he achieved a 98.7 per cent success rate in the Senate, and 94.5 per cent in the House, the highest scores since this calculation was first made in the 1950s.[13] But simultaneously the president's public opinion approval ratings had fallen faster than those of any recently elected president in the first year in office. The Obama administration had initiated health care reforms, passed anti-recession legislation and had foreign policy successes, but the unemployment rate had remained doggedly high in the face of an economic crisis in the west, the country had a jaded perspective on US international policies after ten years of War on Terror, and health care proved a policy area possibly even more controversial than the administration expected.

In an interview published on the eve of the 2010 elections Senate Minority Leader Mitch McConnell said: 'The single most important thing we want to achieve is for President Obama to be a one-term president.'[14] To express this level of single-mindedness is unusual in US politics, but McConnell's stated objective does seem to have informed Republican Party strategy considerably since 2008. The 2009 Obama stimulus bill received no Republican support in the House of Representatives. This was thought unusual in a legislature that commonly has small numbers of members crossing partisan lines on individual issues, but the Republican leadership had decided to define the bill as a profligate expenditure of tax dollars, rather than accept the Democrat view that it was an investment in jobs in the face of recession. In a polity where Republican identifiers have increasingly complained that taxation levels are too high it is hard for an incumbent to support a bill that the leadership are projecting as an attack on taxpayers.

Decisions in the US Senate are generally made by simple majority vote, but there are protections for the minority, and the only way to guarantee avoiding a minority blocking the passage of legislation by use of a filibuster is to wield a 60-vote majority. With the Democrats holding 59 Senate seats, any Republican who supplied the 60th vote would be particularly vulnerable to retribution. In the event three Republican senators supported the stimulus bill, Susan Collins and Olympia Snowe, both of Maine, and Arlen Specter (Pennsylvania), who was shortly to change his party designation to Democrat. Specter commented: 'I think there are a lot of people in the Republican caucus who are glad to see this action taken without their fingerprints, without their participation.'[15]

The health reform battle dominated the first year of the Obama administration. Health care policy attracts the concern of many Americans, but, if some are worried about the breadth of coverage, others feel more threatened by the costs, both individually and as taxpayers. Health care provision in the USA is firmly based on the principle of purchasing insurance, and is not perceived as a social service. Debates about extending the breadth of coverage and controlling costs through government intervention rather than relying on market forces therefore also stir ideological questions about the role of the state in people's lives. The Obama administration's health care review provided a clear and tangible topic around which opposition could organize. The Republicans maintained formidable discipline in Congress and, after Republican Scott Brown unexpectedly won the special election held in Massachusetts to fill the seat previously held by Democrat and staunch health reform supporter Senator Edward Kennedy, the Democrat expectation of 60 relatively reliable votes in the Senate collapsed.

President Obama took the option of moving forward quickly. The Patient Protection and Affordable Care Act, based on the legislation passed in the Senate on 24 December 2009, with some rapidly negotiated adaptations, was signed into law in March 2010, and in parallel with the Health Care and Education Reconciliation Act this constituted the content of the Obama health care reforms. The Obama administration delivered health care reform in line with its campaign promises, but did not receive wholehearted plaudits as a result. Supporters of reform felt that an opportunity to do more had been lost. Opponents felt angered not just by the reform, but by the legislative manipulation by which it had finally been passed. Early polls suggested that, while over 40 per cent of the electorate supported the reforms, more than half the respondents did not. To add more complexity, about two-thirds of opponents felt the reforms went too far, but almost one-third of them thought they had not gone far enough. Once again, while health care had been identified by the electorate as one of the major issues to be tackled, an administration found only electoral punishment in doing so.

At the beginning of the second decade of the twenty-first century both major political parties have developed strategies that attempt to leverage the best results for themselves in a divided government, but both can still hope that recent elections might signal a return to an elections process that results in unified party control of the federal government, and both can envisage being the dominant party in that system.

In 2012 the Republicans attempted to fulfil Mitch McConnell's hope that President Obama would be a one-term president, and, with approval ratings at the beginning of election year as poor as those of one-term President Jimmy Carter, their hopes were high. The fervour that developed over health care legislation still lingered. A perception that any benefits from stimulus legislation were difficult to identify stimulated Republican enthusiasm to see Obama removed, and public opinion polls saying that almost 60 per cent of respondents believed that increasing government spending hurts the economy suggested the possibility of a fertile response to this view.

Before having the opportunity to unseat President Obama the Republicans had to choose their nominee, and this task did not prove simple in the 2012 election season. The formal primary season begins in Iowa in the January of election year, but pre-primary activities have become an increasingly significant part of the nomination process, and the contest has now spread well back into the year before. A gruelling and lengthy programme of television interviews, media investigation and election debates threw a range of hopefuls to the front of the pack, only for them then to withdraw, lose financial support or be wounded by allegations of misconduct, evidence of poor grasp of the issues and other gaffes. The result at the beginning of 2012 was a series of public opinion polls suggesting that respondents preferred 'a Republican' to Obama, but, when a the choice was posited between a Republican named from among the hopefuls, Obama was almost always preferred by a small majority.

In the Senate the Republicans were advantaged by the fact that they held only one-third of the seats up for election in 2012. This time the Democrats offered the large target. In the House the Republicans were defending a solid majority. Public disaffection with Congress was even stronger than with the president, but was more generalized and less partisan. The Republicans hoped that the balance of public opinion on contemporary significant issues would help them to come out of the 2012 elections with unified party control of the presidency and congress, and they looked forward to the potential of carrying that unified control into future elections.

The Democrats hoped that they could successfully defend their electoral positions, particularly through the campaign to re-elect President Obama. This would be likely to result in extending a period of divided party government, but the leadership of the Democratic Party could maintain the hope that any electoral difficulties represented a temporary downturn in an electoral pattern that was steadily moving in the Democrats' favour. In 2008 Obama won 66 per cent of voters under 30, a similar proportion of Hispanics, and 95 per cent of black voters, compared with 54 per cent, 53 per cent and 88 per cent in 2004. Turnout among black and Hispanic voters also grew, reducing the proportion of non-Hispanic white voters from 77 per cent in 2008 to 74 per cent in 2004. Obama's gains magnified those already made by the Democrats in demographic groups that are increasing as a proportion of the population, and with some of those groups, especially the young, indicating more racial tolerance, more support of active government, more anti-war sympathies and more liberal political views.

Ruy Teixeira and John Halpin argue that:

> the shifting demographic composition of the electorate – rising percentages of communities of color, single and highly educated women, Millennial generation voters, secular voters, and educated whites living in more urbanized states or more urbanized parts of states – clearly favors Democrats and has increased the relative strength of the party in national elections in recent years. In contrast, the Republican Party's coalition of older, whiter, more rural, and evangelical voters is shrinking and becoming more geographically concentrated and less important to the overall political landscape of the country.[16]

A report by the Pew Center concentrating on age cohorts confirmed that even in a difficult year the support for the Obama administration remained stronger among the most racially and ethnically diverse Millennial voters (aged 18–30), and weaker among older, less diverse generations.[17]

Political parties and candidates will always bring their strongest efforts to an election campaign, but with both parties feeling within reach of the opportunity to lead federal governments with unified party control those efforts are likely to be even more intense. If there is a return to unified party control – a form of modern realignment – it may not have the same character as the model that disintegrated in the late 1960s. The regional and ideological bases of the parties have altered simultaneously, as conservative southern voters have found a more comfortable political home with the Republican Party, and more liberal Republicans in other regions have deserted their old party.

In the mid-1950s many analysts thought that the emergence of more ideologically coherent political parties would be one route towards the exercise of greater responsibility in politics.[18] The new political parties are more ideologically coherent, and there is some evidence that campaigns and elections are more national in character than in the last century, but former Democratic Speaker Tip O'Neill's dictum that 'All politics is local' remains evident in the relationship between constituent and representative. This relationship has laudable qualities, but it may conflict with a sense of taking seriously collective party responsibility for policy that would otherwise emerge as a political party becomes more disciplined on ideological lines, leading to a party system that is more ideologically driven, but no more responsible in its actions. Voter reaction may, of course, impose the responsibility in time.

Tighter party coalitions, strong party leadership, less cross-partisan courtesy in Congress, the increasing requirement for 60 per cent majorities to get legislation through the US Senate, and the prospect of more close elections as each party attempts to establish its political advantage long-term seem likely to generate a continuing series of fierce election campaigns. Along the way we shall discover whether the divided government system of the last third of the last century is going to continue or whether the fleeting indications of unified party control in a new and contemporary context will coalesce into a long-term structure of federal party politics.

Notes

1 Richard Hofstadter, *The American Political Tradition* (New York: Vintage, 1948).
2 Everett Carll Ladd, 'The 1988 Elections: Continuation of the Post-New Deal System', *Political Science Quarterly*, 104 (1989), 1–18.
3 Jeffrey M. Jones, 'Americans Lack Consensus on Desirability of Divided Government', 2010, http: www.gallup.com/poll/139742/Americans-lack-consensus-desirability-divided-gov.aspx.
4 Philip J. Davies, 'A New Republican Majority', in Iwan Morgan and Philip J. Davies, eds, *Right On? Political Change and Continuity in George W. Bush's America* (London: Institute for the Study of the Americas, 2006).
5 Rhodes Cook, *The Rhodes Cook Letter*, 7(6) (December 2006).
6 See also Philip J. Davies, 'Bush's Partisan Legacy and the 2008 Elections', in Iwan Morgan and Philip J. Davies, eds, *Assessing George W. Bush's Legacy: The Right Man?* (New York: Palgrave Macmillan, 2010).
7 Michael Nelson, 'The Setting: Diversifying the Presidential Talent Pool', in Michael Nelson, ed., *The Elections of 2008* (Washington, DC: CQ Press, 2010).
8 Philip J. Davies, *US Elections Today* (Manchester: Manchester University Press, 1999), 63.
9 John Kenneth White, 'Partisanship in the 1984 Presidential Election: The Rolling Republican Realignment', Paper delivered at the 1985 Northwest Political Science Association Annual Meeting.

10 Karl Rove, 'What Makes a Great President?', 2002, Lecture at the University of Utah Rocco C. Siciliano Forum, http://www.hnn.us/articles/1529.html.
11 Gallup, 'Election 2008 Topics and Trends', 2008, http://www.gallup.com/poll/17785/Election-2008.aspx#3.
12 Pew Research Center, 'Obama's Lead Widens', 21 October 2008, http://people-press.org/reports/pdf/462.pdf, 24.
13 Sarah A. Binder, 'President Obama's Partisan Support in Congress', Brookings Institution, 2010, http://www.brookings.edu/opinions/2010/0113_obama_congress_binder.aspx.
14 Major Garret, 'After the Wave', *National Journal*, 42(43) (October 2010), 60–61.
15 Ryan Grim, 'Specter: Republican Support Stimulus, Don't Want "Fingerprints" on It', *Huffington Post*, http://www.huffingtonpost.com/2009/02/13/specter-republicans-suppo_n_166875.html.
16 Ruy Teixeira and John Halpin, *The Path to 270: Demographics versus Economics in the 2012 Presidential Election* (Washington, DC: Center for American Progress, 2011), http://www.americanprogress.org/issues/2011/11/path_to_270.html.
17 Pew Research Center, 'The Generation Gap and the 2012 Election', 3 November 2011, http://www.people-press.org/2011/11/03/the-generation-gap-and-the-2012-election-3/.
18 American Political Science Association, 'Towards a More Responsible Two-Party System: A Report of the Committee on Political Parties', *American Political Science Review*, 44(3, part 2, supplement) (1950).

11 American campaign finance in comparative perspective

Dean McSweeney

Money for election campaigns is both a necessity and a risk. It is essential to create an informed electorate who turn out to vote in large numbers to confer public legitimacy on the outcome. Printed and electronic communications, campaign events, the specialized campaign techniques such as polling, and professionals who supply them all need money. Yet raising the money to fund these essential expenditures has the potential to warp and undermine democratic processes. Inequalities of money can translate into inequalities of information and persuasiveness, restricting the competitiveness of an election. Suppliers of campaign funds may gain leverage in government as a reward for their donations. In seeking funding, parties and candidates may pander to the interests of individual and organized donors. Elections then risk becoming channels of private advantage rather than a means to securing the public interest.

These dangers lurk in any democracy, and in each country preventative methods have been introduced, particularly in the last 40 years. Several book-length collections have documented these methods, and the political events and controversies surrounding their inception.[1] Such studies are informative about legal regulations and the circumstances in which they were adopted. This approach is less forthcoming about the broader national political and financial environment which shapes the quantities and sources of money available, and the incentives for investing it for political purposes. Campaign finance, I suggest, is better understood if we comprehend who needs funds and for what purposes (demand), and what are the sources and quantities of supply. Demand and supply set challenges for regulators. Their regulatory response, in turn, promotes adaptations in behaviour by those who need money and those who give it.

This chapter illustrates the value of demand, supply and comparison to understanding US campaign finance. It explains why money is needed in such large quantities in the US and by whom. It then shows how money is supplied and the incentives at work in American political giving. There is then a summary of the principal components of US campaign finance law and how it has created innovations in supply and demand. Comparisons are made with other western democracies which show that the US confronts distinctive challenges in controlling supply and demand and its regulatory regime is unusual in both form and effects.

Demand

American elections are notoriously costly, so there is a vast demand for campaign money. One source of high demand is the quantity of elections. Having approximately 525,000 elected positions in federal, state and local government gives the US the highest ratio of elected officials per head of population in the world. That number of general elections is then more than doubled by the parties' primaries which precede them to decide the candidates eligible to contest the election. At federal level in 2008 just 470 officials were chosen: the president, vice president, 33 senators and 435 representatives. Yet the presidential contest alone required over 100 separate primary and caucus contests in states and territories prior to the November election. More than 900 primary elections were needed to select the two major parties' candidates for the general elections for Congress. This volume of election campaigns is without parallel anywhere else in the world.

Demand for campaign money from parties is intensified in the US because they have no formal membership. In most of the other long-established democracies, parties recruit a mass membership. Members provide a supply of year-round activists who become involved in campaigns at election time. They also provide a regular source of income in advance of election campaigns. In contrast, US major parties have never sought to create a fees-paying membership, depriving them of a source of funds. Instead, their funds have had to come exclusively from individuals and groups external to their organizations, much of it raised specifically for campaign purposes.

The large size of American electorates and constituencies is another reason for the expense of campaigns. This is particularly the case in the federal elections. Approximately 200 million Americans were registered voters at the time of the 2008 presidential election. No other country has this many voters eligible to choose one public official. These voters were spread across 3.5 million square miles in the fourth-largest country in the world. Other US elections have electorates far larger than in most other democracies. US senators, governors and other state-wide officials serve populations with a median size of 4.5 million. Larger states like California, Texas and New York contain more people than most of the world's nation states. The average US representative serves a population of more than 700,000. In most European countries, by contrast, there are fewer than 100,000 people per member of parliament. Campaigning effectively in constituencies this size is capital intensive. Candidates travel prodigious distances to meet voters. Expensive communication forms such as television advertising and direct mail are necessary to reach voters in large numbers. Reaching the largest television audiences requires paying the rates charged by popular stations during prime-time viewing hours. The multiplicity of television and radio stations fragments audiences between many broadcasters, compelling campaigns to disperse their advertising across many outlets to reach the electorate.

Whilst television advertising is expensive in all countries, the US is unusual in its availability for use by candidates, parties and interest groups in election campaigns. In contrast, countries including the UK, France, Denmark and Belgium ban television election advertising. Others, including Germany and Australia, confine it to commercial channels, restricting its worth as a means of reaching large numbers of voters because they are barred from state-run channels. Where any television advertising is permitted, it is usually available only to political parties, excluding individual candidates and interest groups. Australia, Canada and Germany are amongst the countries in which television campaign advertising is monopolized by parties. Only Italy and the US, amongst the western democracies, accept advertising from candidates.[2]

Absent from the US are free election broadcasts for political parties. This form of cost containment exists in many advanced industrial democracies, including Australia, the UK, France and Germany. Advertising slots are allocated to political parties, enabling them to reach large numbers of voters with messages entirely under their control without having to pay for air time. Though the parties have to pay production costs, the limited number of slots available contains their total expense. But in the US no such in-kind ben-

Table 11.1 Sources of spending, federal elections 2008

Source	$ m.	%
Candidates (for president and Congress)	3,126	52.3
Parties (national, state, local)	1,631	27.3
Interest groups (PACs, 527s, 501s)	1,221	20.4
Individuals	2	—
Total	5,980	100

Source: David B. Magleby and Anthony Corrado, eds, *Financing the 2008 Election* (Washington, DC: Brookings Institution, 2011).

efit is available. No ads are free to air. Nor is there a restriction on the number that can be purchased, encouraging well-financed campaigns to inundate viewers with ads in the attempt to persuade and mobilize as many as possible. During the 2008 federal and guber-natorial elections over 2.1 million ads were broadcast by candidates, parties and groups. The presidential contest alone accounted for over a million ads, principally sponsored by the candidates. Between June and election day, Obama aired 437,000 ads and McCain, despite the spending restrictions imposed by his acceptance of public funding, broadcast another 337,000. Though fewer in number, ads were plentiful in other contests too. Even the average contest for the House of Representatives deployed close to a thousand ad broadcasts.[3]

In American elections thousands of candidates of the same party spend on simultaneous, separate campaigns. All candidates create their own campaigning organization and mount individual fund-raising efforts. Media advertising is paid for by and promotes individual candidates. Professional campaign services such as polling, ad production, press relations and fund-raising are contracted to each candidate. Nor is it just candidates who prevent parties monopolizing American campaigning, for interest groups and individual citizens are also involved in financing independent campaign activities. As Table 11.1 shows, candidates were the largest source of spending in 2008, more than half the total and close to double the amounts spent by national, state and local parties combined. Although there are separate campaign efforts, some share a common purpose of electing the same candidate or defeat-ing their opponent but through independent activities. In the 2008 presidential election, for example, campaigns aimed at electing Obama or defeating McCain were run by the candi-date's own organization Obama for America, the Democratic National Committee, Demo-cratic Party state committees, interest groups including the Service Employees International Union, the American Federation of Teachers, Health Care for America Now and MoveOn. org, as well as efforts mounted by several individuals.

Candidate-centred campaigns lack the economies of scale of elections dominated by parties. Where parties dominate campaigning, duplication of effort is avoided and costs are curbed. The party name conveys a reputation which attracts votes independent of the identity of its candidates, reducing their need to generate a personal appeal to win office. A party campaign benefits all of its candidates without incurring their individual effort or expense.[4] In addition, professional campaign services are contracted to the party to the benefit of all candidates.

Supply

Lavishly funded US elections are made possible by the number of individuals and groups prepared to invest in campaigns, and the sums they are prepared to expend. This is facilitated by the wealth of the United States and the greatest inequality of income distribution amongst the affluent democracies of the First World, resulting in large numbers of people with large disposable incomes.[5] In addition to saving and spending on luxuries, large sums are donated to others. In his discussion of American exceptionalism, Lipset notes that private philanthropy has gone further there than in any other country in the world.[6] In 2008, Americans donated approximately $200 billion to charitable, educational, religious and other philanthropic activities.[7]

Whilst giving to election campaigns is not philanthropy, the two are related, because they are both dependent upon having large amounts of disposable income, so campaign-giving is particularly widespread amongst the wealthy. For example, over the 2007–08 election cycle, a third of the richest 5 per cent of the population helped to fund an election campaign. Amongst income percentiles 68–95, 18 per cent donated to a campaign. Moreover, those who raise for and give to philanthropic causes overlap with those who perform these functions in election campaigns.[8] Those who solicit for one cause are themselves solicited for others, and giving involves helping friends and associates to promote their favoured causes, whether charitable, religious, educational or political.

Within these money-raising networks, personal relationships facilitate political donations.[9] People are more likely to give if they are asked rather than to take the initiative in making a contribution, and giving is more likely if the request is made by someone known to the donor. Personal interactions between givers to philanthropic causes extend into campaign fund-raising. When requests come from acquaintances whose help in raising money may be needed in future, there is an obligation to give in the expectation of sustaining relationships and reciprocity in responding to solicitation in the future.

This dependence on relationships, and interconnections between different types of giving, hints that motives other than politics can stimulate campaign donations. Rather, givers can be motivated by material or social (solidary) incentives rather than political ends. They are 'investors' or 'intimates' rather than 'ideologues', as Francia *et al.* expressed it in a study of contributors to congressional elections. Investors seek material gains, such as a job or business contact, in exchange for donations. Donors may have expectations of rewards from officeholders they helped to elect. But the expectation of reward may not involve the candidate. Instead it centres on those who solicit funds on the candidate's behalf. Those who respond to their request may do so in the expectation that the fund-raisers will help with a job or business contract if they make a donation. The attraction for donors of this sort of exchange is that a campaign does not even need to win the election to yield the anticipated rewards. Nor are intimates motivated by political objectives; rather they find rewards through their identification and interaction with others by engaging in fund-raising activities. It is only the ideologues who want to advance their political beliefs. Of all donors in the Francia study, approximately a quarter were investors and another quarter were intimates. Only a third of donors were classed as ideologues, animated by political objectives. The remainder had no strong motive of any type.[10]

In addition to individuals, large amounts of US campaign money originates from interest groups which either contribute to candidates and parties or sponsor their own independent campaigns. Group involvement in financing elections is partly a result of the promising potential for their influence, which, compared to other systems of government, is untypically high as a consequence of familiar institutional features such as the fragmentation of government power wrought by the separation of powers, checks and balances, and federalism, which create numerous access points at which groups can insert themselves. A powerful independent legislature in which party discipline is relatively weak and members attentive to constituents also lowers the obstacles to opportunities for group influence in government.

But, to convert potential into influence, groups have to capitalize on all means available, one of which is using money in elections. Though spending on elections is unlikely to buy influence for groups, it does buy access, from which influence can follow. Receptivity to groups also helps individual legislators in the quest for re-election funding. Unable to rely on their parties to fund their campaigns, American legislators need contributions from individuals and interest groups for electoral security. Being accessible to groups, pursuing casework for constituents, proposing bills, sponsoring amendments and obtaining pork-barrel benefits for their constituencies earn incumbents the credit which converts into campaign dollars and votes. Members who sponsor new legislation are rewarded in campaign funds from interest groups: the more bills sponsored, the more donations received from groups.[11] In the congressional session 2009–10, 90 per cent of members obtained at least one earmark (federal funds allocated to companies, organizations, groups and projects without competitive bidding or merit-based criteria). Campaign contributions from individual managers, staff and political action committees associated with the beneficiaries of earmarks were received by 375 members of Congress in 2008–10, ranging from $116,900 to $250.[12]

Threat as well as opportunity stirs groups into financing elections, particularly those connected to business. The US political context is benign for business in many ways, providing greater political assets than those afforded by the structural advantages enjoyed by business in any capitalist system.[13] In the US there is a consensus around the desirability of private enterprise, and no socialist party developed an appeal comparable to that in other western democracies to challenge the capitalist system. In many industries trade union membership never achieved a magnitude to counteract employers' power. But there have been sources of business opposition more vigorous in the US than elsewhere. The legacy of late-nineteenth-century populism is an antagonism towards big businesses for abusing their market position and crushing small-scale entrepreneurship. This was added to from the 1960s with the rise of public interest liberalism, which produced a range of critiques of business practices, including damaging the environment and endangering the health and safety of employees and consumers. The result was new laws, regulations and oversight bodies to impose discipline on business behaviour.

When US business is subjected to law the consequences can be severe. 'Adversarial legalism' characterizes the framework in which US businesses operate. Laws that regulate business are detailed, prescriptive, complex, confusing and difficult to comply with. Violations are resolved by litigation in court rather than by informal negotiation. Severe civil or criminal penalties can be imposed. Relations between regulators and regulated are adversarial rather than cooperative. This style of regulation is not found outside the US. Elsewhere regulation is less detailed. Violations are likely to be followed by remedial action rather than penalties. Negotiation and cooperation characterize relations between regulators and regulated.[14]

This US style of regulation stimulates businesses to political activism. Without political action, the regulatory environment might be even more hostile. For business-oriented political action committees (PACs), campaign spending is a form of protective investment, seeking to restrain adversarial legalism by helping elect sympathetic lawmakers to whom they hope to have access. The connection between legal threat and campaign spending has been signalled in several studies of PACs. They show that firms in industries subject to federal regulation are more likely to form a PAC than those not so regulated, and these firms also donate larger sums.[15]

Campaign finance law

The US, like nearly all advanced industrial democracies, has instituted a set of safeguards to protect against the dangers of campaign financing. Although there many national idiosyncrasies, these safeguards are of three main types: regulation, transparency and subsidization.[16] Regulation covers limits on expenditure, and restrictions on the quantities and sources of donations. Control of contributions caps the amount that can be donated by a single source. Particular sources of money may be entirely prohibited from contributing to campaigns. Transparency covers rules for reporting, disclosure, monitoring and rule-enforcement. Rules can cover either or both of contributions and expenditures which must be reported to a designated body. Either all contributions or those above a specified limit have to be reported. Reports of expenditures may also be required. Subsidization refers to forms of state aid to finance either campaigns specifically or political parties in general. Such subsidies can be in cash or in kind. State funds can be given for parties' year-round activities or for election campaigns. In-kind subsidies include access to free election broadcasts or special tax status for parties.[17]

By international comparison, the US is unusual in its mix of transparency, regulation and subsidization. It is untypically demanding on the first two but light on the third. In contrast, most other democracies are lax on regulation and disclosure but generous in subsidies. As Table 11.2 shows, the US usually appears in the minority of western democracies on many aspects of what it requires, forbids or provides in campaign finance. This particular configuration reflects the political conditions in which American campaign finance law has developed. Issues of campaign finance often divide liberals from conservatives, Democrats from Republicans and senators from representatives. In an institutional system which favours inaction, these divisions have often blocked reforms and muted those which could be introduced. Transparency raises few objections, unlike regulation and subsidization. Conservatives see regulation of spending as an unwarranted intrusion into the right to spend what has been legally obtained. The Supreme Court has given these arguments a constitutional imprimatur, judging restrictions on spending as an infringement of freedom of speech protected by the First Amendment. Conservatives, commonly the opponents of many aspects of public expenditure, have also been reluctant about the use of government

Table 11.2 Political finance laws and regulations in western democracies

Law/regulation	Western democracies* (N=19) %	USA (Y or N)
Disclosure of party income	73.4	Y
Limits on size of contributions	36.8	Y
Ban on corporate contributions	15.8	Y
Ban on union contributions	15.8	Y
Disclosure of party spending	68.4	Y
Limit on party spending	42.1	N
Public funding for parties	94.7	N
Free media for parties	84.2	N
Special tax status for parties	26.3	N

Source: International Institute for Democracy and Electoral Assistance, 'Political Finance Laws and Regulations', http://www.idea.int/resources/databases.cfm#fopp.

Note: * Australia, Austria, Belgium, Canada, Denmark, Finland, France, Germany, Iceland, Ireland, Italy, Netherlands, New Zealand, Norway, Portugal, Spain, Sweden, Switzerland, UK.

funds to finance elections, which is dismissed as 'welfare for politicians'. Conservatives have been joined in this defence by congressional incumbents of both parties, who have been keen to avoid making their own elections more competitive by easing their opponents' access to money.

Since the inception of the current system of US campaign finance in the 1970s in the Federal Election Campaign Act (the FECA system), contributions have been kept low to contain the dependence on a single source. Limits apply to how much individuals, interest groups (in the form of PACs) and parties can donate to a single candidate. Individuals also have ceilings on their total contributions to all candidates, PACs and parties. These controls added to the ban on contributions from companies which had been in place since 1907 and trade unions first introduced in 1943. A loophole through these restrictions, allowing unlimited giving to state parties to use during federal elections ('soft money'), was barred by the Bipartisan Campaign Reform Act of 2002.

Controls on spending are lighter. Limits on overall spending by a campaign apply in only presidential elections and then only to candidates accepting public subsidies. Candidates for their party's presidential nomination who accept public funds are capped in how much they can spend in total and in individual states. Having accepted public funds, a candidate had total spending capped in 2008 at $42.1 million. In the general election major party candidates' campaigns are eligible for complete public funding. As no private donations are permitted, the effect of accepting public funding is to cap the campaign's total spending ($84.1 million in 2008). No spending limits apply to campaigns for House and Senate or to presidential candidates who are not publicly funded.

Transparency requirements are extensive. Since 1976 a specially created body, the Federal Election Commission (FEC), has been responsible for overseeing campaign finance. It collates the data supplied in conformity with the disclosure rules which apply to presidential, Senate and House elections. Campaigns must report all donations, and identify the donors of contributions of $200 and upwards. Reports of campaign expenditures are also required. In presidential campaigns so demanding are these requirements that candidates are allowed to raise money from private sources to cover their legal and accounting compliance costs (known as general election legal and accounting compliance funds, or GELAC). Contribution and spending reports are made public via the Commission website. The Commission also authorizes and records the disbursement of the public subsidies. The Commission provides advice to campaigns to assist their compliance with the law. It is also empowered to punish violations of the law by imposing fines. For example, in the financial year 2008 the Commission resolved 71 cases and imposed penalties amounting to $2.4 million.[18]

US subsidization is meagre compared to that of other democracies. Its cash forms are confined to presidential elections. As mentioned above, public cash subsidies are available to partially fund presidential nomination campaigns and to completely fund the general election in exchange for limiting spending in total and, in the general election, forgoing private contributions. Parties also receive public funds to help finance their national conventions ($16.3 million in 2008). In-kind subsidies include a requirement of broadcasters to price election campaign advertising at their lowest rate, and the US Postal Service charges its lowest rates to deliver election literature. In contrast to the situation in most western democracies, there are no public subsidies to help run political parties or their election campaigns. Nor are there any public funds to help fund candidates running for the House or Senate. In no elections are candidates eligible for the in-kind benefit of free election broadcasts.

Effects of regulation

The inception of the Federal Election Commission, and the use of its enforcement powers, has helped to ensure that campaign finance law is adhered to. Violations do occur, but there is no suggestion that they are widespread, so the FECA system strongly shapes how money is raised and spent. This formative effect registers both in the widespread adherence to the law and also in the ingenuity shown in circumventing its intent without breaching its letter. But the law does matter, because it shapes where and in what forms money finds a way into campaigns. This has generated some unique or uncommon features of American election money compared to that of other western democracies. Amongst these untypical effects are the candidates' financial independence from parties, the small size of donations, the constancy of fund-raising activity by individual candidates, the number of self-financed candidates, the diversity of forms of interest group money and the vast sums spent independently of the candidates.

The trend towards candidate-centred campaigns did not originate from the 1970s campaign finance reforms, but they did give them impetus. Under FECA, parties are restricted in how much they can give their candidates. To improve their election prospects candidates look beyond their parties for additional funds. Many candidates were raising most of their money from non-party sources before FECA, but its inception accelerated and necessitated their independence of party money. FECA capped how much parties could give their candidates for Congress and barred any party contribution to publicly funded candidates in presidential elections. The caps on party giving to congressional candidates were less than half the cost of the average winning campaign when they were introduced. The absence of adjustments for inflation, which campaign spending outpaced, progressively eroded the value of party donations to candidates. In 2008, parties could give House candidates a maximum of $30,000, when the average winning candidate spent $1.7 million. Senate candidates could obtain $40,000 from their parties, when winners spent an average of $7.5 million that year.

FECA sought to prevent candidates' being heavily dependent on any source for fear of its potentially corrupting effect. Parties were conceived of as just like other interests, seeking sectional advantages from which candidates and the public needed protection. This suspicion of party motives was apparently shared by the party politicians in Congress and the White House who enacted the law. It imbued FECA with that distinctively American distrust of parties as enemies rather than agents of the public interest which has been found amongst the country's political elites since the eighteenth century.[19] Other countries, where that anti-party sentiment faded or never appeared, have not sought to give candidates such financial immunity from their parties. To the contrary, parties are often the sole source of campaign funding for candidates in many other advanced industrial democracies.

Self-financed candidates are an extreme version of candidates independent of party funding. No data is available about the frequency of such candidacies in different countries, but they appear more common in the US, where high office is more easily penetrable by the wealthy with political ambitions than in systems where parties are more powerful gatekeepers to candidacy. The use of primaries to make nominations allows political novices to become general election candidates without the approval of party officials, a record of party service or an apprenticeship in a lower public office. Able to fund their lavish campaigns, wealthy candidates seek to start a career at or near the top of government. Conspicuous examples include Malcolm Forbes, who twice campaigned for the Republican presidential nomination, using his own money despite the lack of prior government or electoral experience. Ross Perot ran a self-financed independent campaign for president in 1992, spending approximately

50 per cent more than either of his publicly funded major party opponents. John Corzine successively self-financed his way into the US Senate and the New Jersey governorship. In 2010, 58 candidates for Congress spent over a half a million dollars of their own money.

In US federal elections, small donations are essential, because large ones are illegal. In most western democracies, in the absence of legal caps on contributions, large donations are common, as they were in the US prior to FECA. Whereas one person could give $3 million to Nixon's 1972 general election campaign, 1,300 people, giving the legal maximum, were needed to raise that amount in 2008. In 2008 the maximum legal individual contribution was $28,500 to a party and $2,300 to a candidate. The latter limit on giving to a candidate is low compared to the ceilings on party donations in other countries. Only Belgium sets a lower limit but, unlike the US, it also caps total party spending, so curbing the demand for all forms of donations. In practice, most US contributions are well below the legal maximum. In the 2008 House elections, 22 per cent of donations were under $200, the threshold for campaigns to identify the source of the donation in their reports to the FEC.[20] Small contributions were also important to the candidates for their party's nominations. Obama raised $134 million for his primary campaign in donations under $200, and donations of that size accounted for 62 per cent of the total raised by the Republican Ron Paul.[21]

Low ceilings on donations combined with an unlimited right to spend generate a constant quest by candidates for money. With only two years between elections, for members of the House fund-raising is a permanent activity. They start raising money for the next election as soon as the previous one is over. Many employ a permanent fund-raiser, and during their term of office frequently attend fund-raising events in Washington and their constituencies, and communicate with potential donors to solicit funds. In the 2008 elections, House incumbents had raised an average of $13,000 per week for the preceding two years. Facing far more expensive campaigns, presidential candidates begin fund-raising years before the first caucuses and primaries. Halfway through 2011, 16 months before election day 2012, Obama's re-election campaign had raised over $80 million.

The need for numerous small donors required a professional approach to fund-raising in contrast to the informality of the past. Money had to be sought from numerous givers, most of them strangers to the candidate. Fund-raising firms proliferated, their services available to hire for campaigns intent on raising large sums. Their emergence reflected the need for an expertise and commitment of time that candidates and their campaign treasurers did not possess. Armed with an understanding of the details of campaign finance law, professional fund-raisers supply candidates with lists of potential donors tailored to their party and issue stances. Professionalization has also extended to complying with the law. Accountants and lawyers became essential to campaigns to ensure that the raising, spending and reporting of their finances conformed to the intricacies of the law. The burden of these requirements is exemplified in McCain's GELAC $16 million costs in the 2008 presidential campaign.

As Table 11.2 showed, few western democracies prohibit donations from corporations or trade unions. The US is one of the exceptions, compelling these organizations to create a separate campaign funding body to stay within the law. These restrictions account for the existence of the distinctively American source of campaign money, the political action committee. PACs originated in the 1940s when the temporary Smith–Connally Act (and the later, permanent Taft–Hartley Act) barred trade unions using their funds for financing election candidates. The PAC, a separate body, raising funding for candidates, became the legal vehicle by which unions continued to inject money into campaigns. In the early 1970s there were several hundred PACs. But FECA caused a steep rise in the numbers, a 584 per cent increase, between 1974 and 1986. By the latter year, PACs numbered more than 4,000, as they do to today. In 2008 PACs donated $819 million to candidates and parties as well as spending another $135 million on their own independent campaigns.

FECA stimulated PAC numbers by both easing their formation and capping individual donations, enhancing both the opportunity to create them and their attraction as a means to inject 'interested money' into elections. Until FECA, a PAC had to pay for its own premises, staff and equipment. As a result, substantial sums were expended without reaching election candidates. FECA removed that prohibition, allowing a parent body such as a union or company to pay to set up and administer a PAC. A second prohibition that was removed was that banning federal contractors (those doing business with the federal government) from forming PACs. Suddenly thousands of firms and unions supplying the government with goods and services were eligible to create a PAC.

Caps on individual contributions also added to the appeal of creating a PAC, particularly for companies. In the past, businesses had encouraged employees and shareholders to make individual donations. Some paid bonuses to their executives on the understanding they were to be passed on to favoured candidates. But FECA's caps on the size of individual donations diminished the value of that approach. In comparison, a PAC grew in value, initially being allowed to contribute to a candidate five times more than an individual (closer to two times as a result of the Bipartisan Campaign Reform Act reforms in 2002) and being unlimited in their total donations. Business adapted to these new conditions, as corporate PACs grew from 89 in 1974 to 1,744 in 1986.

Large amounts of independent spending (i.e. expenditures by parties and groups without coordination with the candidate they are designed to help) are another example of American distinctiveness attributable to its system of campaign finance regulation. The caps on donations force groups and individuals who want to aid candidates beyond the legal ceiling to resort to independent campaigning. In 2008 this type of spending accounted for one-seventh of all campaign expenditure. It covers spending on media advertising, contacting voters and communicating with group members. The sums involved indicate that far more money is available for campaign spending than it is legally possible to give to candidates. In 2008, for example, the national parties spent independently 25 times more than they gave to their candidates (see Table 11.3). Spending by groups in the form of 527s and 501(c)s, neither of which are allowed to make donations if they are to preserve their tax status, amounted to $454 million.[22] PACs both made donations and spent $135 million independently.

The scope for independent spending widened in January 2010 when the Supreme Court decided in the *Citizens United* case that companies and unions could draw from their treasuries for such activities, ending a prohibition on the former that had been in place for a century and on the latter since 1943. The decision was followed by the launch of 'super PACs', organizations free from the legal restrictions on campaign activities applying to 527s and 501(c)s, and able to attract uncapped donations from individuals as well as companies and

Table 11.3 Party spending in 2008

Mode of spending	$ m.	%
Donations to candidates	11	3.0
Coordinated with candidates	70	19.3
Independent of candidates	281	77.6
Total	362	99.9

Source: David Magleby, 'Political Parties and the Financing of the 2008 Elections', in David B. Magleby and Anthony Corrado, eds, *Financing the 2008 Election* (Washington, DC: Brookings Institution, 2011).

unions. By early summer 2012, more than 400 'super PACs' were in existence and had already raised over $200 million for the year's elections, supporting the campaigns of candidates, whom in some cases they outraised.

Conclusion

The voracious appetite for campaign funds in the US creates an abnormally dangerous environment in which to run democratic elections. This environment became more dangerous in 2012, as supply and demand changed from 2008. Record amounts seemed likely to be spent, as Obama's example of forgoing public funding was copied by more presidential nomination candidates and both parties in the general election, and the *Citizens United* decision opened up sources of previously forbidden funding. Concern about these developments and, no doubt, the discovery of more loopholes through the law will spark new demands for reform, but short of a major scandal it is unlikely that officeholders will be sufficiently embarrassed to overcome the institutional and partisan obstacles to enact serious innovations. Piecemeal change, if any, is more likely, and greater transparency its likeliest form.

Notes

1 See, for example, Joel Federman and Herbert Alexander, eds, *Comparative Political Finance in the 1980s* (Cambridge: Cambridge University Press, 1989); Arthur B. Gunlicks, ed., *Campaign and Party Finance in North America and Western Europe* (Boulder, CO: Westview Press, 1993); Herbert E. Alexander and Ria Shiratori, eds, *Comparative Political Finance among the Democracies* (Boulder, CO: Westview Press, 1994).

2 Claus H. de Vrees, 'Campaign Communication and Media', in Lawrence LeDuc, Richard G. Niemi and Pippa Norris, eds, *Comparing Democracies 3: Elections and Voting in the 21st Century* (London: Sage, 2010), 118–140.

3 Wisconsin Political Advertising Project, 'Political Advertising in 2008', accessed 23 June 2011 at http://wiscadproject.wisc.edu/wiscads_report_031710.pdf.

4 John Aldrich, *Why Parties?* (Chicago, IL: University of Chicago Press, 1995), 48–50.

5 Joe Soss and Lawrence R. Jacobs, 'The Place of Inequality: Non-Participation in the American Polity', *Political Science Quarterly*, 124(1) (2009), 100–103.

6 Seymour M. Lipset, *American Exceptionalism: A Double-Edged Sword* (New York: Norton, 1996), 67.

7 Center on Philanthropy, 'U.S. Charitable Giving Shows Modest Uptick in 2010 Following Two Years of Declines', Press release, 20 June 2011, accessed 8 October 2011 at http://www.philanthropy.iupui.edu/news/2011/06/pr-GUSA.aspx.

8 Clifford W. Brown, Jr, Lynda W. Powell and Clyde Wilcox, eds, *Serious Money: Fundraising and Contributing in Presidential Nomination Campaigns* (Cambridge: Cambridge University Press, 1995), 61.

9 David B. Magleby, 'Adaptation and Innovation in Financing the 2008 Election', in David B. Magleby and Anthony Corrado, eds, *Financing the 2008 Election* (Washington, DC: Brookings Institution, 2011), 30.

10 Peter L. Francia, John C. Green, Paul S. Herrnson, Lynda W. Powell and Clyde Wilcox, *The Financiers of Congressional Elections: Investors, Ideologues and Intimates* (New York: Columbia University Press, 2003).

11 Janet M. Box-Steffensmeier and J. Tobin Grant, 'All in a Day's Work: The Financial Rewards of Legislative Effectiveness', *Legislative Studies Quarterly*, 24(4) (1999), 511–524.

12 Center for Responsive Politics, '111th Congress Earmarks', accessed 17 July 2011 at http://www.opensecrets.org/bigpicture/earmarks.php.

13 Michael Moran, *Business, Politics and Society* (Oxford: Oxford University Press, 2009), 124–127.

14 Robert Kagan, *Adversarial Legalism* (Cambridge, MA and London: Harvard University Press, 2001).

15 Gary Andreas, 'Business Involvement in Campaign Finance: The Decision to Form a Corporate PAC', *PS: Political Science and Politics*, 18(2) (1985), 223–230; Kevin B. Grier, Michael C. Munger and Brian E. Roberts, 'The Determinants of Industry Political Activity, 1978–1986', *American Political Science Review*, 88(4) (1994), 911–926; David M. Hart, 'Why Do Some Firms Give? Why Do Some Give a Lot? High-Tech PACs, 1977–1996', *Journal of Politics*, 63(4) (2001), 1230–1249.
16 Ingrid van Biezan, 'Party and Campaign Finance', in Lawrence LeDuc, Richard G. Niemi and Pippa Norris, eds, *Comparing Democracies 3: Elections and Voting in the 21st Century* (London: Sage, 2010), 65–97.
17 International Institute for Democracy and Electoral Assistance, 'Political Finance Laws and Regulations', accessed 23 July 2011 at http://www.idea.int/resources/databases.cfm#fopp; Karl-Heinz Nassmacher, *The Funding of Party Competition: Political Finance in 25 Democracies* (Baden-Baden: Nomos, 2009).
18 Federal Election Commission, 'Selected Enforcement Statistics for Fiscal Years 2003–2008', accessed 17 August 2011 at http://www.fec.gov/em/enfpro/enforcestatsfy03-08.pdf.
19 See, for example, Richard Hofstadter, *The Idea of a Party System: The Rise of Legitimate Opposition in the United States, 1780–1840* (Berkeley: University of California Press, 1969); Austin Ranney, *Curing the Mischiefs of Faction: Party Reform in America* (Berkeley: University of California Press, 1975).
20 Paul S. Herrnson and Stephanie Perry Curtis, 'Financing the 2008 Congressional Elections', in David B. Magleby and Anthony Corrado, eds, *Financing the 2008 Election* (Washington, DC: Brookings Institution, 2011), 195.
21 John C. Green and Diana Kingsbury, 'Financing the 2008 Presidential Nominations', in David B. Magleby and Anthony Corrado, eds, *Financing the 2008 Election* (Washington, DC: Brookings Institution, 2011), 96–97.
22 527 and 501(c) refer to the respective sections of the Internal Revenue Service code defining activities which different types of group can engage in whilst remaining exempt from taxation.

12 The ever weakening wall?

The Roberts Supreme Court and the church–state debate

Emma Long

The Establishment Clause of the First Amendment to the US Constitution states: 'Congress shall make no law respecting an establishment of religion.' Since *Everson v. Board of Education* in 1947, the Supreme Court has been committed to defining the meaning of the terms 'respecting' and 'establishment' as they apply to the modern United States. While most commentators agree that the Clause was intended to regulate the relationship between the institutions of the state and those of the nation's churches, beyond this agreement is difficult to find. Exactly where the line should be drawn between church and state is unclear and controversial, based on different interpretations of the nation's history, the views and intentions of the Founding Fathers, the significance of the Founders' views in judging modern issues, and the 'proper' method for approaching constitutional interpretation.[1]

The Roberts Court's early Religion Clause cases were closely watched. For at least two decades critics from within and from outside the Court had argued that Establishment Clause jurisprudence was hopelessly muddled and confused, leading to inconsistent results and an incomprehensible body of precedent that did more harm than good to the church–state relationship.[2] The question was whether the Court could begin to find a way to develop a more coherent approach to the Establishment Clause or whether it would remain mired in the muddled jurisprudence of the past. A second area of interest for commentators was which approach to Establishment Clause jurisprudence the Court would favour. Would the Court continue the long-noted trend of the Rehnquist Court towards greater accommodation of religion and religious belief – a lowering of the wall of separation according to critics – or would the Justices seek to follow a path that would provide greater obstacles to the interaction of church and state?

A note on the 'Roberts Court'

Any discussion of the 'Roberts Court' in the period from October 2005 to July 2011 is, in part, misleading. The convention of naming periods of the Supreme Court's history for the Chief Justice who presided makes for easy identification of eras, but too often implies a consistency of membership, thinking, rationale and approach that belies the changes wrought on the Court. The appointment of John Roberts to replace Chief Justice William Rehnquist was followed by the appointments of Justice Samuel Alito in January 2006, Justice Sonia Sotomayor in August 2009 and Justice Elena Kagan in August 2010. While such regular arrival of new personnel is not unusual in the Court's history, the average appointment to the Court coming once every two years, it stands in stark contrast to the final 11 years of the Rehnquist Court, which saw no retirements from the bench. It also ensures that any discussion of the 'Roberts Court' must be undertaken with an understanding that the term be seen as an identification of a time period rather than a statement regarding the ideology, approaches or methods of the Justices who constituted it.

The cases

Between October 2005, when John Roberts began his first term as Chief Justice, and July 2011, when Elena Kagan concluded her freshman year as the Court's junior Associate Justice, the Court heard and decided four major Religion Clause cases. Two directly involved the Establishment Clause; two implicated the Clause only indirectly. All four, however, presented questions and issues that the Court had dealt with in previous cases, allowing Court commentators to begin to assess the impact of the new Justices on Establishment Clause jurisprudence.

Hein v. Freedom from Religion Foundation, Inc. (2007) and *Arizona Christian School Tuition Organization v. Winn* (2011) both raised the question of state financial aid for religion and religious organizations. The issue dominated the Supreme Court's Establishment Clause jurisprudence from 1971 when in *Lemon v. Kurtzman* the Burger Court created a three-part test to judge the constitutionality of government programmes which provided benefits to religious organizations.[3] It was also the issue around which criticisms of inconsistency coalesced. Varying opinions – which upheld loans to religious school students of textbooks but not of maps, globes, tape recorders and overhead projectors, which struck down but then later upheld programmes of remedial education provided to religious school students on religious school campuses, and which held that the direct grant of financial resources to religious organizations violated the Establishment Clause, but upheld the reimbursement of printing costs for a student religious magazine – fuelled concerns both that the Court was incapable of developing a consistent jurisprudence and that its conservative majority was slowly eroding the scope of the provision.[4] *Hein* and *Winn* offered the opportunity of a first glimpse of the Roberts Court's approach to such issues.

Hein v. Freedom from Religion Foundation involved a challenge to a series of conferences, organized by the executive branch of the federal government, to publicize and support the activities of the Office of Faith-Based and Community Initiatives. Created by President George W. Bush in 2001, the purpose of the Office was to 'ensure that private and charitable community groups, including religious ones . . . have the fullest opportunity permitted by law to compete on a level playing field [for federal assistance], so long as they achieve valid public purposes'.[5] The Office was controversial from the beginning; advocates of strict separation asserted that its purpose undermined the traditional separation of church and state by permitting, and in some cases encouraging, the distribution of public funds to religious organizations. The Freedom from Religion Foundation (FFRF), a non-profit organization of 'freethinkers, atheists, agnostics, and sceptics', which 'works to educate the public on matters relating to non-theism, and to promote the constitutional principle of separation between church and state', challenged these conferences on the grounds that they used public funds to promote religious groups over secular groups, violating the Establishment Clause.[6] If the Court found for FFRF, a major initiative of the Bush administration would be under threat; if the Court found for the government, precedent for direct public funding of religious groups was a possibility. In *Hein*, the Court avoided either ruling and decided the case on a legal technicality.

The Supreme Court does not issue advisory opinions; neither does it decide hypothetical cases. In order for a case to come before the Court it must represent an actual judiciable controversy, one in which there is a conflict of rights or interests that can legitimately be addressed and redressed by the Court.[7] One of the ways in which the Court ensures this is through the rule of 'standing': plaintiffs must show actual harm to their interests by the challenged actions. In *Hein*, Justice Alito, writing for the plurality of three, argued that FFRF did not have standing to bring the case. The Foundation argued that, as taxpayers, it and its members had the right to challenge what they saw as the use of government funds for unconstitutional purposes. Traditionally the Court did not allow such cases on the grounds that the harm to taxpayers from any individual use of tax-raised funds was so 'generalized and attenuated' as to undermine any claims for redress. However, in *Flast v. Cohen* in 1968, the Warren Court carved out a narrow exception to the rule for taxpayers in Establishment Clause cases on the grounds that such challenges alleged congressional violation of an express constitutional limitation on its actions.[8] While claiming not to challenge *Flast*, Alito asserted that the circumstances of *Hein* did not fall within the bounds of the exception created in the earlier case, because the expenditure at issue was undertaken not by Congress but by the executive branch.[9] Expansion of the *Flast* exception to executive actions, Alito argued, 'would raise serious separation-of-powers concerns' by 'enlist[ing] the federal courts to superintend, at the behest of any federal taxpayer, the speeches, statements, and myriad daily activities of the President, his staff, and other Executive Branch officials'.[10] Rejecting calls by Justices Antonin Scalia and Clarence Thomas in concurrence to 'repudiate' and 'overrule' *Flast*, Alito claimed the ruling 'leave[s] *Flast* as we found it', but refused to extend it beyond its natural bounds.[11]

Because of the nature of the challenge in *Hein*, the case left open the question of whether the Court would be prepared to narrow further the *Flast* exception by preventing taxpayer challenges to legislative actions at state or federal level. *Arizona Christian School Tuition Organization v. Winn* addressed this, at least indirectly. Arizona permitted individuals to claim dollar-for-dollar tax credits, to a maximum of $500, for donations made to school tuition organizations (STOs) which used the contributions to provide scholarships to students attending private schools, including religious schools. As the four dissenters noted, although the STOs were private organizations, their existence, and the structure through which they worked, was created and encouraged by the state. The law was challenged by Kathleen Winn and other residents, who charged that the programme permitted the use of state funds for religious education. The fact that the programme used tax credits rather than a tax deduction was, they argued, irrelevant, since the dollar-for-dollar reimbursement meant such distinctions were little more than form over substance. Equally, since certain STOs encouraged donations by arguing that this was not individuals' money but state money, the validity of the distinction, Winn and others argued, was further undermined.

Once again the Court, in a majority opinion written by Justice Anthony Kennedy, sought to reaffirm the narrowness of the *Flast* exception and distinguish it from the case before them. Winn and the others, Kennedy asserted, did not have standing to challenge the Arizona law, since they could show no financial injury as a result of the programme. They had not shown, nor could they show, that their current tax burden was higher as a consequence of this programme than it would have been without it. Equally, there was no guarantee that forcing the programme's abandonment would result in a lesser tax burden on individuals; in fact it might lead to higher taxes, as the state was forced to pay to educate students who could no longer afford to attend private schools.[12] Thus there was no evidence of harm caused, nor any judicial remedy within the Court's authority – both basic requirements for standing to bring a case. In addition, so the majority argued, there was a substantial difference between a tax and a tax credit. In the latter case, the state permitted private individuals to make their own decisions about how to spend their money; in this case, the choice was between donations to an STO and payment of the equivalent in state taxes to the government. But the state did not force that choice; it merely made the choice an available option by establishing the STO framework. Scholarships to religious schools were thus funded by the private donations of individuals, and not by the tax framework of the state. As such, no Establishment Clause violation could be perceived.

Whereas *Hein* and *Winn* raised the issues of standing and government financing of religious organizations, the Roberts Court's two other Religion Clause cases addressed a second area of controversy: the place of religion in public spaces that may be associated with the state. *Pleasant Grove City, Utah v. Summum* (2009) involved Pioneer Park in Pleasant Grove City, a public park which contained 11 permanent, privately donated displays and monuments, including a Ten Commandments monument donated to the city in 1971 by the Fraternal Order of Eagles. Summum, a religious organization, sought to erect a stone monument in the park containing the Seven Aphorisms of Summum.[13] The city rejected the application, asserting a policy of accepting only those monuments which directly related to the city's history or which were donated by organizations with long-standing community ties. Summum charged that the refusal to accept their monument violated the Free Speech Clause of the First Amendment by limiting the expression of views in the park to certain groups. The claim rested on the Court's 'public forum' doctrine, which held that the state may create a forum for public speech but may not then discriminate against speakers within that forum on the basis of the content of their speech. Summum argued that the rejection of their monument, while permitting the display of the Ten Commandments monument, unconstitutionally discriminated against Summum on the basis of the content of their speech.

The Court unanimously rejected Summum's complaint, arguing that, while the park was a public forum, the monuments represented government speech, not private speech, and thus were not subject to First Amendment limitations. 'The Free Speech Clause', Justice Alito wrote for the majority, 'restricts government regulation of private speech; it does not regulate government speech. . . . A government entity may exercise this same freedom to express its views when it receives assistance from private sources for the purpose of delivering a government-controlled message.'[14] The limited space in the park and the permanence of the monuments distinguished this from a typical public forum, in which an almost unlimited number of speakers may be accommodated because of the impermanence of their occupying the space. As such, the park, so far as it applied to the display of the monuments, was not a forum for public speech but a forum for private government speech: and the government, like any private speaker, was not required to express all points of view. The government's policy for accepting monuments for the park reflected reasonable grounds for managing limited space, and thus Summum's claims were rejected.

Significant by its absence from the Court's reasoning was the Establishment Clause, which appeared only in concurrences by Justices Scalia and David Souter. As both noted, the case had been litigated 'in the shadow of', and 'with one eye on', the Establishment Clause.[15] For Scalia, a long-time advocate for government accommodation of religion, the display simply represented the government's recognition of the role of Christianity in American history and thus did not present an Establishment Clause difficulty.[16] For Souter, although the particular circumstances of *Pleasant Grove City* did not raise Establishment difficulties, other cases might do so. 'In such an instance', he suggested:

> there will be safety in numbers, and it will be in the interest of a careful government to accept other monuments to stand nearby, to dilute the appearance of adopting whatever particular religious position the single example alone might stand for.[17]

Souter thus restated what has come to be known as the 'plastic reindeer rule': religious displays on or in government property may be permissible if they are accompanied by other, secular, seasonal displays, because such additional features reduce the likelihood that a 'neutral observer' will perceive in the display an endorsement or favouring of the religious message.[18]

Neither Scalia nor Souter expanded existing Establishment Clause jurisprudence regarding public displays with religious content, but their addressing the issue highlighted more clearly the majority's sidestepping of it. On the one hand there was no need to address the issue: the Establishment Clause was not directly raised by the parties to the case, and the case, as the majority showed, could easily be decided without reference to the religious issue. Deciding the case on one constitutional principle rather than two also allowed for simplicity and clarity that might be undermined by the mixing of elements of the First Amendment. Yet, on the other hand, the situation at issue in *Pleasant Grove City*, where two religious monuments were under discussion (one accepted, the other rejected), clearly echoed circumstances the Court had addressed before. The absence of even the barest recognition of this was notable.

The Court could not, however, duck the issue so easily the following year when hearing argument in *Salazar v. Buono* (2010). The case involved a long-running dispute about a plain white Latin cross, first erected by Veterans of Foreign Wars (VFW) in 1934 as a memorial to those who died during the First World War. The cross was challenged as a violation of the Establishment Clause, because it was displayed on federal government land that was part of the Mojave National Preserve. Earlier versions of the case had found that the display violated the Establishment Clause; as a result, the cross had been covered by a wooden box since 2002. Following this, the federal government had entered into negotiations with a local resident, Henry Sandoz, to transfer the land on which the cross was displayed to the ownership of the VFW in exchange for a parcel of Sandoz's land nearby. Frank Buono challenged the land transfer on the grounds that it was an attempt to circumvent the earlier ruling that the display of the cross violated the Establishment Clause. Because the terms of the land transfer required VFW to continue to display the cross, Buono argued that this was continued government support for a religious symbol. In support, he pointed to congressional actions which prevented the use of federal funds for dismantling the cross and which designated it as 'a national memorial commemorating United States participation in World War One and honoring the American veterans of that war'.[19] Under the Court's extant jurisprudence, which made reference to the perceptions of a 'neutral observer', the government's actions violated the Establishment Clause, Buono asserted, because they represented continued government support for the display of a religious symbol.

Buono divided the Justices along political lines over both the meaning of the cross and the meaning of the government's actions with regard to it. For the plurality of Kennedy, Roberts and Alito, the cross was not a religious symbol, but a war memorial that happened to be in the shape of a Latin cross. Its history, the time since its initial erection, and its use all combined to make it more than simply a Christian symbol. 'Here, one Latin cross in the desert evokes far more than religion', wrote Kennedy. 'It evokes thousands of small crosses in foreign fields marking the graves of Americans who fell in battles, battles whose tragedies are compounded if the fallen are forgotten.'[20] Alito in concurrence agreed: 'the symbol that was selected, a plain unadorned white cross, no doubt evoked the unforgettable image of the white crosses, row on row, that marked the final resting places of so many American soldiers who fell in that conflict'.[21] Respect for the meaning invested in the cross as a memorial meant that dismantling of the cross was not an option; it would imply disrespect for the veterans honoured by the memorial.[22] Rather than permit the cross to remain, but covered, Congress had sought the best possible compromise, one which permitted the memorial to remain but addressed the Establishment Clause concerns of the earlier case. 'The land transfer statute embodies Congress's legislative judgment that this dispute is best resolved through a framework and policy of accommodation for a symbol that . . . has complex meaning beyond the expression of religious views.'[23] The plurality's portrayal of the memorial as more than a religious symbol provided the grounding for the deference to congressional action. Congress's motives were not the illicit ones of circumventing the earlier Court ruling but the legitimate, honourable motives of wishing to maintain respect for those who had given their lives in defence of their country. Downplaying the religious element of the memorial and focusing on its symbolism permitted the plurality to portray Congress's actions as a well-meaning attempt to find a compromise between memorialization and the Establishment concerns raised by Buono.

For the dissenters this was little more than obfuscation. 'Making a plain, unadorned Latin cross a war memorial does not make the cross secular. It makes the war memorial sectarian', blasted Justice John Paul Stevens in dissent with Justices Ruth Bader Ginsburg and Sonia Sotomayor.[24] The legitimate ends of recognizing the sacrifice of those fallen in battle cannot, and should not, be achieved by unconstitutional methods, Stevens argued. Presenting the memorial as primarily a religious symbol revealed congressional actions in a different light. Thus the land transfer statute was little more than the government's attempts to maintain the display of a religious symbol, in violation of the Establishment Clause and the earlier ruling. Congressional actions designating the cross a national memorial, as well as the ban on federal funds being used to dismantle the cross, built an image of a series of governmental actions designed to protect, and by implication endorse, the religious display. Seen in this light the land transfer statute, with its requirement that the memorial be maintained, was revealed as little more than the latest in a long line of measures designed to ensure the cross remained on display. 'The reasonable observer who knows all the pertinent facts and circumstances surrounding the symbol and its placement . . . would perceive the government had endorsed the cross' as a result of its 'herculean efforts' to preserve its display, argued Stevens.[25] The plurality's failure to recognize this misrepresented not only the circumstances at issue, but the meaning of the earlier case.

The meaning and significance of *Hein, Winn, Pleasant Grove City* and *Buono*

Four cases in an area of constitutional jurisprudence are not many on which to build a definitive understanding of the direction in which the Court is heading. However, the unusual way in which *Hein* and *Winn* were decided, combined with the approaches taken in *Pleasant Grove City* and *Buono* and the Justices' own statements about the role of the Court in these cases, provides some grounds on which to begin an analysis of the Roberts Court and the Establishment Clause.

Justice Louis Brandeis famously commented on the role of the Court that 'The most important thing we do is not doing.'[26] 'Judicial restraint' is a term, and an idea, that has become increasingly politicized. However, its foundation – the view that the courts should only do as much as necessary to deal with the case at bar – has deep roots in American legal history. In their respective hearings before Congress, both Roberts and Alito indicated support for the concept of a restrained, cautious judiciary. Might it then be possible to suggest that the Roberts Court's approach to Establishment Clause cases indicates judicial restraint in action, or if not restraint at least judicial minimalism? This would go some way to explaining the lower number of cases that the Court has heard since Roberts's appointment. In June 2006,

Charles Lane in the *Washington Post* commented that 'Going Out of Business' might be a more accurate inscription for the Court's front door, while in December the same year Linda Greenhouse commented on 'the case of the dwindling docket'.[27] In the 2005/06 term, the first under Roberts, the Court issued only 69 opinions; two years later, that number had dropped to 67, the lowest since the Court's 1953/54 term; and in the 2010/11 term the Court's 82 opinions represented only slightly more than half the number of cases the Court was deciding in the mid-1980s. Even allowing for the reduced number of cases heard by the Rehnquist Court in its later years, this is a sharp drop. Other trends have played a role in this decline, including fewer cases filed by the Solicitor General's office, a declining number of laws passed by Congress, and fewer losses for the federal government in the lower courts.[28] The political divide on the Court might also provide some of the explanation, as those who fear they may be on the losing side of a case look for alternative methods to achieve their goals. None of these, however, exclude judicial restraint, or minimalism, as a factor in the Court's decision-making.

The approach taken to *Flast* by the *Hein* plurality and the *Winn* majority suggested concern with judicial restraint. Both refused to extend the *Flast* exception beyond what was seen as its natural bounds. In *Hein*, the plurality expressed concern that extending *Flast* to expenditures by the executive branch 'would deputize federal courts as virtually continuing monitors of the wisdom and soundness of Executive action, and that, most emphatically, is not the role of the judiciary'.[29] In *Winn*, the majority made explicit its concern for the separation of powers:

> For the federal courts to decide questions of law arising outside of cases and controversies would be inimical to the Constitution's democratic character. And the resulting conflict between the judicial and the political branches would not, in the long run, be beneficial to either.[30]

In both cases the rulings held that no standing existed, because the challenged actions fell outside the narrow exception established in *Flast*, and the lack of concrete injury, combined with the danger of pushing the courts into decisions made by the other branches of government, provided good reason for the Court to reject any such expansion.

The results in all four cases can be seen in light of judicial restraint. On the surface, at least, none substantially changed the existing Establishment Clause jurisprudence. The Court had not previously addressed executive actions in Establishment terms, and tax credits, as well as other forms of tuition payment schemes, had previously been held constitutional.[31] Public displays with religious messages, whether monuments or in other forms, had also been accepted by the Court; and in *Salazar v. Buono* the Court remanded the case for further consideration, refraining from deciding the merits of the case as Justice Alito had urged in concurrence.[32] Thus a radical overhaul of Establishment Clause jurisprudence was not forthcoming, and in fact was explicitly rejected in the approach to *Flast*. The Court rested on previously developed doctrine, such as 'government speech' in *Pleasant Grove City*, referred decisions to the lower courts, or claimed to 'leave [precedent] where we found it' by refusing to expand its application – all hallmarks of judicial restraint.

A closer look, particularly at the Court's rulings on standing, reveals a much different picture, however. In *Winn*, the majority argued that the Court's prior Establishment cases were not relevant to the decision: 'those cases do not mention standing. . . . When a potential jurisdictional defect is neither noted nor discussed in a federal decision, the decision does not stand for the proposition that no defect existed.'[33] Effectively the majority argued that, even though in previous cases the Court had heard Establishment Clause challenges brought by taxpayers, that did not mean that the Court had accepted that those taxpayers had legitimate standing. Instead, the Court simply failed to mention the issue. At best this is misleading and at worst disingenuous. As the dissenters argued in a forceful opinion by Justice Kagan, for nearly half a century the Court had been accepting and deciding Establishment cases brought by taxpayers: '[W]e considered and decided all these cases, because we thought taxpayer standing existed. The majority shrugs off these decisions because they did not discuss what was taken as obvious.'[34] The cases were heard, the dissenters argued, because it was understood that *Flast* permitted exactly the kind of taxpayer standing at issue in *Winn*; it was not discussed because it was not necessary. To read anything more into previous cases was to rest more on them than could be justified. The result of the majority opinion was to undermine a large proportion of the Court's prior Establishment Clause cases without recognizing that this was occurring. Such a fundamental reinterpretation of previous cases does not fit within the bounds of judicial restraint.

Even more significantly, the combined results in *Hein* and *Winn* threatened huge implications for future Establishment Clause challenges. '[T]he Court's arbitrary distinction', Kagan argued, 'threatens to eliminate *all* occasions for a taxpayer to contest the government's monetary support of religion.'[35] Despite the majority's claim that cases which could show 'real injury to particular individuals' would and could still be litigated, the reason for the *Flast* exception, as the dissenters pointed out, was that in Establishment cases often taxpayers are the only ones in a position to bring a challenge, and the very nature of the tax system militates against being able to show concrete, direct injury.[36] The Court's decision potentially threatens to close the door completely to taxpayer challenges under the Establishment Clause.[37] Thus government actions which raise Establishment questions may in future only be challenged through the political system, rather than the courts. While, on the one hand, this would respect judicial minimalism, removing the Court from the arena of church–state cases, it would also represent a significant shift away from the Court's previous approach. This implies activism rather than restraint. If it results, as many strict separationists fear, in the greater interaction of church and state because fewer challenges are possible, then *Hein* and *Winn* would represent far greater activism than is presently perceived.

Speaking at a 2009 conference on 'The Future of the First Amendment', Erwin Chemerinsky, legal scholar and founding dean of the School of Law at the University of California, Irvine, identified three themes emerging from the Roberts Court's treatment of First Amendment cases. The third theme he identified as 'the triumph of majoritarianism', 'leaving the protection of religious freedom, leaving the enforceable walls separating church and state, entirely to what the government does'.[38] Such an approach has fundamental implications for the second Religion Clause of the First Amendment, protecting freedom of religion, in that it suggests religious minorities must rely on majorities to protect their rights.[39] But the implications for the Establishment Clause are less clear, especially since the one area of broad agreement among scholars of the Clause is that it prevents government establishing or favouring one religion over others, even if that is the religion of the majority.

Some of the potential implications, however, are hinted at in *Pleasant Grove City* and *Salazar*. Majority religions are far more likely to be represented in the history, politics and culture of a society. Thus, in the case of the Pioneer Park memorials, those with links to majority faiths were more likely to be accepted than those from minority faiths, not as a result of any religious motivation but because the majority faith is more likely to have been active in the community over time. The Ten Commandments, as a central element of Christianity, have a far stronger claim to historical roots than the Seven Aphorisms of Summum.

Recognition based on non-religious factors may, in effect, end up favouring those faiths adhered to for the longest time or by the most people in a community. The plurality's approach to the Latin cross at issue in *Salazar* also contained hints of majoritarianism. The frequent references to congressional action implied deference to the will of the majority as enacted by the legislature, an argument made explicitly by Scalia in concurrence.[40] And the suggestion that the Latin cross sends a message of heroism and sacrifice over and above any religious message is a view that is more easily taken by those who share that faith than by those who do not. The danger is that viewing such symbols, activities and practices through the eyes of the majority blinds others to the messages that are sent to those outside of that majority. Neither *Pleasant Grove City* nor *Salazar* suggests that the Court is inclined to follow the route of majoritarianism as the sole determining factor in Establishment Clause jurisprudence, but the echoes of that approach in both cases provide indications of potential results should such a view become dominant.

One clear element in all four Establishment cases from the Roberts Court is deference to the government. Such deference has links to majoritarianism, although it also fits with an approach that emphasizes judicial restraint. In *Hein* the Court was unwilling to challenge spending decisions by the executive branch, and in *Winn* saw no reason to strike down the Arizona programme without concrete evidence of harm. In *Pleasant Grove City*, the 'government speech' doctrine recognized the state's ability to express views on a variety of issues, and in *Salazar* both the plurality and the concurrences emphasized the importance of congressional judgement in assessing the validity of the land transfer statute. None of this would be surprising from a Court dedicated to the idea of judicial restraint or judicial minimalism. In all cases the majority recognized the legitimate role of the legislature in making decisions in areas which touch on the Establishment Clause. Deference to the legislature may be a result of a genuine belief in judicial restraint or may obscure policy preferences that can be reached by simply leaving legislative judgments in place. Any assessment of such a position, however, requires substantially more evidence than, to date, the Roberts Court has provided.

Writing in 2008, noted Establishment Clause scholar Carl Esbeck interpreted the Court's decision in *Hein* as reflecting an older battle between rights and structure in the Constitution. '[T]he Court in *Flast* weakened the requirement of standing to sue, which in turn weakened the doctrine of separation of powers. It was a trade off.'[41] In Esbeck's interpretation the Establishment Clause does not actively protect the rights of the individual, but rather acts as a restraint on government power which, indirectly, protects the rights of individuals. Such a view gives equal responsibility for maintaining the provisions of the Constitution to the executive and legislative branches of government. Viewing these branches as partners in the endeavour offers the possibility that the Court can withdraw from an area of jurisprudence which has been so heavily criticized in recent years. There are grounds for the Justices to see this as an appealing option. The long-standing separationist–accommodationist divide on the Court does not lend itself to the kind of radical overhaul of Establishment Clause jurisprudence that those who accuse the Court of inconsistency would like to see. Equally, more than 60 years of Establishment Clause jurisprudence have not settled the issue of the 'proper' line between church and state: that debate continues to divide politicians, legal scholars, religious groups and historians. Withdrawing from the issue offers the possibility that a more general consensus may emerge, or at the least that the Court may use its time to consider other issues, while allowing precedent to govern any new Establishment cases. The Court's standing decisions in *Hein* and *Winn*, reducing access to the courts in such cases, might well indicate the Court's decision to withdraw from this area of jurisprudence for the time being.

This, in turn, reinforces an image of the Roberts Court as one of restraint and minimalism, accepting the equal role of the other branches of government in interpreting the meaning of the Establishment Clause.

When viewed out of the broader context of such cases, such withdrawal might suggest restraint. However, when seen in the light of the Court's previous approach, such actions suggest at the very least a substantial change in the Court's thinking, if not a kind of activism. The actions of the Burger Court in Establishment cases, especially in those involving government benefits to religious organizations, implied that the Court saw the Establishment Clause as protecting a right, one that could be litigated through the courts as a result of challenges by individuals. If the majority of the Roberts Court now see the Clause as a structural issue, that is a significant change of approach with potentially major implications for Establishment Clause doctrine. Viewed in the context of the Court's long history of involvement with the Establishment Clause, the Court deciding 'not to decide' in such cases represents not judicial minimalism, but a major jurisprudential shift.

Concluding thoughts

The reality is that it is still much too early in the development of the Roberts Court definitively to state how the Court will approach the Establishment Clause. There are simply too few cases to be confident of any particular interpretation. There are hints of particular views, but they are little more than hints. Even the consequences of the Court's decisions in *Hein* and *Winn*, with their potentially major restriction on who may bring Establishment challenges, remain in the realm of possibility; the rulings are still too recent to be able to see how their implications will work out in practice. It is entirely possible that, by restricting standing, the Court is aiming to permit greater accommodation of religion without actively ruling that way. It is equally possible, however, that the Court, seeking to limit its role in a way fitting with judicial restraint, is simply limiting the kinds of cases it will hear by more strictly interpreting its own rules. Unless or until the Court accepts more cases in this field, or until the broader political consequences of greater focus on the legislative and executive branches are evident, the Court's exact motives remain unclear.

Notes

1 This is a large body of scholarship. However, good introductions to the different perspectives include: Thomas Berg, 'Religion Clause Anti-Theories', *Notre Dame Law Review*, 72 (1997), 693; Robert Cord, 'Church–State Separation: Restoring the "No Preference" Doctrine of the First Amendment', *Harvard Journal of Law and Public Policy*, 9 (1986), 129; Mark DeWolfe Howe, *The Garden and the Wilderness: Religion and Government in American Constitutional History* (Chicago, IL: University of Chicago Press, 1965); Isaac Kramnick and R. Laurence Moore, *The Godless Constitution: The Case against Religious Correctness* (New York and London: W. W. Norton, 1996); Leonard Levy, *The Establishment Clause: Religion and the First Amendment*, 2nd rev. edn (London and Chapel Hill: University of North Carolina Press, 1994); Michael Malbin, *Religion and Politics: The Intentions of the Authors of the First Amendment* (Washington, DC: American Enterprise Institute for Public Policy Research, 1978).

2 The most recent criticism came from Justice Clarence Thomas, dissenting from the Court's decision to refuse to hear *Utah Highway Patrol Association v. American Atheists* (no. 10-1276) and *Davenport v. American Atheists* (no. 10-1297) in October 2011. The cases involved a challenge to the roadside display of 12- by 6-foot white crosses by the Utah Highway Patrol Association to memorialize patrol officers killed in the line of duty. Declaring that 'we should not now abdicate our responsibility to clean up our mess', Thomas referred to 'an Establishment Clause jurisprudence in shambles' (p. 1), commented on the 'superficiality and irrationality' of the Court's precedent (p. 7) and stated: 'our

Establishment Clause precedents remain impenetrable . . . it is difficult to imagine an area of the law more in need of clarity' (p. 17). See 565 US __ (2011), slip opinion (Justice Thomas, dissenting).

3 'First, the statute must have a secular legislative purpose; second, its principal or primary effect must be one that neither advances nor inhibits religion . . . finally, the statute must not foster an excessive government entanglement with religion.' *Lemon v. Kurtzman* 403 US 602, 612–3 (1971) (internal references and quotation marks omitted).

4 See, for example, *Lemon v. Kurtzman* 403 US 602 (1971); *Committee for Public Education and Religious Liberty v. Nyquist* 413 US 756 (1973); *Meek v. Pittenger* 421 US 349 (1975); *Wolman v. Walter* 433 US 229 (1977); *Aguilar v. Felton* 473 US 402 (1985); *Grand Rapids School District v. Ball* 473 US 373 (1985); *Rosenberger v. The Rector and Visitors of the University of Virginia* 515 US 819 (1995); *Agostini v. Felton* 521 US 203 (1997).

5 *Hein v. Freedom from Religion Foundation* 551 US 587, 594 (2007), slip opinion, p. 2 (plurality).

6 Freedom from Religion Foundation website, accessed 10 December 2011 at http://ffrf.org/.

7 'A plaintiff must allege personal injury fairly traceable to the defendant's allegedly unlawful conduct and likely to be redressed by the requested relief.' *Allen v. Wright* 468 US 737, 751 (1984).

8 *Flast v. Cohen* 392 US 83, 102–6 (1968).

9 'The link between congressional action and constitutional violation that supported taxpayer standing in *Flast* is missing here. Respondents do not challenge any specific congressional action or appropriation. . . . Those expenditures resulted from executive discretion, not congressional action. . . . We have never found taxpayer standing under such circumstances.' *Hein v. Freedom from Religion Foundation* 551 US 587, 605 (2007), slip opinion, p. 14 (plurality).

10 *Hein v. Freedom from Religion Foundation* 551 US 587, 589 (2007), slip opinion, pp. 20, 21 (plurality).

11 *Hein v. Freedom from Religion Foundation* 551 US 587, 618 (2007), slip opinion, pp. 1, 21 (Justice Scalia, with Justice Thomas, dissenting); p. 24 (plurality).

12 *Arizona Christian School Tuition Organization v. Winn* 563 US __ (2011), slip opinion, pp. 8–10 (Opinion of the Court).

13 The Court opinion describes Summum as a religious organization. The group, however, describe themselves as 'an informal gathering of people who are seeking to understand themselves, to know who they truly are inside. Summum is not about doctrine, dogma, or beliefs, but about gaining the experiences that will awaken us to the spirit within and to our place in the matrix of Creation's formulations.' From the Summum website, accessed 11 December 2011 at http://www.summum.us/about/.

14 *Pleasant Grove City v. Summum* 555 US 460, 467, 468 (2009), slip opinion, pp. 4, 5 (Opinion of the Court).

15 *Pleasant Grove City v. Summum* 555 US 460, 482 (2009), slip opinion, p. 1 (Justice Scalia, concurring); p. 2 (Justice Souter, concurring in judgment).

16 *Pleasant Grove City v. Summum* 555 US 460, 483 (2009), slip opinion, p. 2 (Justice Scalia, concurring). See *Van Orden v. Perry* 545 US 677 (2005).

17 *Pleasant Grove City v. Summum* 555 US 460, 486 (2009), slip opinion, p. 2 (Justice Souter, concurring in judgment).

18 The 'plastic reindeer rule' developed as a result of challenges to crèches and similar Christmas displays that were accompanied by Santas, Christmas trees and reindeer. See *Lynch v. Donnelly* 465 US 688 (1984) and *County of Allegheny v. ACLU* 492 US 573 (1989).

19 *Salazar v. Buono* 559 US __ (2010), slip opinion, p. 5 (plurality).

20 *Salazar v. Buono* 559 US __ (2010), slip opinion, p. 17 (plurality).

21 *Salazar v. Buono* 559 US __ (2010), slip opinion, p. 3 (Justice Alito, concurring).

22 'The 2002 injunction thus presented the government with a dilemma. It could not maintain the cross without violating the injunction, but it could not remove the cross without conveying disrespect for those the cross was seen as honoring.' *Salazar v. Buono* 559 US __ (2010), slip opinion, p. 12 (plurality).

23 *Salazar v. Buono* 559 US __ (2010), slip opinion, p. 13 (plurality).

24 *Salazar v. Buono* 559 US __ (2010), slip opinion, p. 14 (Justice Stevens, with Justices Ginsburg and Sotomayor, dissenting).

25 *Salazar v. Buono* 559 US __ (2010), slip opinion, p. 17 (Justice Stevens, with Justices Ginsburg and Sotomayor, dissenting) (internal references and quotation marks omitted).

26 Quoted in Alexander Bickel, *The Least Dangerous Branch: The Supreme Court at the Bar of Politics*, 2nd edn (New Haven, CT: Yale University Press, 1986), 71.

27 Charles Lane, 'Plenty of Room on the Fall Docket', *Washington Post*, 5 June 2006, p. A13; Linda Greenhouse, 'Case of the Dwindling Docket Mystifies the Supreme Court', *New York Times*, 7 December 2006, p. A1.

28 Greenhouse, 'Case of the Dwindling Docket', A1.

29 *Hein v. Freedom from Religion Foundation* 551 US 587, 612 (2007), slip opinion, p. 21 (plurality) (internal references and quotations omitted).

30 *Arizona Christian School Tuition Organization v. Winn* 563 US __ (2011), slip opinion, p. 5 (Opinion of the Court) (internal quotation marks omitted).

31 See *Mueller v. Allen* 463 US 388 (1983); *Zelman v. Simmons-Harris* 536 US 639 (2002).

32 *Salazar v. Buono* 559 US __ (2010), slip opinion, p. 1 (Justice Alito, concurring).

33 *Arizona Christian School Tuition Organization v. Winn* 563 US __ (2011), slip opinion, p. 17 (Opinion of the Court).

34 *Arizona Christian School Tuition Organization v. Winn* 563 US __ (2011), slip opinion, p. 10 (Justice Kagan, with Justices Ginsburg, Breyer and Sotomayor, dissenting).

35 *Arizona Christian School Tuition Organization v. Winn* 563 US __ (2011), slip opinion, p. 2 (Justice Kagan, with Justices Ginsburg, Breyer and Sotomayor, dissenting).

36 *Arizona Christian School Tuition Organization v. Winn* 563 US __ (2011), slip opinion, p. 18 (Opinion of the Court); p. 3 (Justice Kagan, with Justices Ginsburg, Breyer and Sotomayor, dissenting).

37 This trend has been noted across the Court's jurisprudence. 'The Court's conservatives have been on a campaign to close the courthouse door to people with legitimate legal claims. They have expanded a variety of doctrines to send wronged parties away empty-handed.' 'The Supreme Court's New Term', *New York Times*, 6 October 2008, p. A28.

38 The two other themes he identified were deference to the government (see discussion below) and the triumph of conservative values. Erwin Chemerinsky, 'The Future of the First Amendment', *Willamette Law Review*, 46 (2010), 623, 638.

39 Chemerinsky, 'Future of the First Amendment', 623, 639–642.

40 'In this case Congress has determined that transferring the memorial to private hands best serves the public interest and complies with the Constitution. . . . Federal courts have no warrant to revisit that decision – *and to risk replacing the people's judgment with their own* – unless and until a proper case is brought before them.' *Salazar v. Buono* 559 US __ (2010), slip opinion, p. 7 (Justice Scalia, with Justice Thomas, concurring in judgment).

41 Carl Esbeck, 'What the *Hein* Decision Can Tell Us about the Roberts Court and the Establishment Clause', *Mississippi Law Journal*, 78 (2008), 199, 213.

Index